MINOTAUR PRESS, A TOP COW PRODUCTIONS COMPANY, PRESENTS...

THINK TANK™

CREATED BY
MATT HAWKINS
&
RAHSAN EKEDAL

TOP COW PRODUCTIONS, INC.®

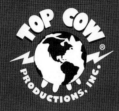

published by
Top Cow Productions, Inc.
Los Angeles

THINK TANK

MATT HAWKINS
CO-CREATOR & WRITER

RAHSAN EKEDAL
CO-CREATOR & ARTIST

TROY PETERI
LETTERER

COVER ART BY
**RAHSAN EKEDAL
& BRIAN REBER**

EDITED BY
**BRYAN ROUNTREE
& MATT HAWKINS**

BOOK DESIGN AND LAYOUT BY
JANA COOK

"DEDICATED TO YOU, THE READER."
— MATT HAWKINS & RAHSAN EKEDAL

To find the comic shop
nearest you, call:
1-888-COMICBOOK

Want more info? Check out:
www.topcow.com
for news & exclusive Top Cow merchandise!

TOP COW PRODUCTIONS, INC.

Marc Silvestri - CEO
Matt Hawkins - President & COO
Bryan Rountree - Managing Editor
Elena Salcedo - Operations Manager
Betsy Gonia - Production Assistant

IMAGE COMICS, INC.
Robert Kirkman - chief operating officer
Erik Larsen - chief financial officer
Todd McFarlane - president
Marc Silvestri - chief executive officer
Jim Valentino - vice-president
Eric Stephenson - publisher
Ron Richards - director of business development
Jennifer de Guzman - pr & marketing director
Branwyn Bigglestone - accounts manager
Emily Miller - accounting assistant
Jamie Parreno - marketing assistant
Jenna Savage - administrative assistant
Kevin Yuen - digital rights coordinator
Jonathan Chan - production manager
Drew Gill - art director
Tyler Shainline - print manager
Monica Garcia - production artist
Vincent Kukua - production artist
Jana Cook - production artist
www.imagecomics.com

THINK TANK Volume 1

ISBN: 978-1-60706-660-6

JUNE 2013. SECOND PRINTING.

Published by Image Comics, Inc. Office of Publication: 2001 Center Street, 6th Floor, Berkeley, CA 94704. $14.99 USD.
THINK TANK © & ™ 2013 Self Loathing Narcissist, Inc. All rights reserved. Originally published in single issue format
as THINK TANK 1-4. "THINK TANK", The THINK TANK logos, and the likeness of all characters (human and otherwise)
featured herein are trademarks of Self Loathing Narcissist, Inc. SUNSET © & ™ 2012 Christos Gage and Top Cow
Productions, Inc. ECHOES © & ™ 2013 Joshua Hale Filkov and Top Cow Productions, Inc. Image Comics and the Image
Comics logo are trademarks of Image Comics, Inc. The characters, events, and stories in this publication are entirely
fictional. Any resemblance to actual persons, (living or dead), events, institutions, or locales, without satirical intent, is
coincidental. No portion of this publication may be reproduced or transmitted, in any form or by any means, without
the express written permission of Top Cow Productions, Inc. Printed in the U.S.A. For information regarding the CPSIA
on this printed material call: 203-595-3636 and provide reference # RICH - 489096

TABLE OF CONTENTS

DISCARDED

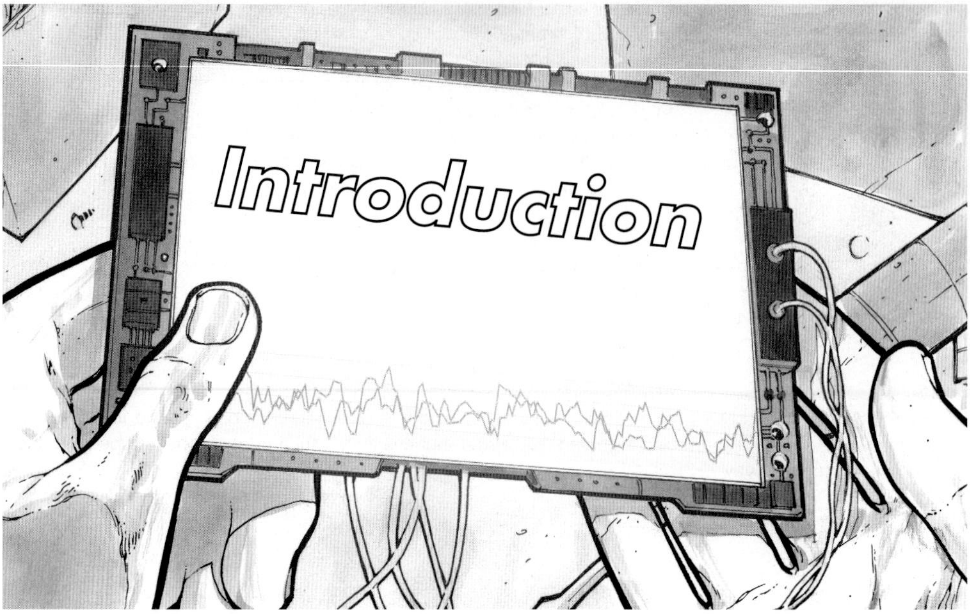
Introduction

I've seen Matt Hawkins pick a door lock, know for certain he once cracked a safe, and am quite positive that he can get in and out of a locked office by crawling over the ceiling tiles, dropping in, and then getting out like a ninja (when he was a younger man, anyway). I'm reasonably sure that these sorts of swashbuckling exploits are part of Matt's past and not his present way of life.

My point is I know from firsthand experience that my friend, Matt, is quite capable of thinking like a spy. He thinks even more about Science.

Matt and I met nearly two decades ago when we were both totally immersed in the comic book business. It was 1993 and smack dab in the middle of the chaotic early days of the Image Comics revolution. I was hired to put a steady hand on the steering wheel of the Image Central office. Matt was in the upper echelon of Extreme Studios. Our offices were on the same floor in those days.

It was clear to me, from the get-go, that Matt wasn't your average comic book guy. His interests were wider and more varied than most of the kids his age working at Extreme. We became friends. We hung out a lot. We talked about anything and everything. It was one long, ongoing conversation that sprawled out over many years. The topics ranged from the comics business, comics creator gossip, history, politics, religion, entertainment, mythology, and science.

My obsession was mythology. Matt's was science. We traded facts and opinions about both disciplines secure in the belief that when it comes to science and mythology: one is yin to the other's yang.

It's funny when I look back that the first creator owned book of Matt's that I helped shepherd through Image Comics was *Lady Pendragon*, a riff on Arthurian myth and legend.

A few years ago we were somewhere having a bite or a coffee and Matt made this off-handed comment that he believed one of the missing sweet spots in today's comics marketplace is fiction based on scientific facts. You know, something like Michael Crichton's *Andromeda Strain*.

I understood immediately what he meant and I think I might have blurted out something like "Hurry up before someone else figures that out!"

Now that I've read *Think Tank*, I'm confident no one else could have conceived and written this book except Matt. Everything about this book is refracted through the lens of Matt Hawkins: his mind, his quirks, his personality.

A causal mention of a lens is my inelegant cue to comment on a hidden player in *Think Tank*: Sir Isaac Newton. Newton's book on light and color, *Opticks*, was his second most important work. Newton's greatest work was *Mathematical Principles of Natural Philosophy*, generally known as *Principia*, the foundation work upon which modern physics was built.

At some point doing research for my own comic book, *Beanworld*, I became interested in alchemy. Not the pop culture caricature of alchemy, that of the wizened cranky old coot trying to turn lead into gold. Nothing like that. I became fascinated with the literature describing the connections between alchemical narrative drawings and symbols to the psychology of art and dreams.

So you can imagine my shock when I read that Sir Isaac Newton was also one of the last great alchemists before he became one of the first great modern scientists. I've read that Newton allegedly wrote over a million words on alchemy. The Royal Society of London for Improving Natural Knowledge, "the invisible college of natural philosophers," is said to have judged Newton's alchemy papers "not fit to be printed." Newton had been the President of this super group of physicians, philosophers, and scientists, so the Royal Society was probably embarrassed by Newton's obsession for research taking place outside of the rules of the Scientific Method. To apparently protect Newton's reputation after his death in 1727 they decided it was better for everyone concerned to hide those papers and write that stuff out of out of Sir Isaac's scientific continuity. When the papers were rediscovered in the last century, it became clear that it was in the midst of Newton's alchemical research that his line of work transmogrified into his scientific discoveries.

The take away here is that Newton was identified as a potential genius at a young age and entered into Trinity College, Cambridge as a teen where he immediately excelled outside of the curriculum. He was smarter than his teachers. He was also a head case. In his youth he was boisterous, opinionated, a real pain in the ass to his friends and patrons. I see a lot of Sir Isaac in Dr. David Loren, the lead character in *Think Tank*.

And why not? Sir Isaac acts as a bit of a narrator in the book. Every scene transition is signaled by the caption: F=ma. Hell, I'll be the first to admit I didn't remember what it means. Looked it up and it is Sir Isaac Newton's second law of physics. The one that describes acceleration. Matt's using it as a signal to the reader that the story's shifting gears, putting pedal to the metal, and the action is about to get really crazy.

David's internal dialogue reads the way Matt talks. Rapid and to the point. The character's name might be Dr. David Loren but it's Matt's voice I hear in my head.

Matt says that the gizmos, theories, and applications in *Think Tank* are nuts on. It already exists. For real. He got some of it from his science buddies and scouring the corners of the Internet. Makes you wonder what the Government Brain Boys working in the belly of the Military Industrial Beast are really cooking up for the Spooks and Soldiers. Probably best not to dwell on it. We'll know soon enough. Or will we?

There are some seriously disturbing ideas presented in the pages of *Think Tank*, particularly those describing the potential loss of the sanctity of our own thoughts. That someone else in the not-so-far future will be able to scan our thoughts and discern our beliefs puts us on the edge of a paradigm shift that, quite frankly, I can't quite get my head wrapped around. "Our thoughts are the last vestige of our privacy in an increasingly connected and public world," says David as he's discovering how to crack into the human mind and tap into the consciousness of other human beings.

This got me thinking about the future of the First Amendment (freedom of speech and expression), the Fourth Amendment (freedom from unreasonable search and seizure) and the crazy nature of scientific work-made-for-hire.

Pretty much when pure scientific research is absconded by the powers-paying-for-it a lot of wackiness follows. Think the Manhattan Project, gathering perhaps the most extraordinary league of the world's finest physicists and engineers since the early days of the original Royal Society. For years these people worked, ate, drank, even partied together, all dedicated to seeing if their crazy-assed theories really had practical applications. They drilled deep into the question of nuclear physics, chopping it all up into little projects, solving small problem after small problem, all the while inventing new processes and machines. Most of them were just delighted to have the funding and facilities to accelerate their research on How-Everything-Works-And-Fits-Together-With-Everything-Else.

The result was The Bomb.

This heavy stuff was immediately deemed way too important to be in the hands of nutty dreamers and egghead scientists. And once again, as had happened so many times before, the men and women who made it all happen were reminded that their output was all work-made-for-hire and the property of The Government.

The arms race that resulted from the fruits of the Manhattan Project is truly mindboggling. Most of it is so deeply classified that we, the ordinary citizens, are barely aware that there are weapon systems that can kill gazillions of people and destroy acres of property in the blink of an eye. The people who are in charge of wielding such powerful weapons always talk in deliberately unemotional, military-industrial techno-speak using bland phrases like "collateral damage" and "friendly fire." Living breathing human beings become "assets" and "unilaterals." Locations where people are just living their lives become "hard targets."

This is the world in which we meet our protagonist, Dr. David Loren, as he finds himself confronting his place in a world that he has clearly outgrown and is ready to escape from.

I don't want to shortchange co-creator and artist, Rahsan Ekedal. His artwork is totally appropriate to the subject matter. Rahsan's line and tone work is as clear, uncluttered, and terse as Matt's dialogue. A great mesh of story and art.

So f=ma, my friends. *Think Tank* is about to take over your brain and guide you onto one hell of a joyride! And as the caution elsewhere in these pages says; DANGER: reading this book will make you smarter.

Larry Marder
Newport Coast CA
2012

CHAPTER 1

THINK TANK

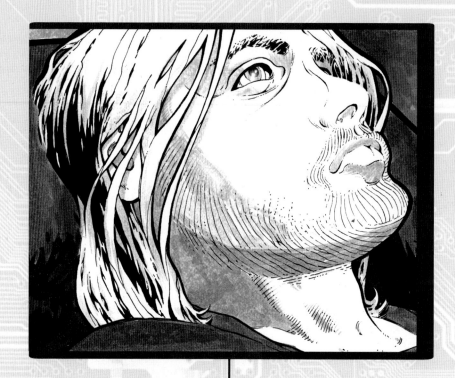

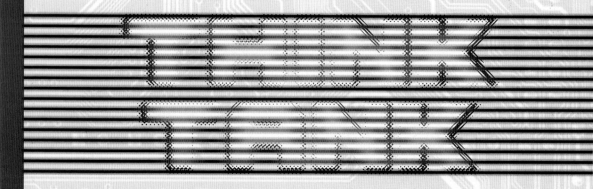

$$\oint \vec{E} \cdot d\vec{A} = \frac{1}{\varepsilon_0} q_{in} \qquad \oint \vec{B} \cdot d\vec{A} = 0 \qquad \oint \vec{E} \cdot d\vec{\ell} = -\frac{d}{dt} \int \vec{B} \cdot d\vec{A}$$

$$\oint \vec{B} \cdot d\vec{\ell} = \mu_0 i_{in} \qquad \vec{F} = q(\vec{v} \times \vec{B} + \vec{E}) \qquad i = \frac{dq}{dt}$$

point charge $\quad E = \frac{1}{4\pi\varepsilon_0} \frac{q}{r^2} \qquad V = \frac{1}{4\pi\varepsilon_0} \frac{q}{r} \qquad p = qd$

$$V_f - V_i = -\int_i^f \vec{E} \cdot d\vec{s} \qquad E_x = -\frac{\partial V}{\partial x} \qquad \vec{\tau} = \vec{p} \times \vec{E}$$

$$C = \frac{Q}{V} \qquad U_E = \frac{1}{2} Q V = \frac{1}{2} C V^2 = \frac{1}{2} \frac{Q^2}{C} \qquad C = \varepsilon_0 \frac{A}{d}$$

$$R = \frac{V}{i} \qquad P = Vi \qquad P = i^2 R = \frac{V^2}{R} \qquad R = \rho \frac{L}{A}$$

"SCIENCE IS A WONDERFUL THING IF ONE DOES NOT HAVE TO EARN ONE'S LIVING AT IT." ~ALBERT EINSTEIN

$$R_{eq} = R_1 + R_2 + \cdots \qquad \frac{1}{C_{eq}} = \frac{1}{C_1} + \frac{1}{C_2} + \cdots$$

$$\frac{1}{R_{eq}} = \frac{1}{R_1} + \frac{1}{R_2} + \cdots$$

$$d\vec{B} = \frac{\mu_0}{4\pi} \frac{i \, d\vec{s} \times \hat{r}}{r^2} \qquad B = \frac{\mu_0}{2\pi} \frac{i}{r} \qquad B = \mu_0 n i \qquad \vec{\tau} = \vec{\mu} \times \vec{B}$$

$$\varepsilon = -\frac{d\Phi}{dt} \qquad \varepsilon = -N \frac{d\Phi}{dt} \qquad L = \frac{|\varepsilon|}{\left|\frac{di}{dt}\right|} = \frac{N\Phi}{i}$$

$$u_E = \frac{1}{2} \varepsilon_0 E^2 \qquad u_B = \frac{1}{2} \frac{B^2}{\mu_0} \qquad U_B = \frac{1}{2} L i^2$$

$$q \cdot e^{-t/\tau_c} \qquad q = C\varepsilon(1 - e^{-t/\tau_c}) \qquad i = i_0 e^{-t/\tau_L} \qquad i = \frac{\varepsilon}{R}(1 - e^{-t/\tau_L})$$

$$\frac{L}{R} \qquad \tau_c = RC \qquad \mu = NiA \qquad \frac{1}{4\pi\varepsilon_0} = 9 \times 10^9 \qquad \frac{\mu_0}{4\pi} = 10^{-7}$$

means $10^6 \qquad \mu$ means 10^{-6}

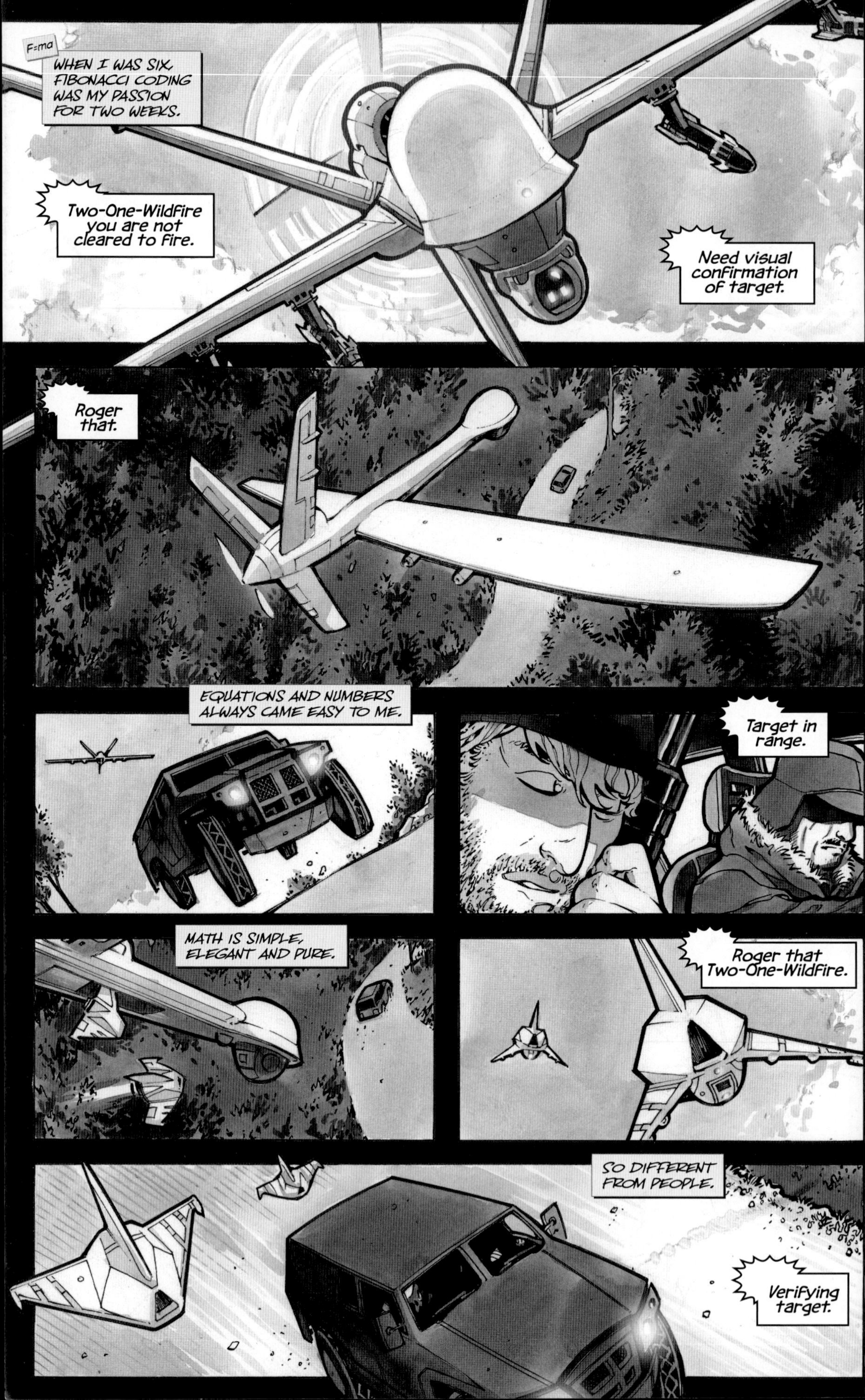
F=ma
WHEN I WAS SIX, FIBONACCI CODING WAS MY PASSION FOR TWO WEEKS.
Two-One-Wildfire you are not cleared to fire.
Need visual confirmation of target.
Roger that.
EQUATIONS AND NUMBERS ALWAYS CAME EASY TO ME.
Target in range.
MATH IS SIMPLE, ELEGANT AND PURE.
Roger that Two-One-Wildfire.
SO DIFFERENT FROM PEOPLE.
Verifying target.

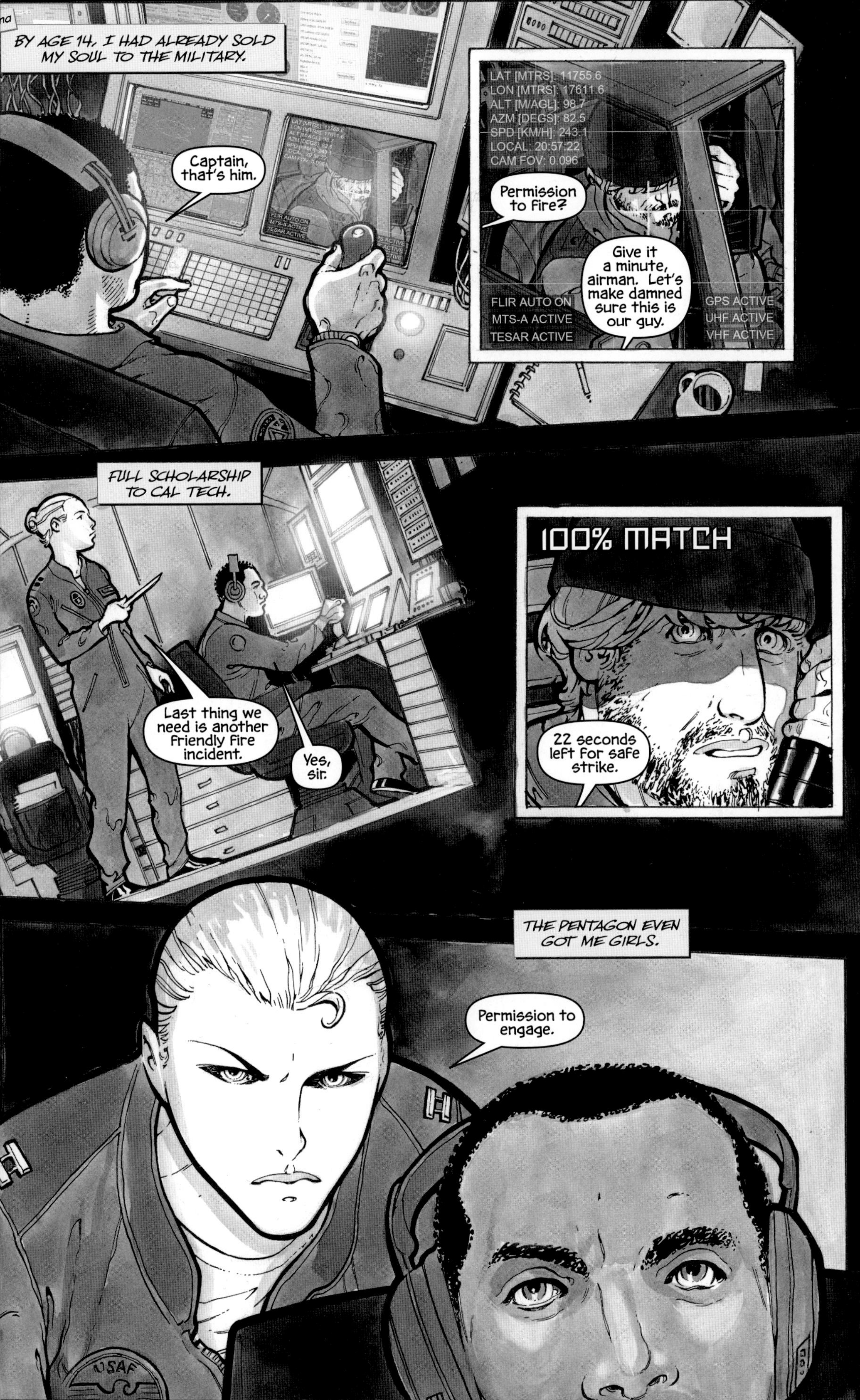

BY AGE 14, I HAD ALREADY SOLD MY SOUL TO THE MILITARY.
Captain, that's him.
LAT [MTRS]: 11755.6
LON [MTRS]: 17611.6
ALT [M/AGL]: 98.7
AZM [DEGS]: 82.5
SPD [KM/H]: 243.1
LOCAL: 20:57:22
CAM FOV: 0.096
Permission to fire?
Give it a minute, airman. Let's make damned sure this is our guy.
FLIR AUTO ON
MTS-A ACTIVE
TESAR ACTIVE
GPS ACTIVE
UHF ACTIVE
VHF ACTIVE
FULL SCHOLARSHIP TO CAL TECH.
Last thing we need is another friendly fire incident.
Yes, sir.
100% MATCH
22 seconds left for safe strike.
THE PENTAGON EVEN GOT ME GIRLS.
Permission to engage.
USAF

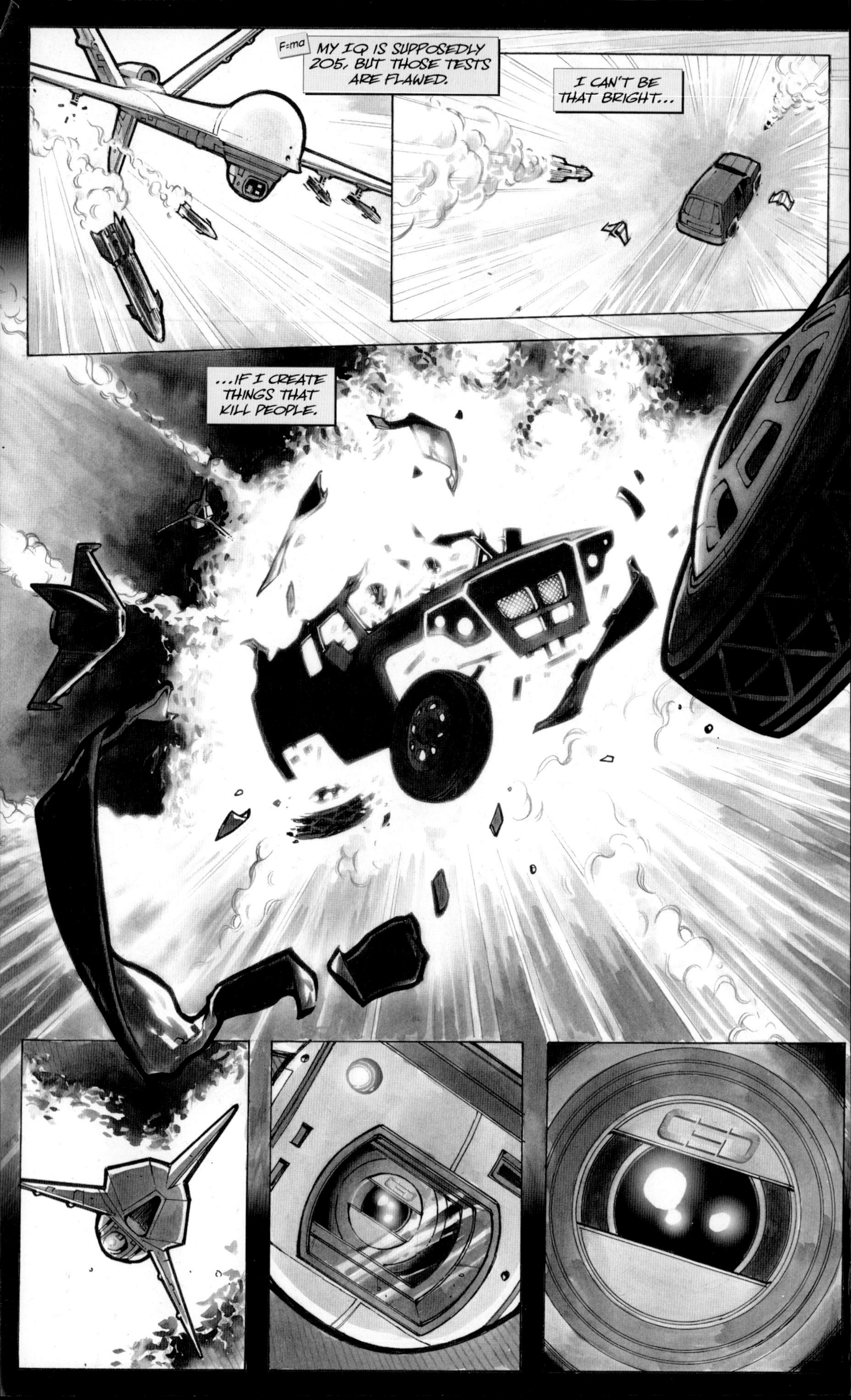
F=ma
MY IQ IS SUPPOSEDLY 205, BUT THOSE TESTS ARE FLAWED.
I CAN'T BE THAT BRIGHT...
...IF I CREATE THINGS THAT KILL PEOPLE.

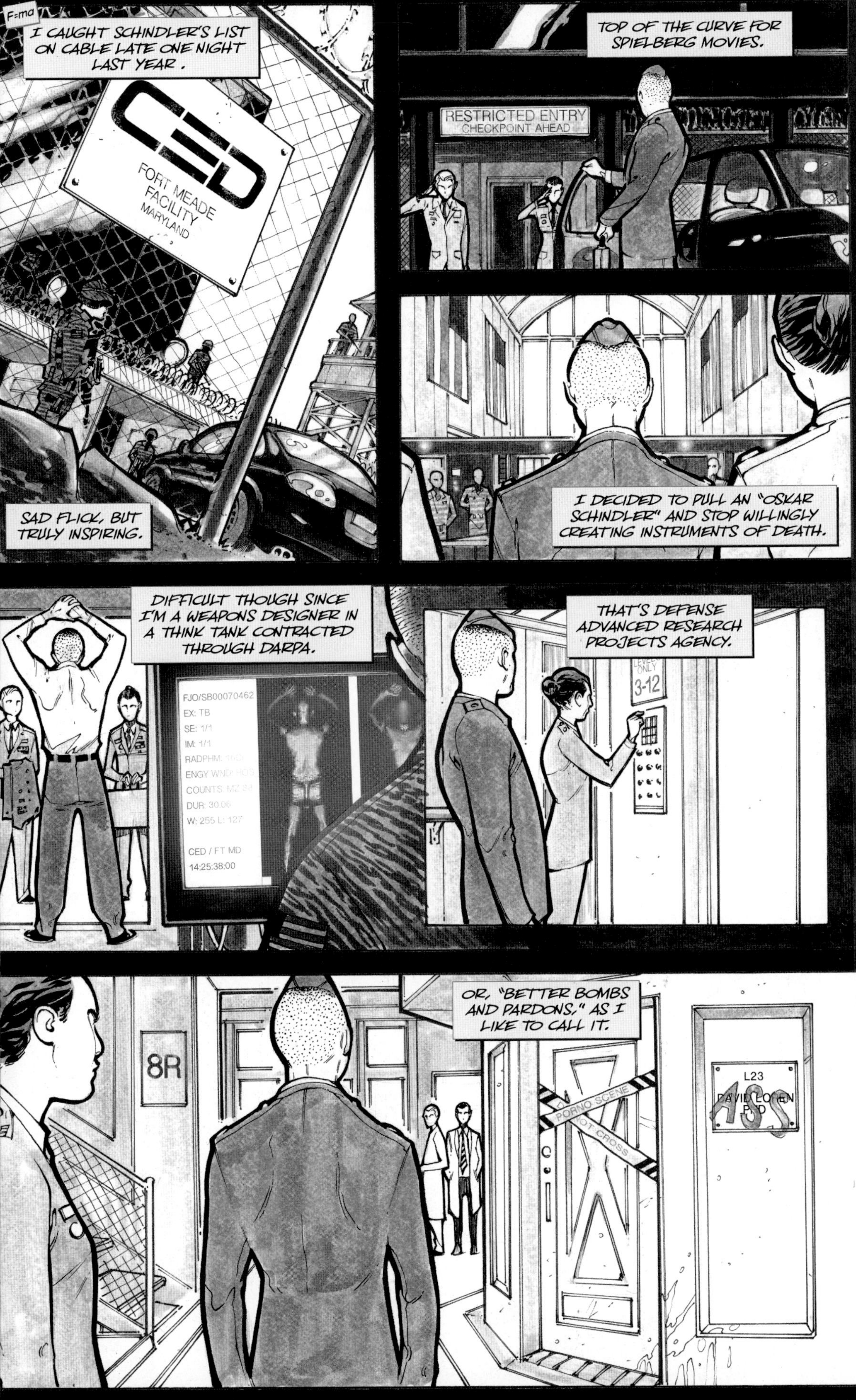
F=ma
I CAUGHT SCHINDLER'S LIST ON CABLE LATE ONE NIGHT LAST YEAR.
CED
FORT MEADE FACILITY MARYLAND
SAD FLICK, BUT TRULY INSPIRING.
TOP OF THE CURVE FOR SPIELBERG MOVIES.
RESTRICTED ENTRY
CHECKPOINT AHEAD
I DECIDED TO PULL AN "OSKAR SCHINDLER" AND STOP WILLINGLY CREATING INSTRUMENTS OF DEATH.
DIFFICULT THOUGH SINCE I'M A WEAPONS DESIGNER IN A THINK TANK CONTRACTED THROUGH DARPA.
FJO/SB00070462
EX: TB
SE: 1/1
IM: 1/1
DUR: 30.06
W: 255 L: 127
CED / FT MD
14:25:38:00
THAT'S DEFENSE ADVANCED RESEARCH PROJECTS AGENCY.
LEVELS ONLY
3-12
OR, "BETTER BOMBS AND PARDONS," AS I LIKE TO CALL IT.
8R
PORNO SCENE
DO NOT CROSS
L23
ASS

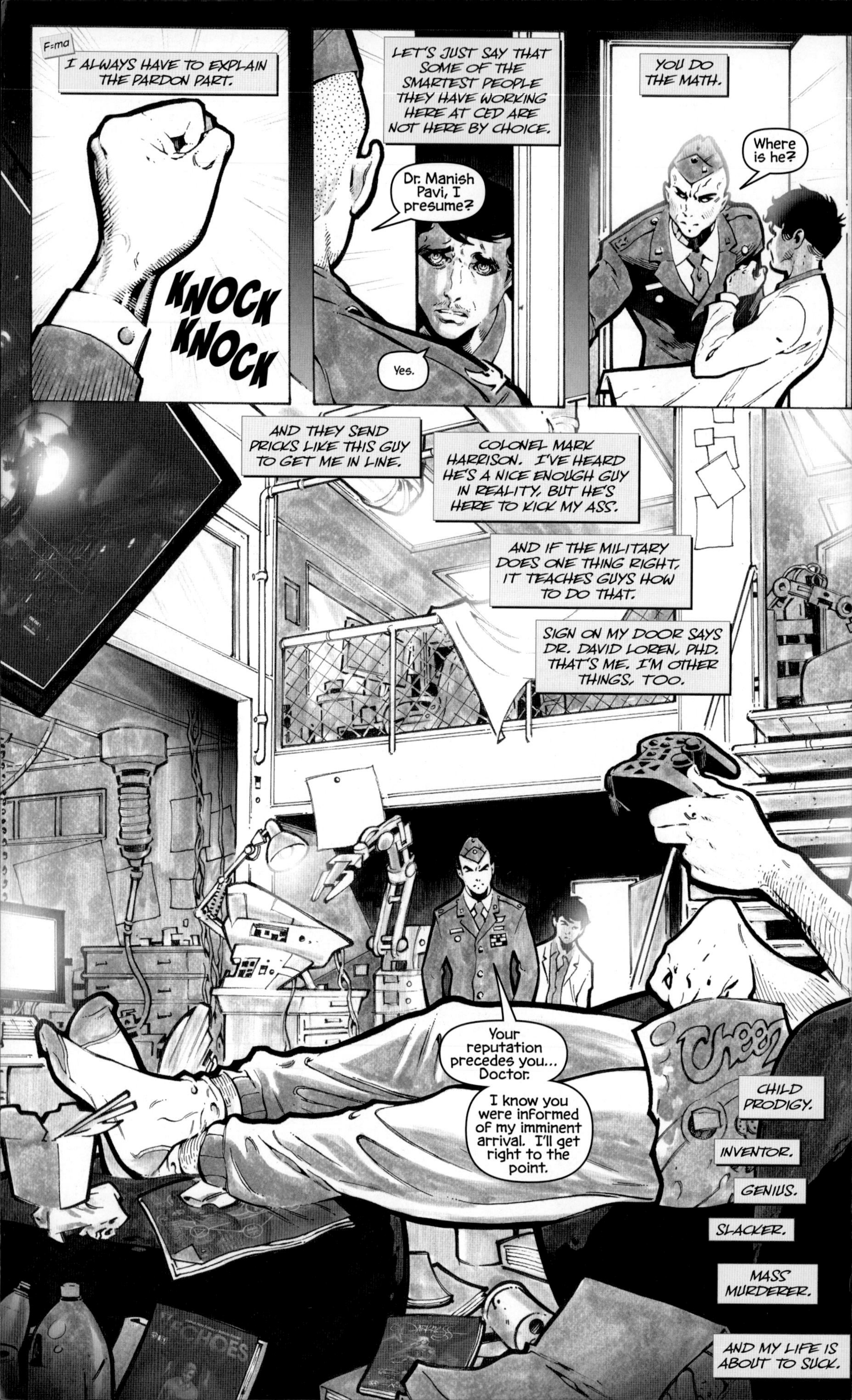
F=ma
I ALWAYS HAVE TO EXPLAIN THE PARDON PART.
KNOCK KNOCK
LET'S JUST SAY THAT SOME OF THE SMARTEST PEOPLE THEY HAVE WORKING HERE AT CED ARE NOT HERE BY CHOICE.
Dr. Manish Pavi, I presume?
Yes.
YOU DO THE MATH.
Where is he?
AND THEY SEND PRICKS LIKE THIS GUY TO GET ME IN LINE.
COLONEL MARK HARRISON. I'VE HEARD HE'S A NICE ENOUGH GUY IN REALITY, BUT HE'S HERE TO KICK MY ASS.
AND IF THE MILITARY DOES ONE THING RIGHT, IT TEACHES GUYS HOW TO DO THAT.
SIGN ON MY DOOR SAYS DR. DAVID LOREN, PHD. THAT'S ME. I'M OTHER THINGS, TOO.
Your reputation precedes you... Doctor.
I know you were informed of my imminent arrival. I'll get right to the point.
CHILD PRODIGY.
INVENTOR.
GENIUS.
SLACKER.
MASS MURDERER.
AND MY LIFE IS ABOUT TO SUCK.

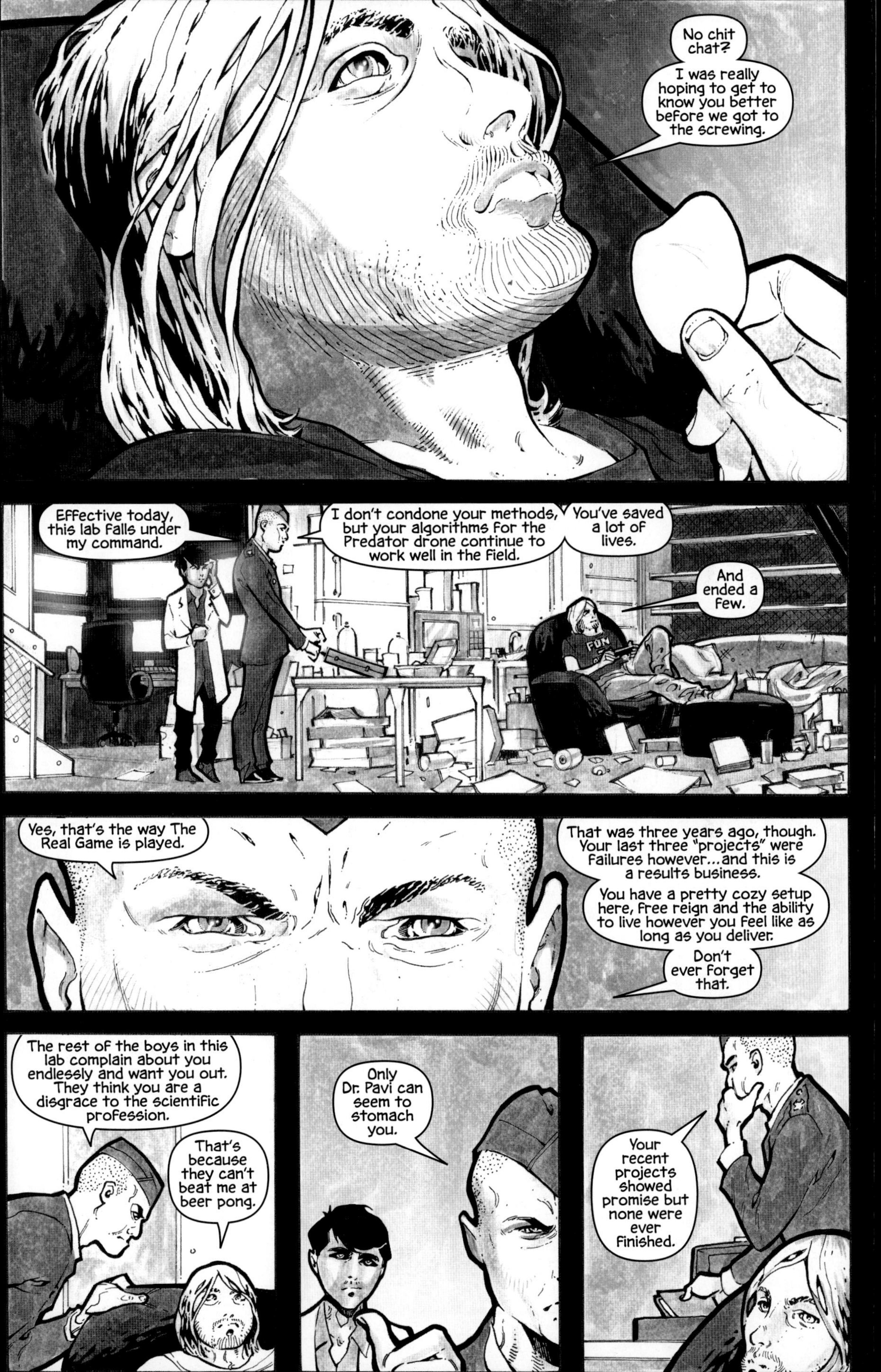
No chit chat?
I was really hoping to get to know you better before we got to the screwing.
Effective today, this lab falls under my command.
I don't condone your methods, but your algorithms for the Predator drone continue to work well in the field.
You've saved a lot of lives.
And ended a few.
Yes, that's the way The Real Game is played.
That was three years ago, though. Your last three "projects" were failures however...and this is a results business.
You have a pretty cozy setup here, free reign and the ability to live however you feel like as long as you deliver.
Don't ever forget that.
The rest of the boys in this lab complain about you endlessly and want you out. They think you are a disgrace to the scientific profession.
That's because they can't beat me at beer pong.
Only Dr. Pavi can seem to stomach you.
Your recent projects showed promise but none were ever finished.

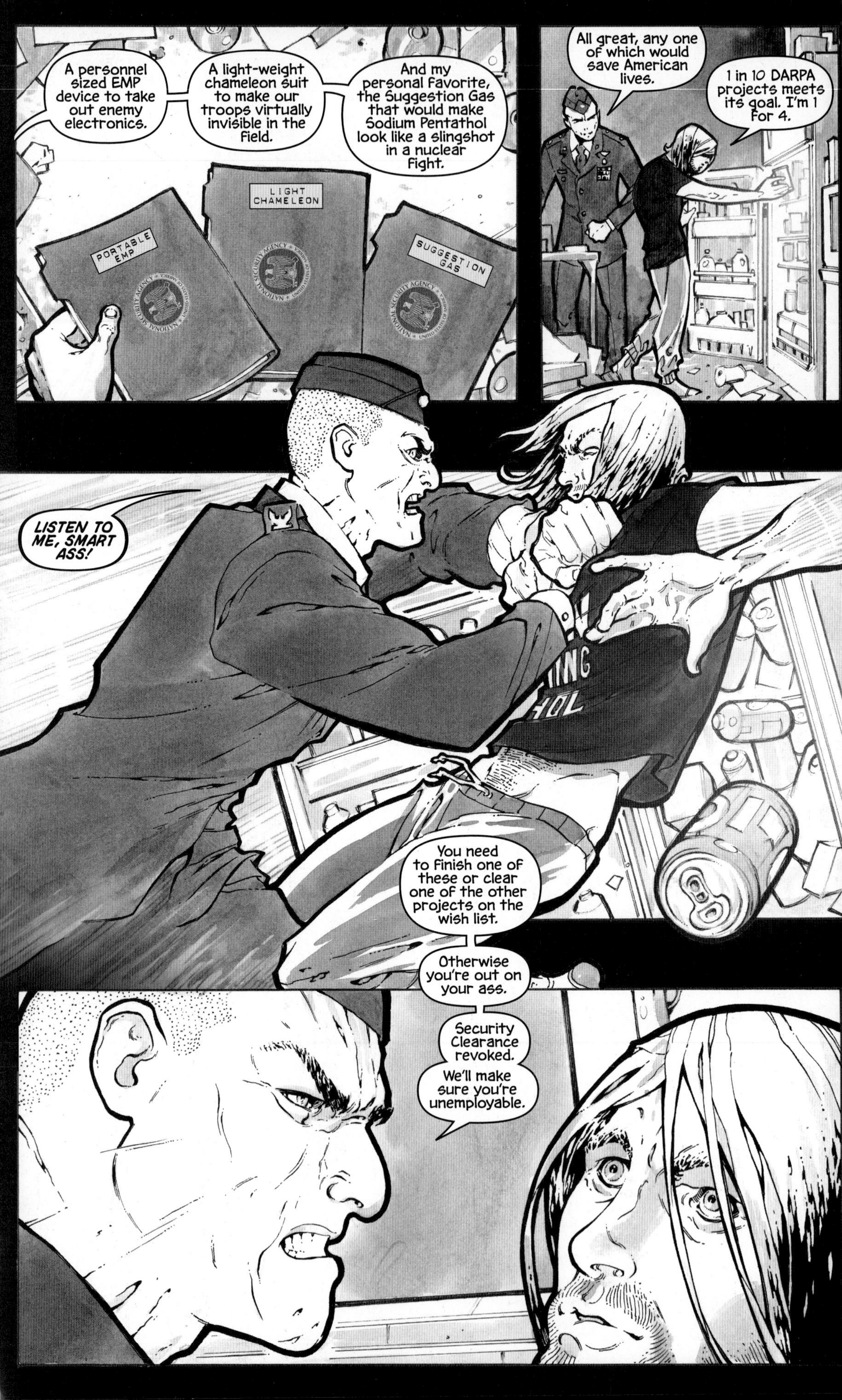
A personnel sized EMP device to take out enemy electronics.
A light-weight chameleon suit to make our troops virtually invisible in the field.
And my personal favorite, the Suggestion Gas that would make Sodium Pentathol look like a slingshot in a nuclear fight.
PORTABLE EMP
LIGHT CHAMELEON
SUGGESTION GAS
All great, any one of which would save American lives.
1 in 10 DARPA projects meets its goal. I'm 1 for 4.
LISTEN TO ME, SMART ASS!
You need to finish one of these or clear one of the other projects on the wish list.
Otherwise you're out on your ass.
Security Clearance revoked.
We'll make sure you're unemployable.

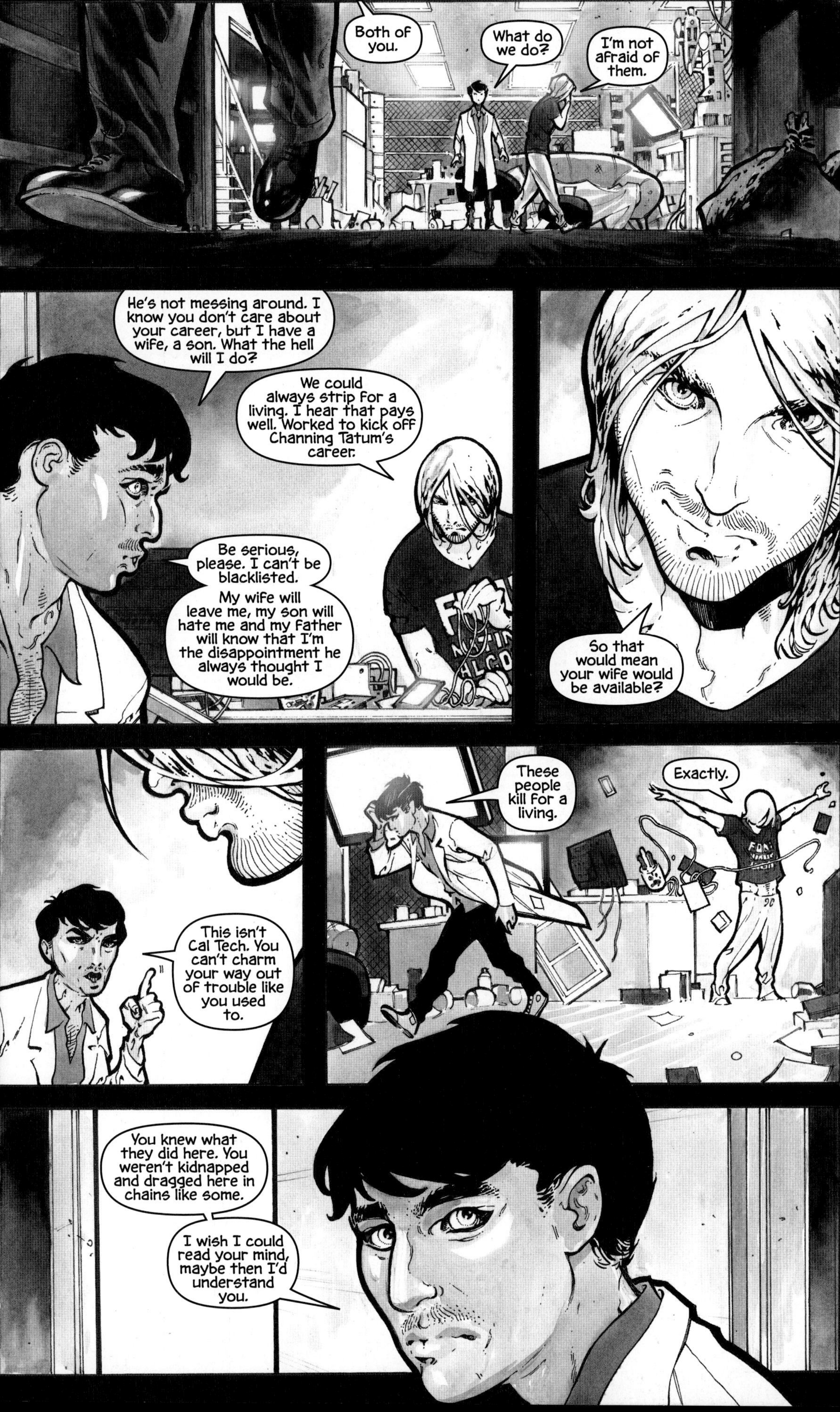
Both of you.
What do we do?
I'm not afraid of them.
He's not messing around. I know you don't care about your career, but I have a wife, a son. What the hell will I do?
We could always strip for a living. I hear that pays well. Worked to kick off Channing Tatum's career.
Be serious, please. I can't be blacklisted.
My wife will leave me, my son will hate me and my father will know that I'm the disappointment he always thought I would be.
So that would mean your wife would be available?
This isn't Cal Tech. You can't charm your way out of trouble like you used to.
These people kill for a living.
Exactly.
You knew what they did here. You weren't kidnapped and dragged here in chains like some.
I wish I could read your mind, maybe then I'd understand you.

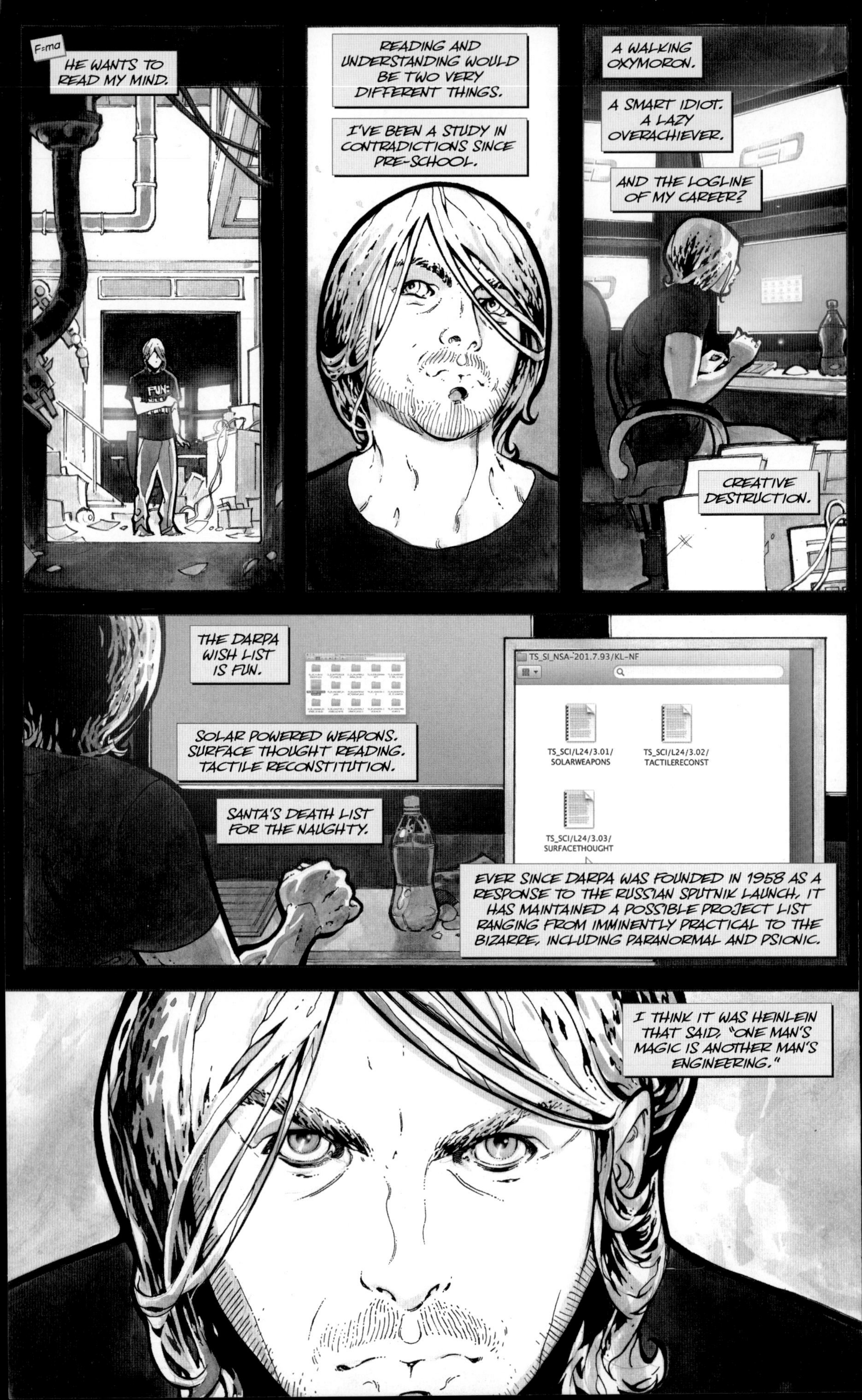
F=ma
HE WANTS TO READ MY MIND.
READING AND UNDERSTANDING WOULD BE TWO VERY DIFFERENT THINGS.
I'VE BEEN A STUDY IN CONTRADICTIONS SINCE PRE-SCHOOL.
A WALKING OXYMORON.
A SMART IDIOT. A LAZY OVERACHIEVER.
AND THE LOGLINE OF MY CAREER?
CREATIVE DESTRUCTION.
THE DARPA WISH LIST IS FUN.
SOLAR POWERED WEAPONS. SURFACE THOUGHT READING. TACTILE RECONSTITUTION.
SANTA'S DEATH LIST FOR THE NAUGHTY.
TS_SI_NSA-201.7.93/KL-NF
TS_SCI/L24/3.01/ SOLARWEAPONS
TS_SCI/L24/3.02/ TACTILERECONST
TS_SCI/L24/3.03/ SURFACETHOUGHT
EVER SINCE DARPA WAS FOUNDED IN 1958 AS A RESPONSE TO THE RUSSIAN SPUTNIK LAUNCH, IT HAS MAINTAINED A POSSIBLE PROJECT LIST RANGING FROM IMMINENTLY PRACTICAL TO THE BIZARRE, INCLUDING PARANORMAL AND PSIONIC.
I THINK IT WAS HEINLEIN THAT SAID, "ONE MAN'S MAGIC IS ANOTHER MAN'S ENGINEERING."

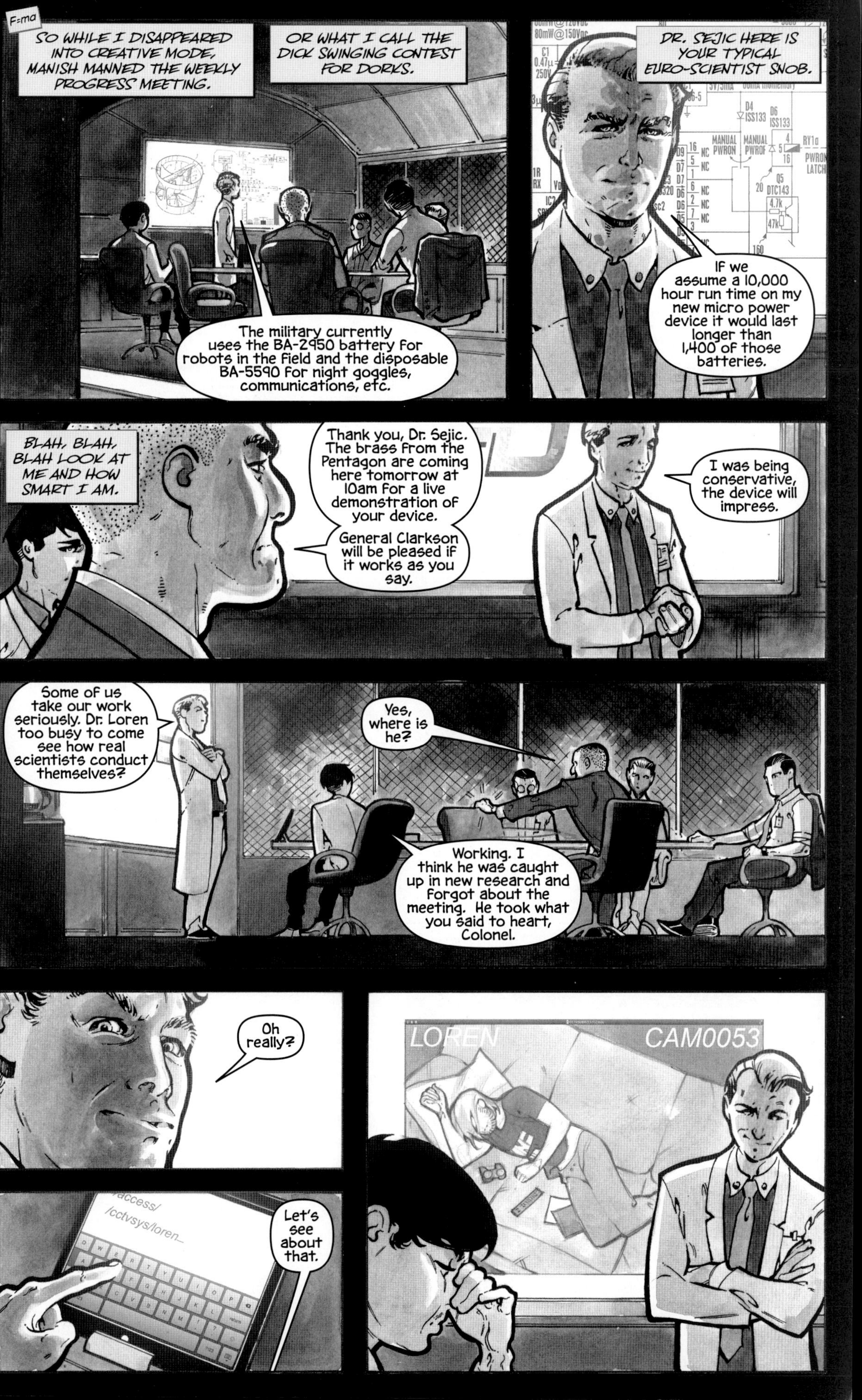

F=ma
SO WHILE I DISAPPEARED INTO CREATIVE MODE, MANISH MANNED THE WEEKLY PROGRESS MEETING.
OR WHAT I CALL THE DICK SWINGING CONTEST FOR DORKS.
The military currently uses the BA-2950 battery for robots in the field and the disposable BA-5590 for night goggles, communications, etc.
DR. SEJIC HERE IS YOUR TYPICAL EURO-SCIENTIST SNOB.
If we assume a 10,000 hour run time on my new micro power device it would last longer than 1,400 of those batteries.
BLAH, BLAH, BLAH LOOK AT ME AND HOW SMART I AM.
Thank you, Dr. Sejic. The brass from the Pentagon are coming here tomorrow at 10am for a live demonstration of your device.
General Clarkson will be pleased if it works as you say.
I was being conservative, the device will impress.
Some of us take our work seriously. Dr. Loren too busy to come see how real scientists conduct themselves?
Yes, where is he?
Working. I think he was caught up in new research and forgot about the meeting. He took what you said to heart, Colonel.
Oh really?
/access/
/cctvsys/loren_
Let's see about that.
LOREN
CAM0053

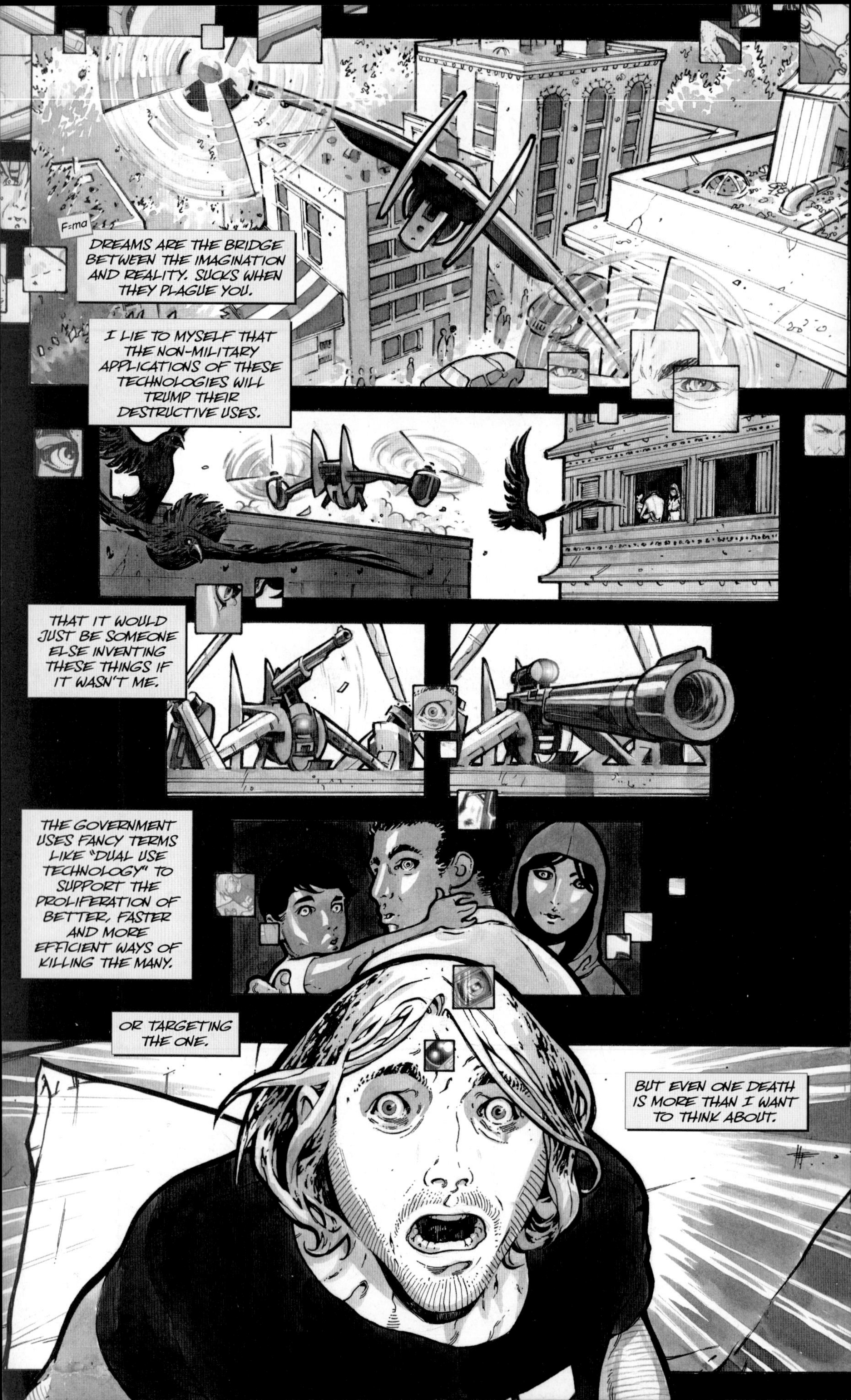
F=ma
DREAMS ARE THE BRIDGE BETWEEN THE IMAGINATION AND REALITY. SUCKS WHEN THEY PLAGUE YOU.
I LIE TO MYSELF THAT THE NON-MILITARY APPLICATIONS OF THESE TECHNOLOGIES WILL TRUMP THEIR DESTRUCTIVE USES.
THAT IT WOULD JUST BE SOMEONE ELSE INVENTING THESE THINGS IF IT WASN'T ME.
THE GOVERNMENT USES FANCY TERMS LIKE "DUAL USE TECHNOLOGY" TO SUPPORT THE PROLIFERATION OF BETTER, FASTER AND MORE EFFICIENT WAYS OF KILLING THE MANY.
OR TARGETING THE ONE.
BUT EVEN ONE DEATH IS MORE THAN I WANT TO THINK ABOUT.

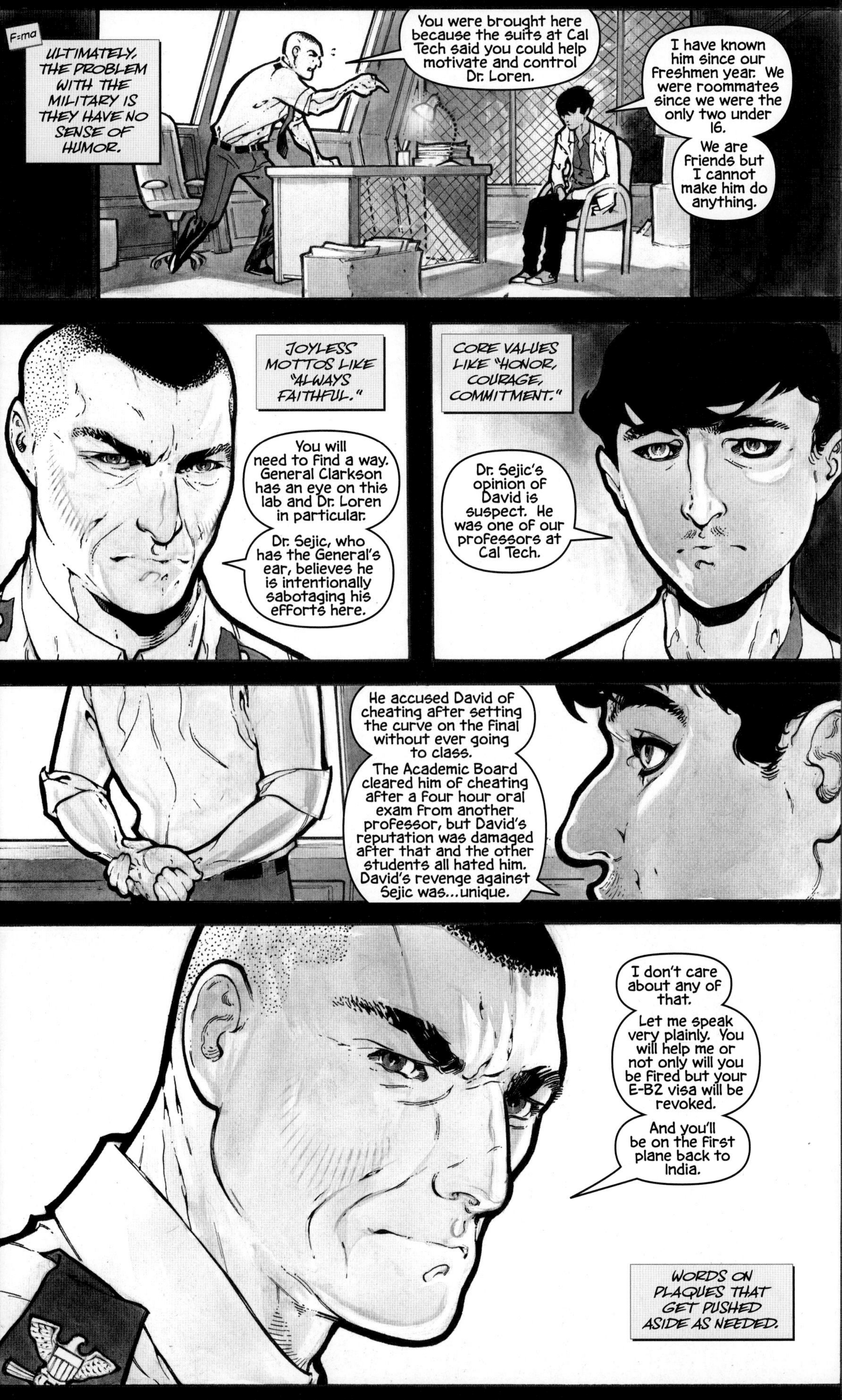
F=ma
ULTIMATELY, THE PROBLEM WITH THE MILITARY IS THEY HAVE NO SENSE OF HUMOR.
You were brought here because the suits at Cal Tech said you could help motivate and control Dr. Loren.
I have known him since our freshmen year. We were roommates since we were the only two under 16.
We are friends but I cannot make him do anything.
JOYLESS MOTTOS LIKE "ALWAYS FAITHFUL."
You will need to find a way. General Clarkson has an eye on this lab and Dr. Loren in particular.
Dr. Sejic, who has the General's ear, believes he is intentionally sabotaging his efforts here.
CORE VALUES LIKE "HONOR, COURAGE, COMMITMENT."
Dr. Sejic's opinion of David is suspect. He was one of our professors at Cal Tech.
He accused David of cheating after setting the curve on the final without ever going to class.
The Academic Board cleared him of cheating after a four hour oral exam from another professor, but David's reputation was damaged after that and the other students all hated him. David's revenge against Sejic was...unique.
I don't care about any of that.
Let me speak very plainly. You will help me or not only will you be fired but your E-B2 visa will be revoked.
And you'll be on the first plane back to India.
WORDS ON PLAQUES THAT GET PUSHED ASIDE AS NEEDED.

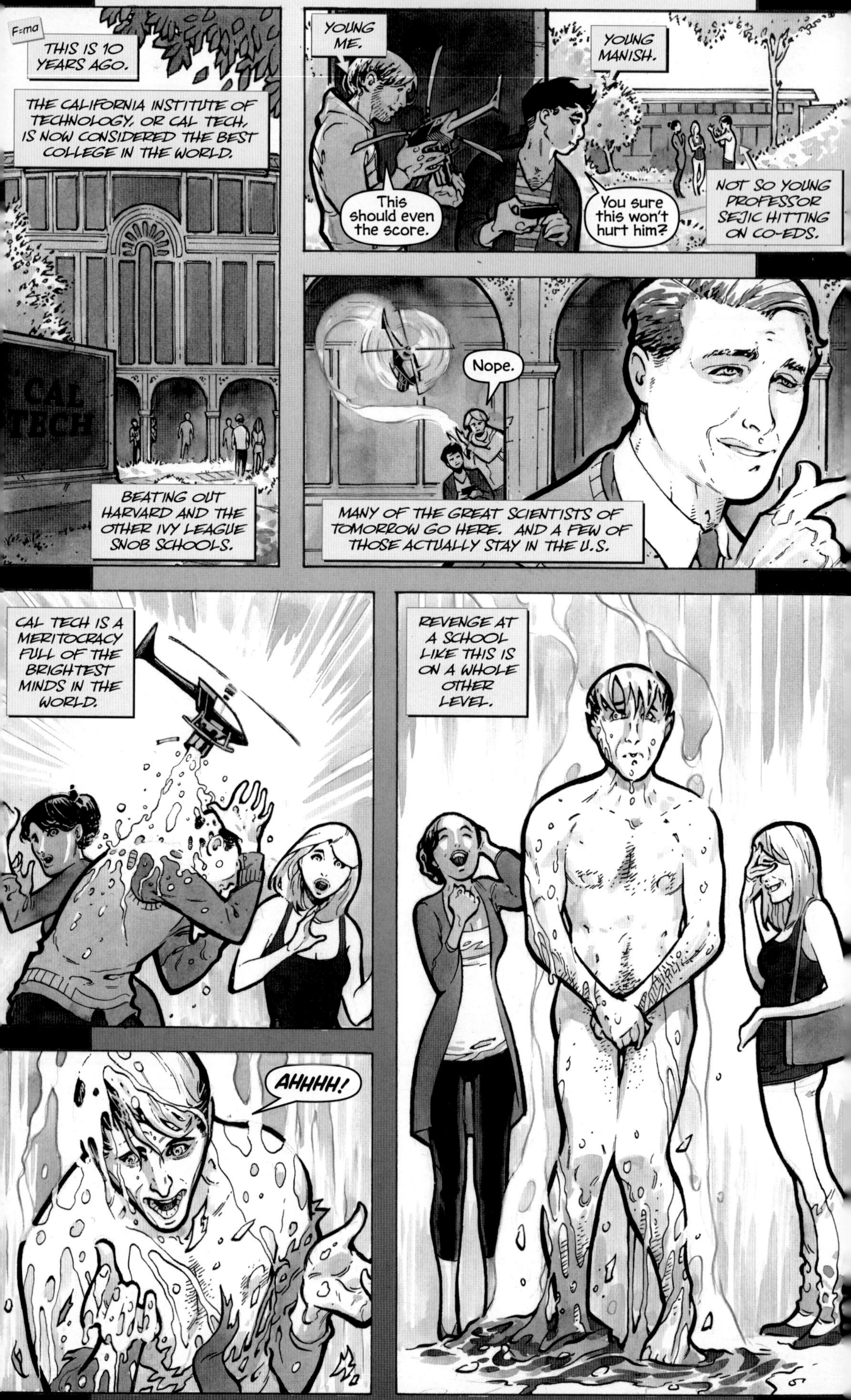
F=ma
THIS IS 10 YEARS AGO.
THE CALIFORNIA INSTITUTE OF TECHNOLOGY, OR CAL TECH, IS NOW CONSIDERED THE BEST COLLEGE IN THE WORLD.
CAL TECH
BEATING OUT HARVARD AND THE OTHER IVY LEAGUE SNOB SCHOOLS.
YOUNG ME.
This should even the score.
YOUNG MANISH.
You sure this won't hurt him?
NOT SO YOUNG PROFESSOR SEJIC HITTING ON CO-EDS.
Nope.
MANY OF THE GREAT SCIENTISTS OF TOMORROW GO HERE. AND A FEW OF THOSE ACTUALLY STAY IN THE U.S.
CAL TECH IS A MERITOCRACY FULL OF THE BRIGHTEST MINDS IN THE WORLD.
AHHHH!
REVENGE AT A SCHOOL LIKE THIS IS ON A WHOLE OTHER LEVEL.

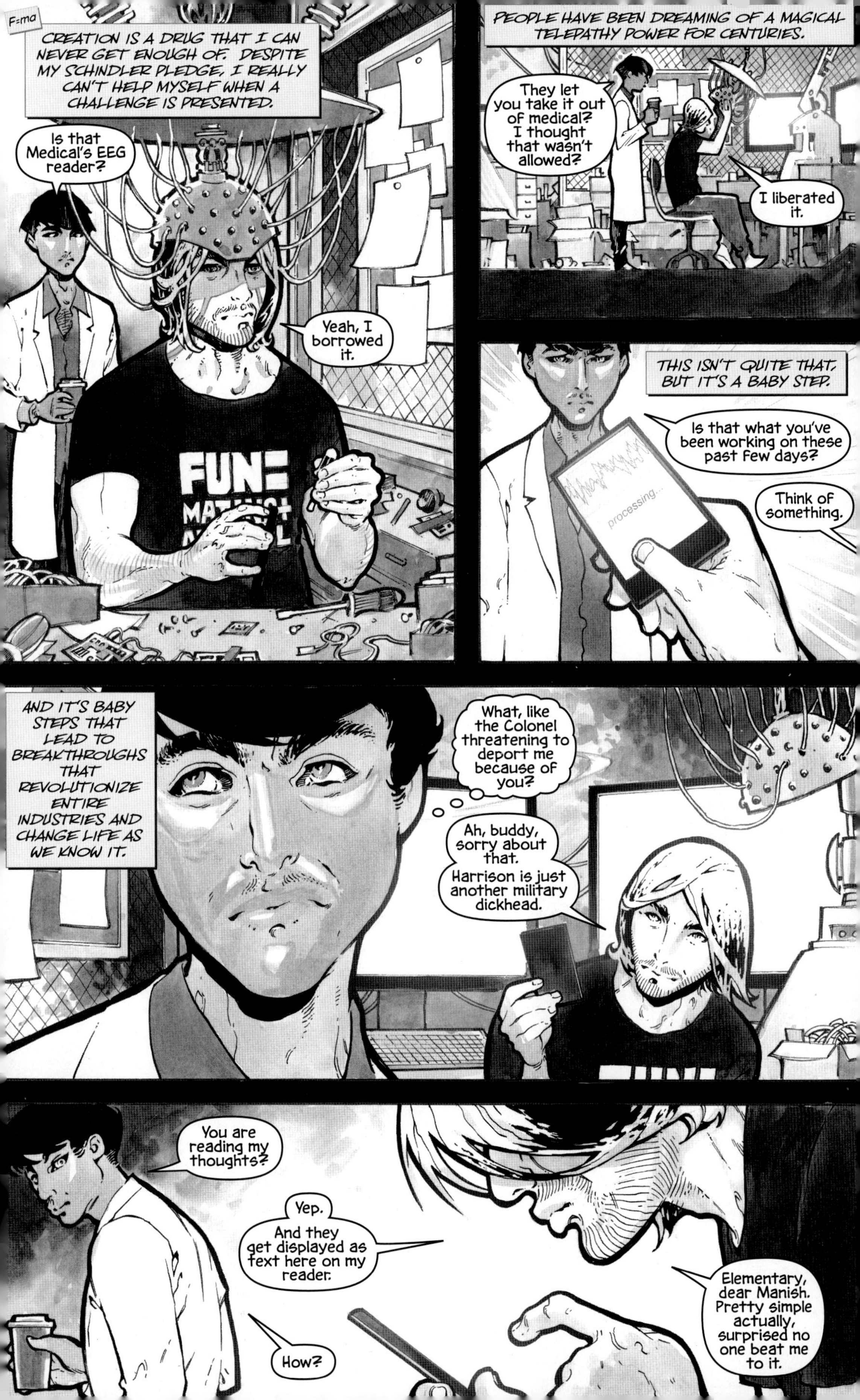
F=ma
CREATION IS A DRUG THAT I CAN NEVER GET ENOUGH OF. DESPITE MY SCHINDLER PLEDGE, I REALLY CAN'T HELP MYSELF WHEN A CHALLENGE IS PRESENTED.
Is that Medical's EEG reader?
FUN=
Yeah, I borrowed it.
PEOPLE HAVE BEEN DREAMING OF A MAGICAL TELEPATHY POWER FOR CENTURIES.
They let you take it out of medical? I thought that wasn't allowed?
I liberated it.
THIS ISN'T QUITE THAT, BUT IT'S A BABY STEP.
Is that what you've been working on these past few days?
processing...
Think of something.
AND IT'S BABY STEPS THAT LEAD TO BREAKTHROUGHS THAT REVOLUTIONIZE ENTIRE INDUSTRIES AND CHANGE LIFE AS WE KNOW IT.
What, like the Colonel threatening to deport me because of you?
Ah, buddy, sorry about that. Harrison is just another military dickhead.
You are reading my thoughts?
Yep. And they get displayed as text here on my reader.
How?
Elementary, dear Manish. Pretty simple actually, surprised no one beat me to it.

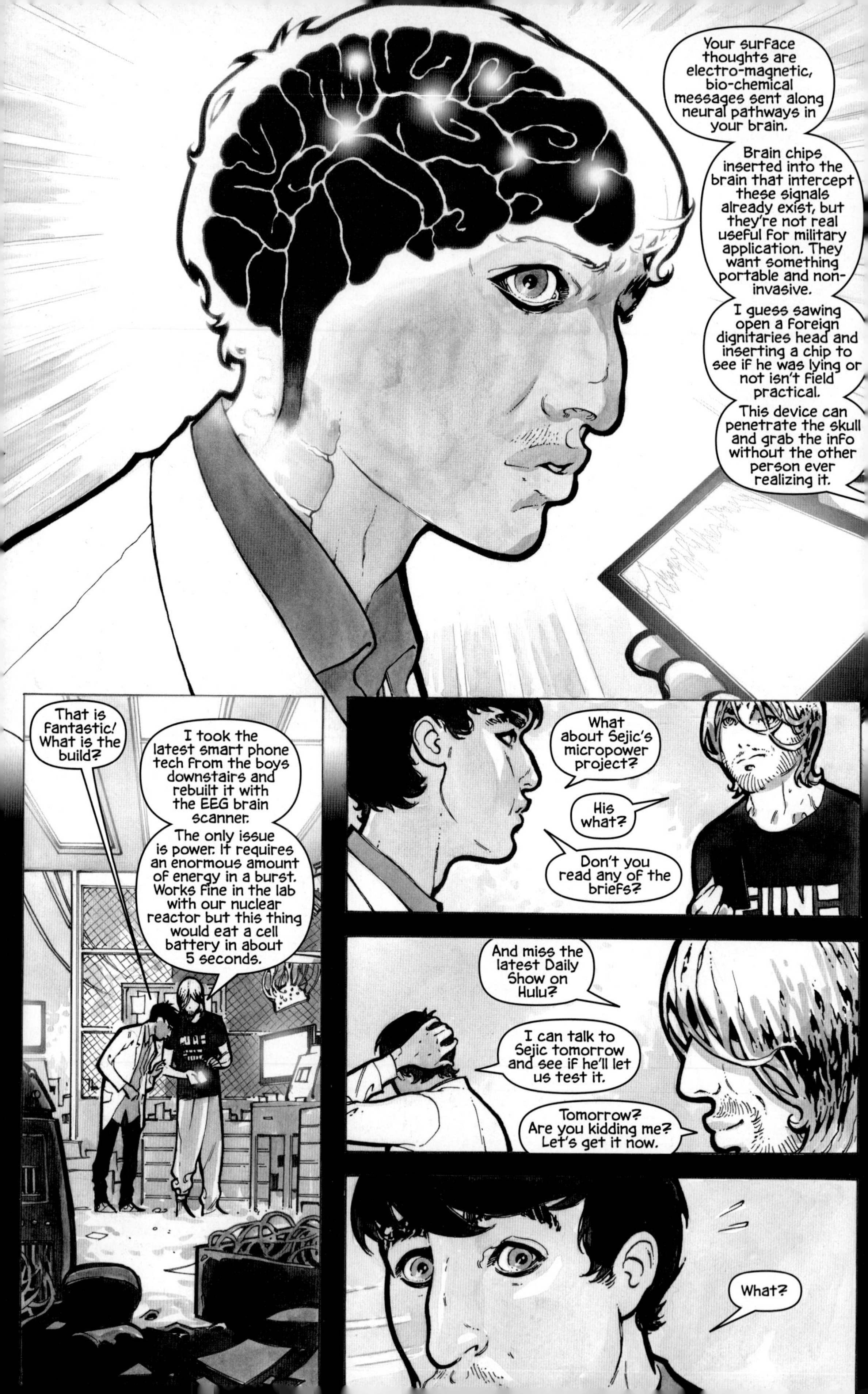
Your surface thoughts are electro-magnetic, bio-chemical messages sent along neural pathways in your brain.
Brain chips inserted into the brain that intercept these signals already exist, but they're not real useful for military application. They want something portable and non-invasive.
I guess sawing open a foreign dignitaries head and inserting a chip to see if he was lying or not isn't field practical.
This device can penetrate the skull and grab the info without the other person ever realizing it.
That is fantastic! What is the build?
I took the latest smart phone tech from the boys downstairs and rebuilt it with the EEG brain scanner.
The only issue is power. It requires an enormous amount of energy in a burst. Works fine in the lab with our nuclear reactor but this thing would eat a cell battery in about 5 seconds.
What about Sejic's micropower project?
His what?
Don't you read any of the briefs?
And miss the latest Daily Show on Hulu?
I can talk to Sejic tomorrow and see if he'll let us test it.
Tomorrow? Are you kidding me? Let's get it now.
What?

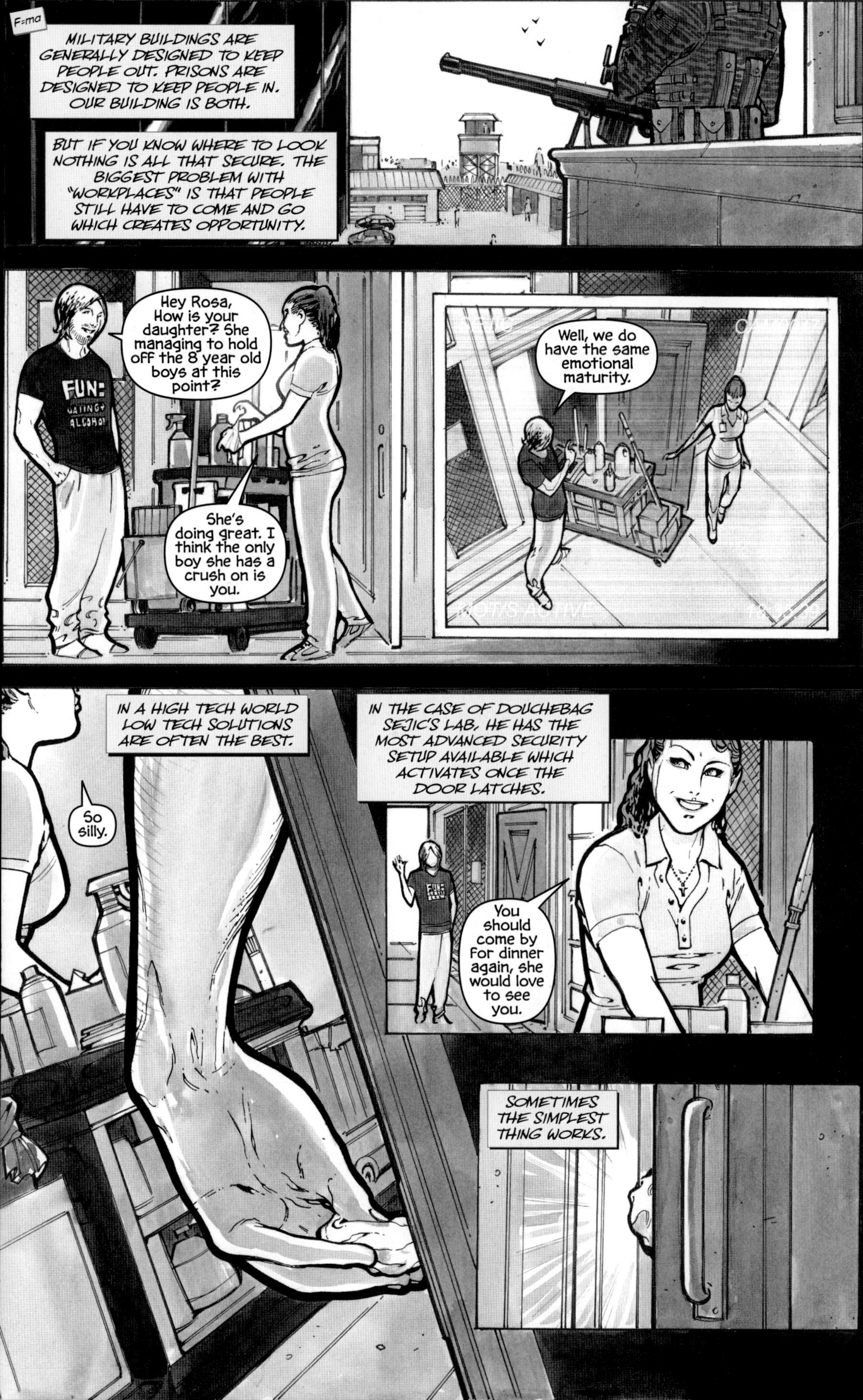
F=ma
MILITARY BUILDINGS ARE GENERALLY DESIGNED TO KEEP PEOPLE OUT. PRISONS ARE DESIGNED TO KEEP PEOPLE IN. OUR BUILDING IS BOTH.
BUT IF YOU KNOW WHERE TO LOOK NOTHING IS ALL THAT SECURE. THE BIGGEST PROBLEM WITH "WORKPLACES" IS THAT PEOPLE STILL HAVE TO COME AND GO WHICH CREATES OPPORTUNITY.
Hey Rosa, How is your daughter? She managing to hold off the 8 year old boys at this point?
She's doing great. I think the only boy she has a crush on is you.
Well, we do have the same emotional maturity.
IN A HIGH TECH WORLD LOW TECH SOLUTIONS ARE OFTEN THE BEST.
So silly.
IN THE CASE OF DOUCHEBAG SEJIC'S LAB, HE HAS THE MOST ADVANCED SECURITY SETUP AVAILABLE WHICH ACTIVATES ONCE THE DOOR LATCHES.
You should come by for dinner again, she would love to see you.
SOMETIMES THE SIMPLEST THING WORKS.

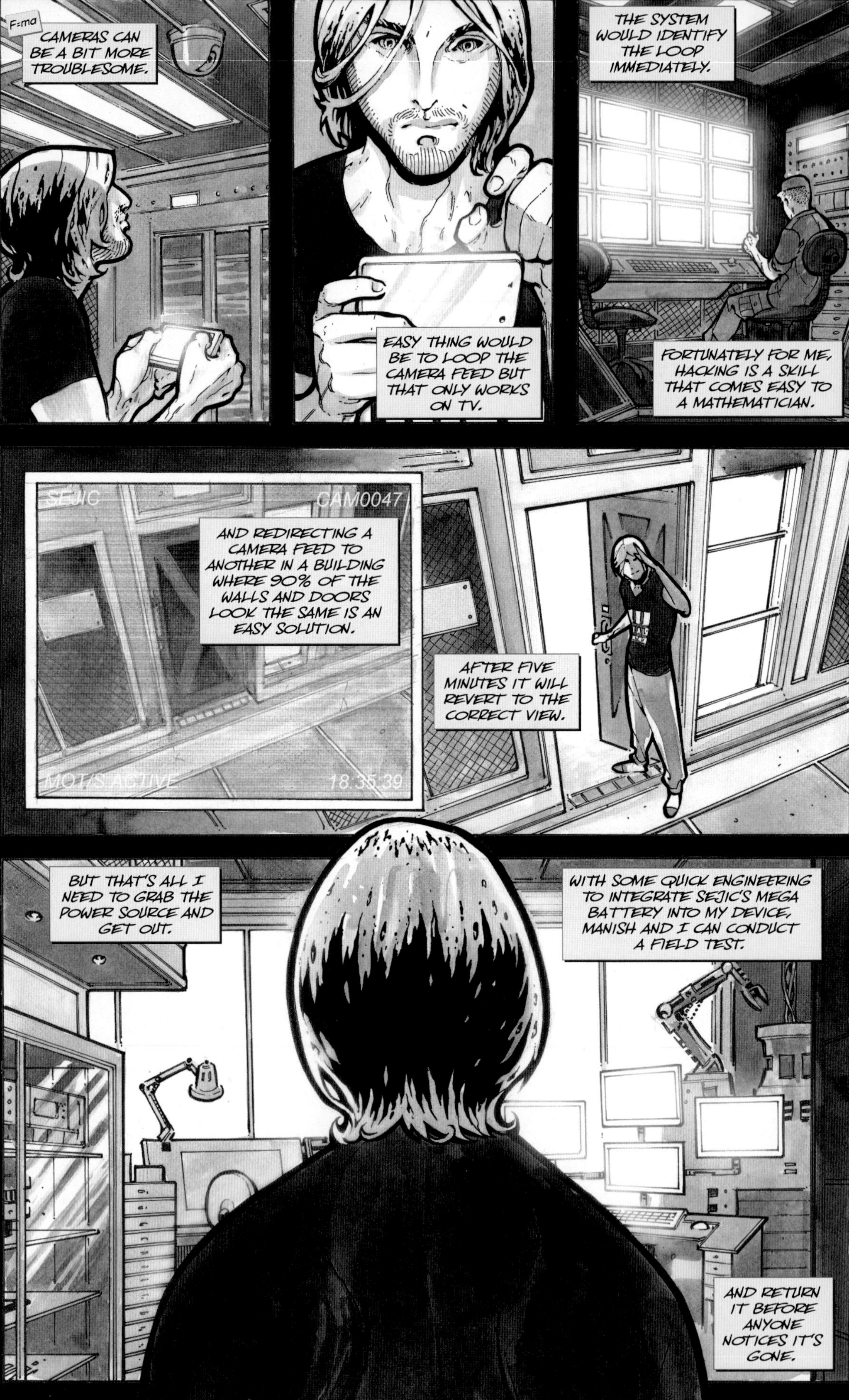
F=ma
CAMERAS CAN BE A BIT MORE TROUBLESOME.
EASY THING WOULD BE TO LOOP THE CAMERA FEED BUT THAT ONLY WORKS ON TV.
THE SYSTEM WOULD IDENTIFY THE LOOP IMMEDIATELY.
FORTUNATELY FOR ME, HACKING IS A SKILL THAT COMES EASY TO A MATHEMATICIAN.
SEJIC
CAM0047
AND REDIRECTING A CAMERA FEED TO ANOTHER IN A BUILDING WHERE 90% OF THE WALLS AND DOORS LOOK THE SAME IS AN EASY SOLUTION.
MOT/S ACTIVE
18:35:39
AFTER FIVE MINUTES IT WILL REVERT TO THE CORRECT VIEW.
BUT THAT'S ALL I NEED TO GRAB THE POWER SOURCE AND GET OUT.
WITH SOME QUICK ENGINEERING TO INTEGRATE SEJIC'S MEGA BATTERY INTO MY DEVICE, MANISH AND I CAN CONDUCT A FIELD TEST.
AND RETURN IT BEFORE ANYONE NOTICES IT'S GONE.

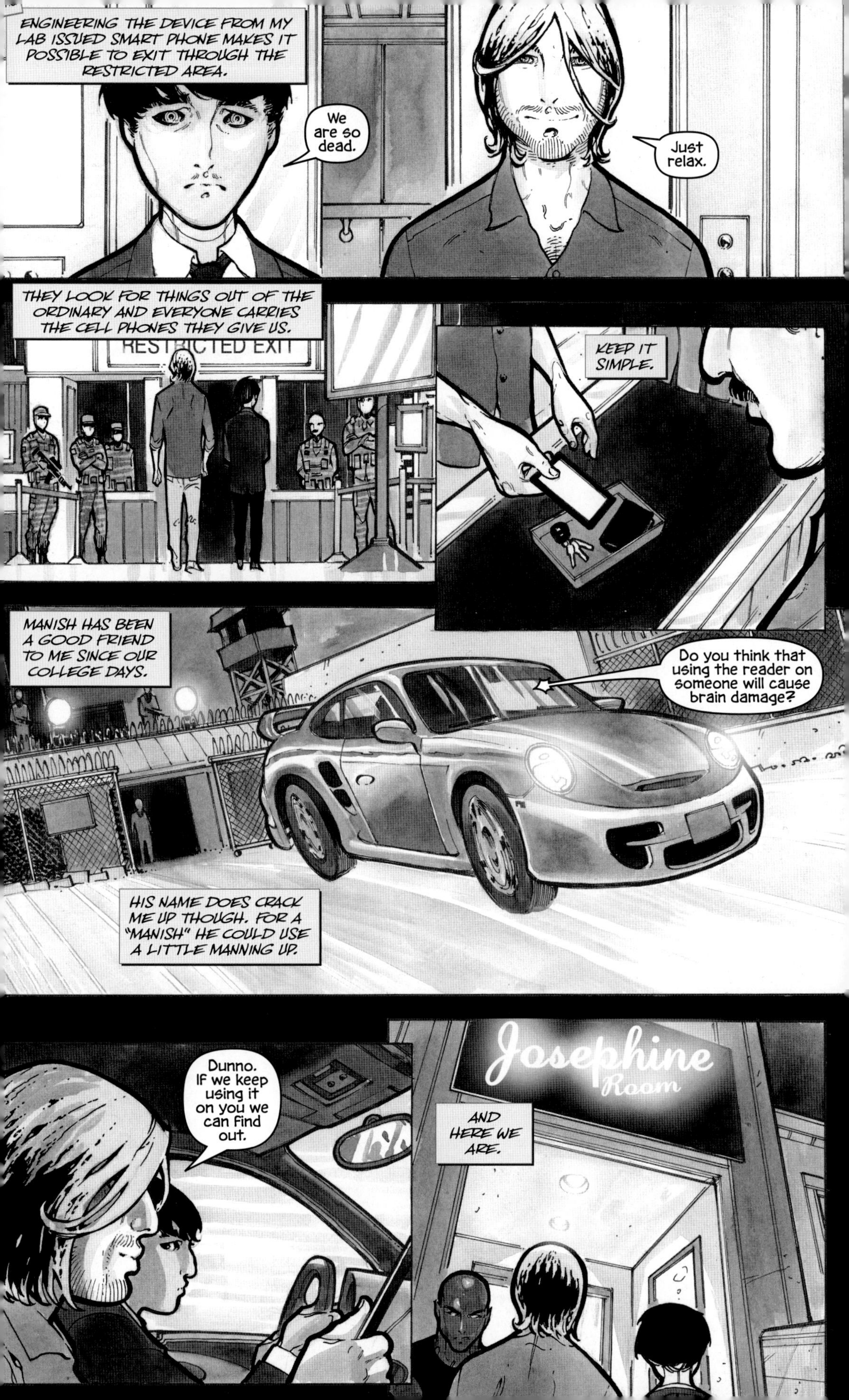
ENGINEERING THE DEVICE FROM MY LAB ISSUED SMART PHONE MAKES IT POSSIBLE TO EXIT THROUGH THE RESTRICTED AREA.
We are so dead.
Just relax.
THEY LOOK FOR THINGS OUT OF THE ORDINARY AND EVERYONE CARRIES THE CELL PHONES THEY GIVE US.
RESTRICTED EXIT
KEEP IT SIMPLE.
MANISH HAS BEEN A GOOD FRIEND TO ME SINCE OUR COLLEGE DAYS.
Do you think that using the reader on someone will cause brain damage?
HIS NAME DOES CRACK ME UP THOUGH. FOR A "MANISH" HE COULD USE A LITTLE MANNING UP.
Dunno. If we keep using it on you we can find out.
Josephine Room
AND HERE WE ARE.

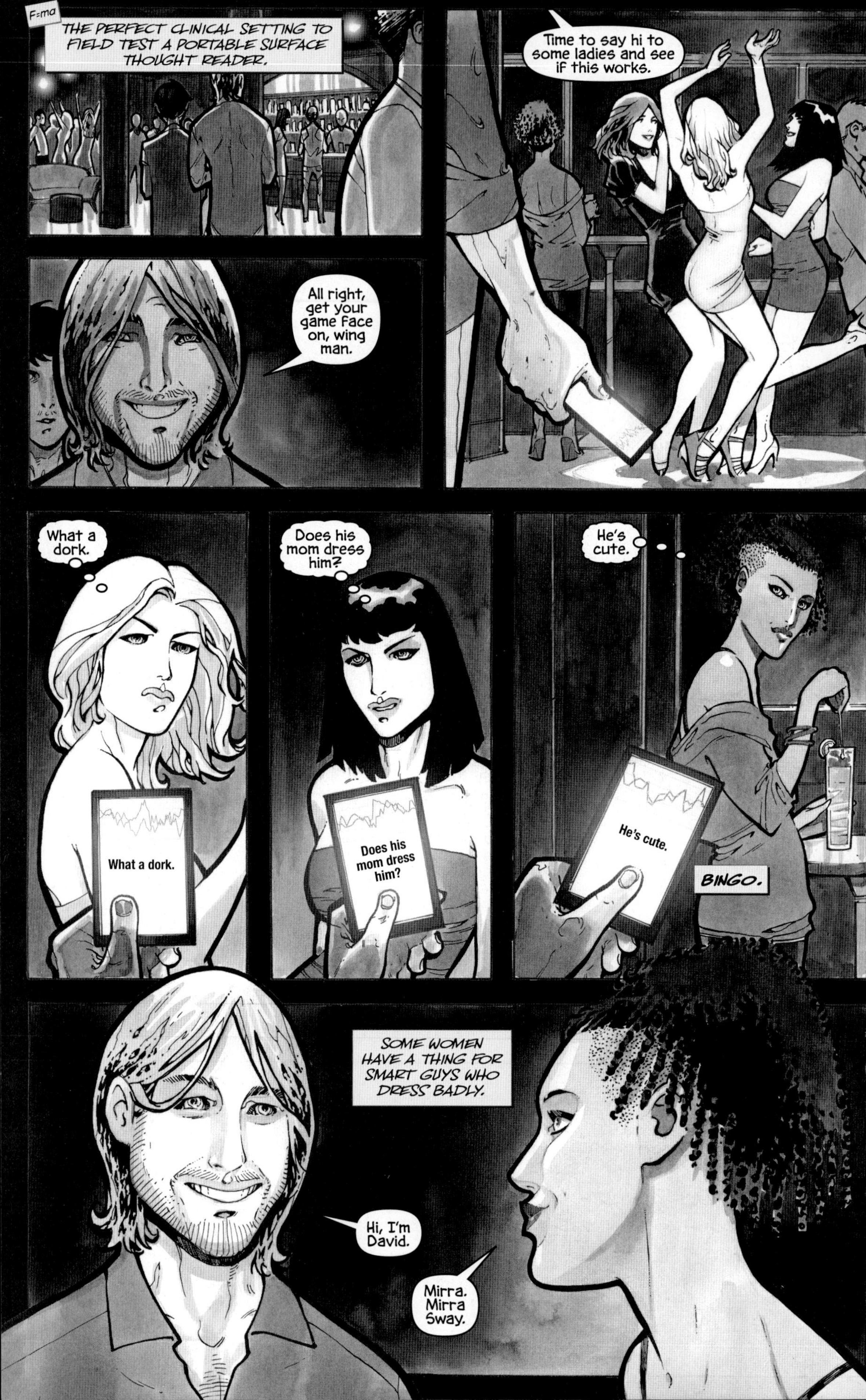
F=ma
THE PERFECT CLINICAL SETTING TO FIELD TEST A PORTABLE SURFACE THOUGHT READER.
Time to say hi to some ladies and see if this works.
All right, get your game face on, wing man.
What a dork.
What a dork.
Does his mom dress him?
Does his mom dress him?
He's cute.
He's cute.
BINGO.
SOME WOMEN HAVE A THING FOR SMART GUYS WHO DRESS BADLY.
Hi, I'm David.
Mirra. Mirra Sway.

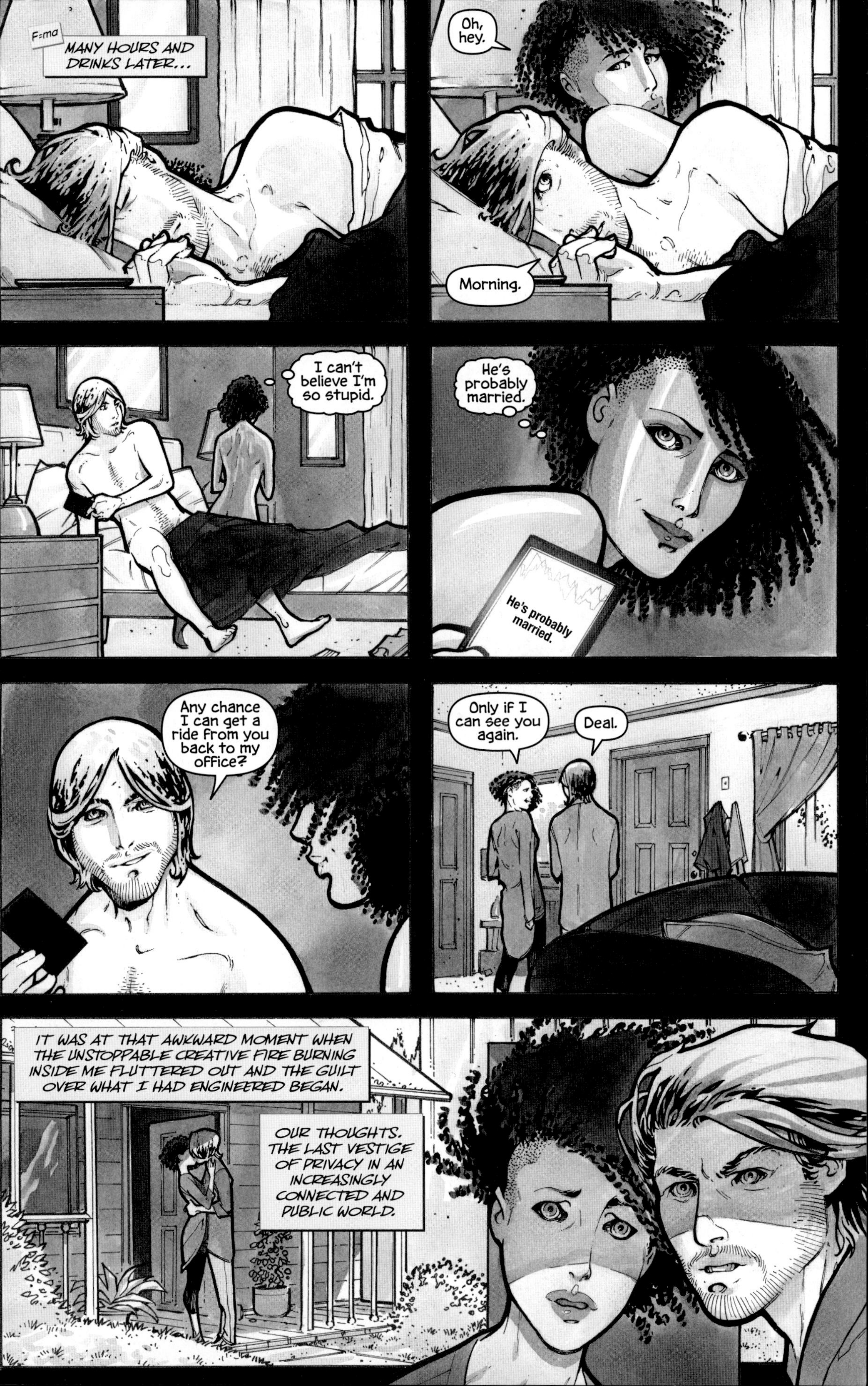
F=ma
MANY HOURS AND DRINKS LATER...
Oh, hey.
Morning.
I can't believe I'm so stupid.
He's probably married.
He's probably married.
Any chance I can get a ride from you back to my office?
Only if I can see you again.
Deal.
IT WAS AT THAT AWKWARD MOMENT WHEN THE UNSTOPPABLE CREATIVE FIRE BURNING INSIDE ME FLUTTERED OUT AND THE GUILT OVER WHAT I HAD ENGINEERED BEGAN.
OUR THOUGHTS. THE LAST VESTIGE OF PRIVACY IN AN INCREASINGLY CONNECTED AND PUBLIC WORLD.

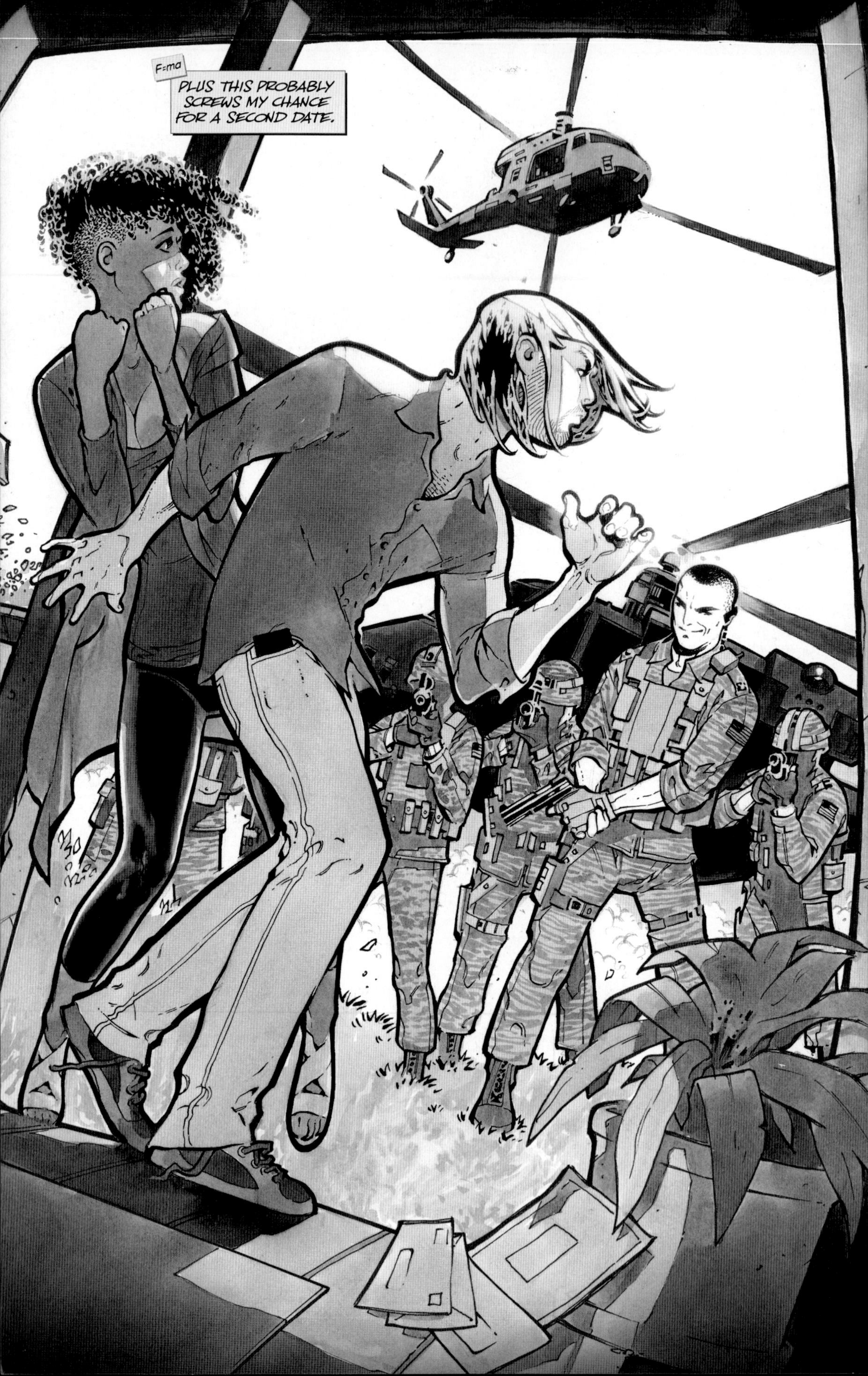
F=ma
PLUS THIS PROBABLY SCREWS MY CHANCE FOR A SECOND DATE.

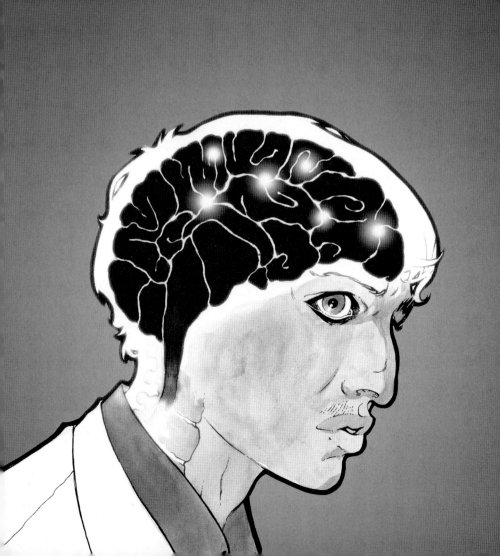

CHAPTER 2

THINK TANK

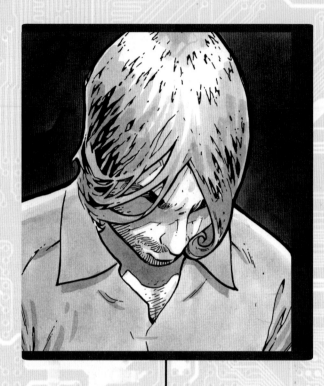

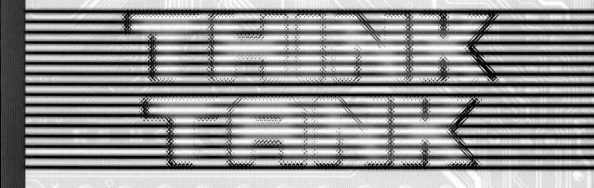

$$\vec{E} \cdot d\vec{A} = \frac{1}{\varepsilon_0} q_{in} \qquad \oint \vec{B} \cdot d\vec{A} = 0 \qquad \oint \vec{E} \cdot d\vec{\ell} = -\frac{d}{dt}\int B \, dA$$

$$\vec{B} \cdot d\vec{\ell} = \mu_0 I_{in} \qquad \vec{F} = q(\vec{v} \times \vec{B} + \vec{E}) \qquad i = \frac{dq}{dt}$$

nt charge
$$E = \frac{1}{4\pi\varepsilon_0}\frac{q}{r^2} \qquad V = \frac{1}{4\pi\varepsilon_0}\frac{q}{r} \qquad p = qd$$

$$V_f - V_i = -\int_i^f \vec{E} \cdot d\vec{s} \qquad E_x = -\frac{\partial V}{\partial x} \qquad \vec{\tau} = \vec{p} \times \vec{E}$$

$$C = \frac{Q}{V} \qquad U_E = \frac{1}{2}QV = \frac{1}{2}CV^2 = \frac{1}{2}\frac{Q^2}{C} \qquad C = \varepsilon_0 \frac{A}{d}$$

$$R = \frac{V}{i} \qquad P = Vi \qquad P = i^2 R = \frac{V^2}{R} \qquad R = \rho\frac{L}{A}$$

R_{eq}

"ANY INTELLIGENT FOOL CAN MAKE THINGS BIGGER, MORE COMPLEX, AND MORE VIOLENT. IT TAKES A TOUCH OF GENIUS--AND A LOT OF COURAGE-- TO MOVE IN THE OPPOSITE DIRECTION." ~ALBERT EINSTEIN

$$\frac{1}{R_{eq}} = \frac{1}{R_1} + \frac{1}{R_2} + \cdots \qquad C_{eq}$$

$$d\vec{B} = \frac{\mu_0}{4\pi}\frac{i \, d\vec{s} \times \hat{r}}{r^2} \qquad B = \frac{\mu_0}{2\pi}\frac{i}{r} \qquad B = \mu_0 n i \qquad \vec{\tau} = \vec{\mu} \times \vec{B}$$

$$= -\frac{d\Phi}{dt} \qquad \mathcal{E} = -N\frac{d\Phi}{dt} \qquad L = \frac{|\mathcal{E}|}{\left|\frac{di}{dt}\right|} = \frac{N\Phi}{i}$$

$$u_E = \frac{1}{2}\varepsilon_0 E^2 \qquad u_B = \frac{1}{2}\frac{B^2}{\mu_0} \qquad U_B = \frac{1}{2}Li^2$$

$$q_0 e^{-t/\tau_c} \qquad q = C\mathcal{E}(1 - e^{-t/\tau_c}) \qquad i = i_0 e^{-t/\tau_L} \qquad i = \frac{\mathcal{E}}{R}(1 - e^{-t/\tau_L})$$

$$\frac{L}{R} \qquad \tau_c = RC \qquad \mu = NiA \qquad \frac{1}{4\pi\varepsilon_0} = 9\times10^9 \qquad \frac{\mu_0}{4\pi} = 10^{-7}$$

means 10^6 \qquad μ means 10^{-6}

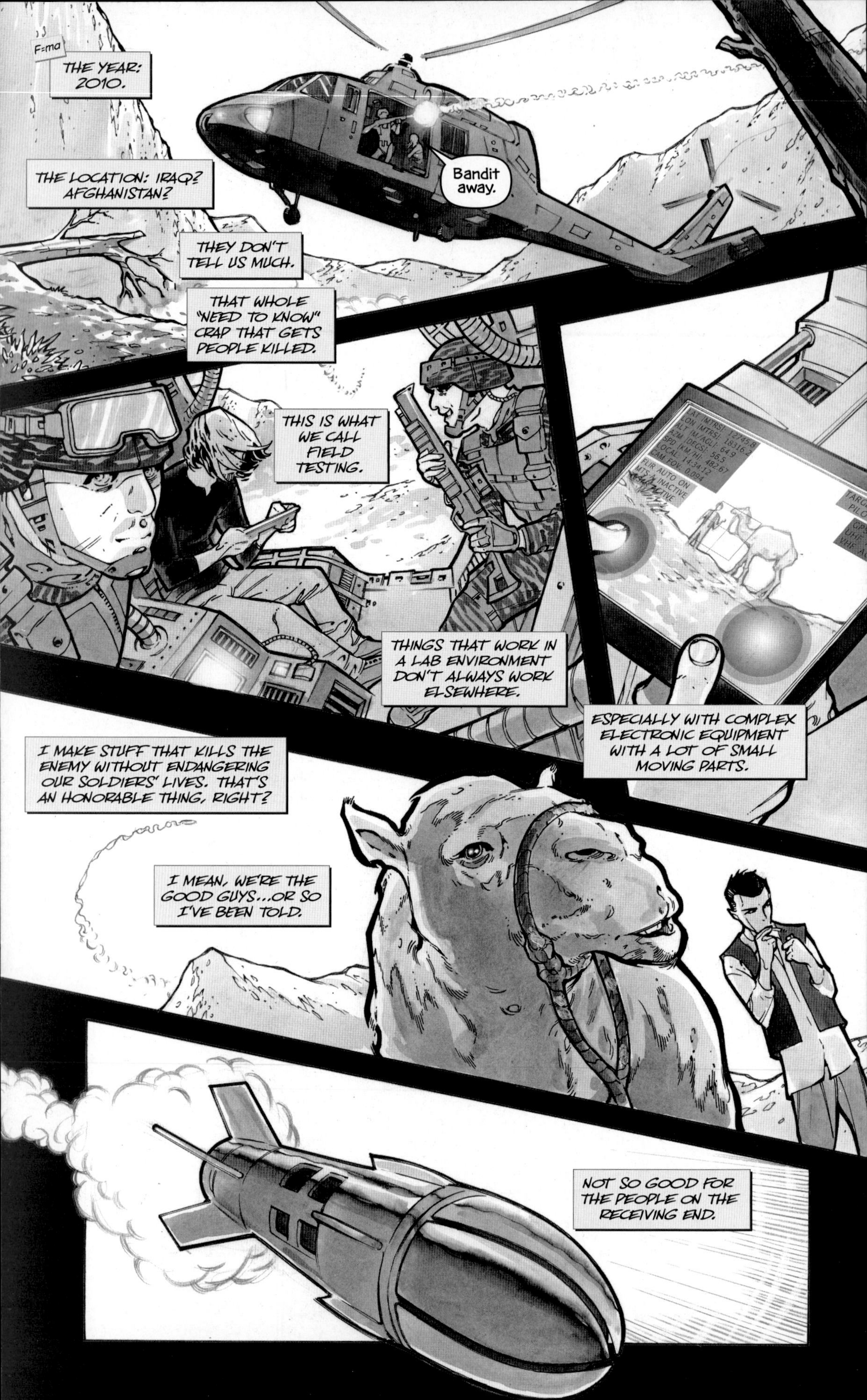
F=ma
THE YEAR: 2010.
THE LOCATION: IRAQ? AFGHANISTAN?
Bandit away.
THEY DON'T TELL US MUCH.
THAT WHOLE "NEED TO KNOW" CRAP THAT GETS PEOPLE KILLED.
THIS IS WHAT WE CALL FIELD TESTING.
THINGS THAT WORK IN A LAB ENVIRONMENT DON'T ALWAYS WORK ELSEWHERE.
ESPECIALLY WITH COMPLEX ELECTRONIC EQUIPMENT WITH A LOT OF SMALL MOVING PARTS.
I MAKE STUFF THAT KILLS THE ENEMY WITHOUT ENDANGERING OUR SOLDIERS' LIVES. THAT'S AN HONORABLE THING, RIGHT?
I MEAN, WE'RE THE GOOD GUYS...OR SO I'VE BEEN TOLD.
NOT SO GOOD FOR THE PEOPLE ON THE RECEIVING END.

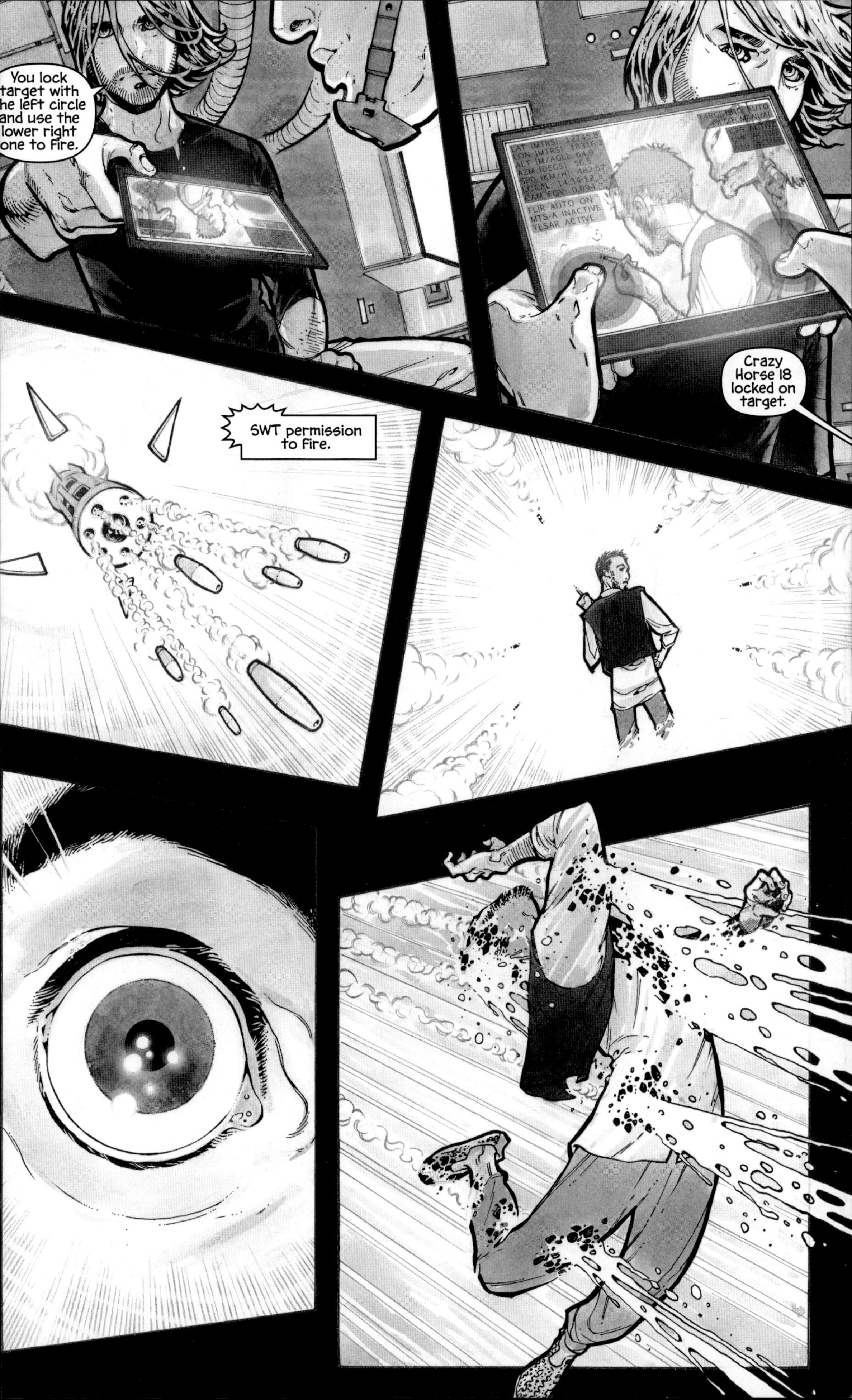
You lock target with the left circle and use the lower right one to fire.
LAT (MTRS): 12745.8
LON (MTRS): 18316.2
ALT (M/AGL): 64.9
AZM (DEGS): 56.5
SPD (KM/H): 482.67
LOCAL: 14:34:12
CAM FOV: 0.094
FLIR AUTO ON
MTS-A INACTIVE
TESAR ACTIVE
PILOT MANUAL
GPS ACTIVE
Crazy Horse 18 locked on target.
SWT permission to fire.

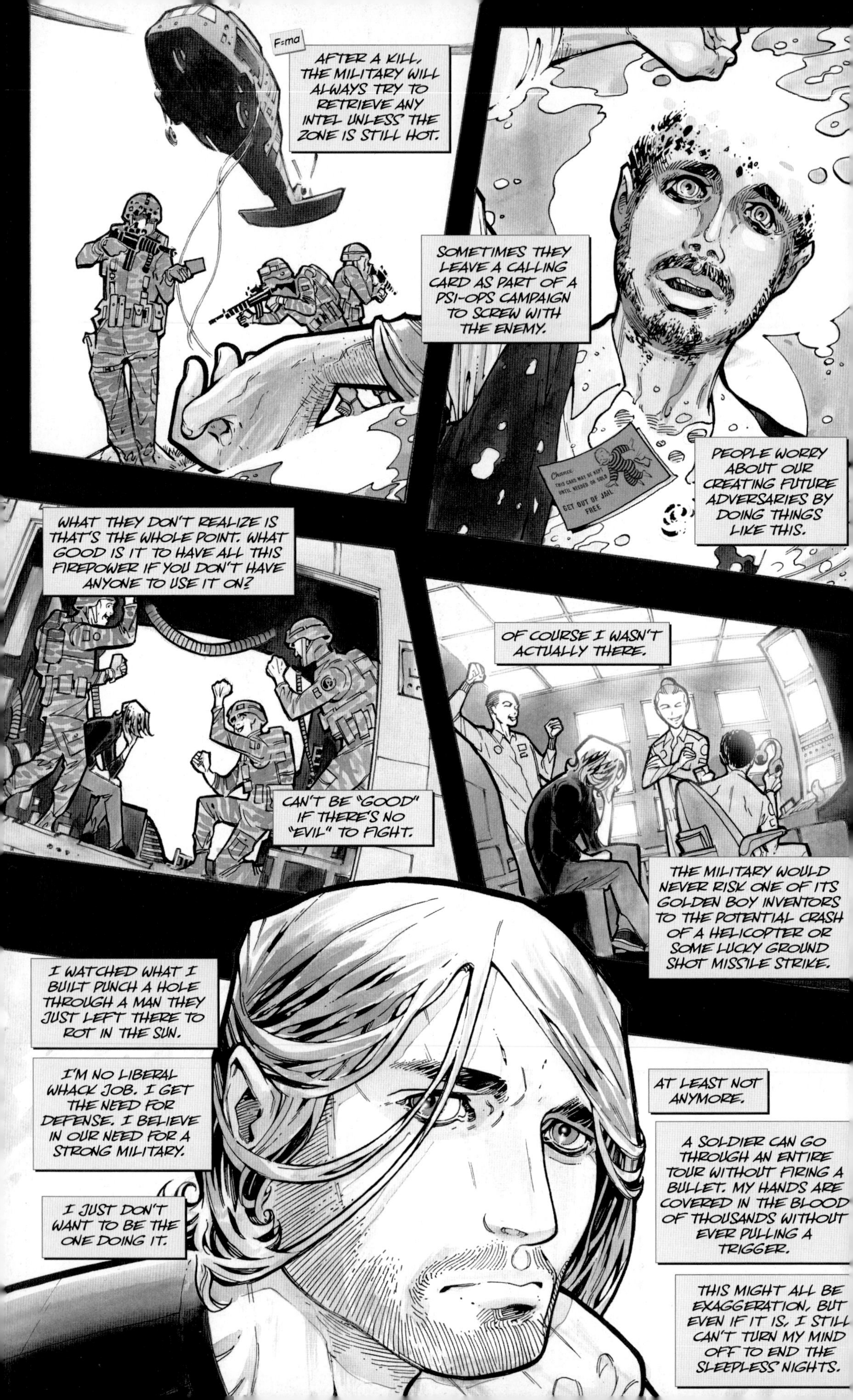
F=ma
AFTER A KILL, THE MILITARY WILL ALWAYS TRY TO RETRIEVE ANY INTEL UNLESS THE ZONE IS STILL HOT.
SOMETIMES THEY LEAVE A CALLING CARD AS PART OF A PSI-OPS CAMPAIGN TO SCREW WITH THE ENEMY.
Chance.
THIS CARD MAY BE KEPT UNTIL NEEDED OR SOLD
GET OUT OF JAIL FREE
PEOPLE WORRY ABOUT OUR CREATING FUTURE ADVERSARIES BY DOING THINGS LIKE THIS.
WHAT THEY DON'T REALIZE IS THAT'S THE WHOLE POINT. WHAT GOOD IS IT TO HAVE ALL THIS FIREPOWER IF YOU DON'T HAVE ANYONE TO USE IT ON?
CAN'T BE "GOOD" IF THERE'S NO "EVIL" TO FIGHT.
OF COURSE I WASN'T ACTUALLY THERE.
THE MILITARY WOULD NEVER RISK ONE OF ITS GOLDEN BOY INVENTORS TO THE POTENTIAL CRASH OF A HELICOPTER OR SOME LUCKY GROUND SHOT MISSILE STRIKE.
I WATCHED WHAT I BUILT PUNCH A HOLE THROUGH A MAN THEY JUST LEFT THERE TO ROT IN THE SUN.
I'M NO LIBERAL WHACK JOB. I GET THE NEED FOR DEFENSE. I BELIEVE IN OUR NEED FOR A STRONG MILITARY.
I JUST DON'T WANT TO BE THE ONE DOING IT.
AT LEAST NOT ANYMORE.
A SOLDIER CAN GO THROUGH AN ENTIRE TOUR WITHOUT FIRING A BULLET. MY HANDS ARE COVERED IN THE BLOOD OF THOUSANDS WITHOUT EVER PULLING A TRIGGER.
THIS MIGHT ALL BE EXAGGERATION, BUT EVEN IF IT IS, I STILL CAN'T TURN MY MIND OFF TO END THE SLEEPLESS NIGHTS.

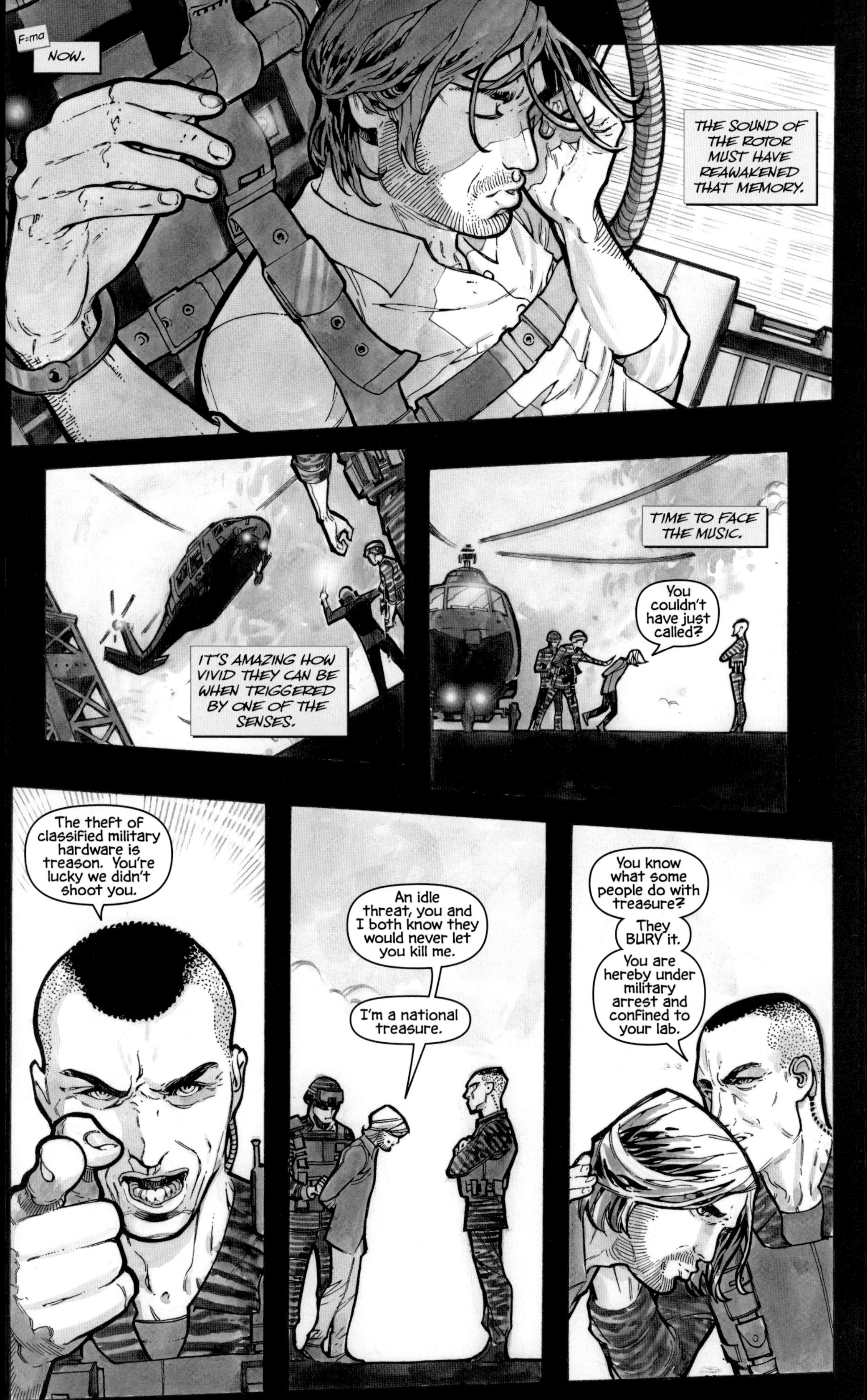
F=ma
NOW.
THE SOUND OF THE ROTOR MUST HAVE REAWAKENED THAT MEMORY.
IT'S AMAZING HOW VIVID THEY CAN BE WHEN TRIGGERED BY ONE OF THE SENSES.
TIME TO FACE THE MUSIC.
You couldn't have just called?
The theft of classified military hardware is treason. You're lucky we didn't shoot you.
An idle threat, you and I both know they would never let you kill me.
I'm a national treasure.
You know what some people do with treasure?
They BURY it.
You are hereby under military arrest and confined to your lab.

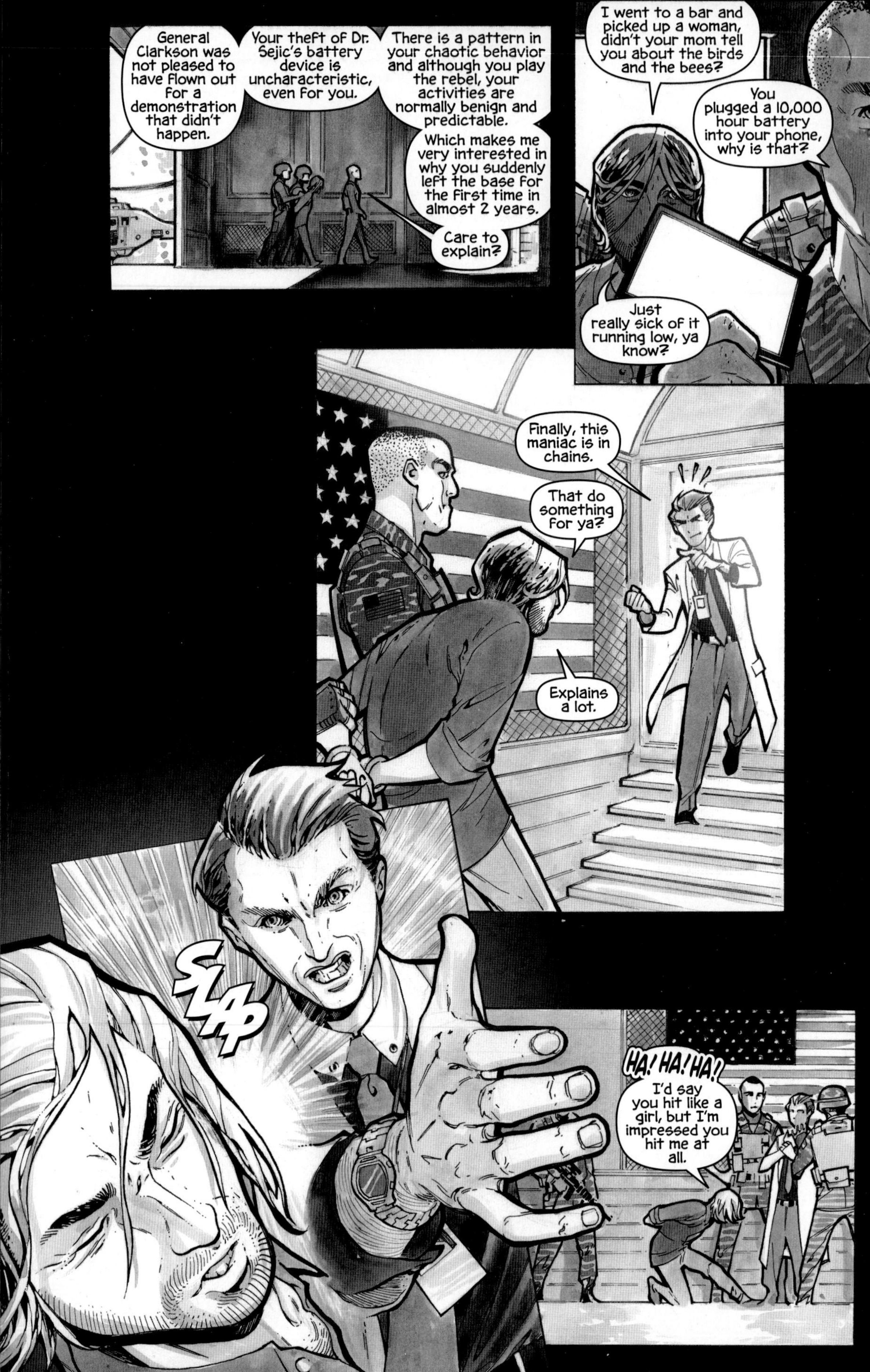
General Clarkson was not pleased to have flown out for a demonstration that didn't happen.
Your theft of Dr. Sejic's battery device is uncharacteristic, even for you.
There is a pattern in your chaotic behavior and although you play the rebel, your activities are normally benign and predictable.
Which makes me very interested in why you suddenly left the base for the first time in almost 2 years.
Care to explain?
I went to a bar and picked up a woman, didn't your mom tell you about the birds and the bees?
You plugged a 10,000 hour battery into your phone, why is that?
Just really sick of it running low, ya know?
Finally, this maniac is in chains.
That do something for ya?
Explains a lot.
SLAP
HA! HA! HA!
I'd say you hit like a girl, but I'm impressed you hit me at all.

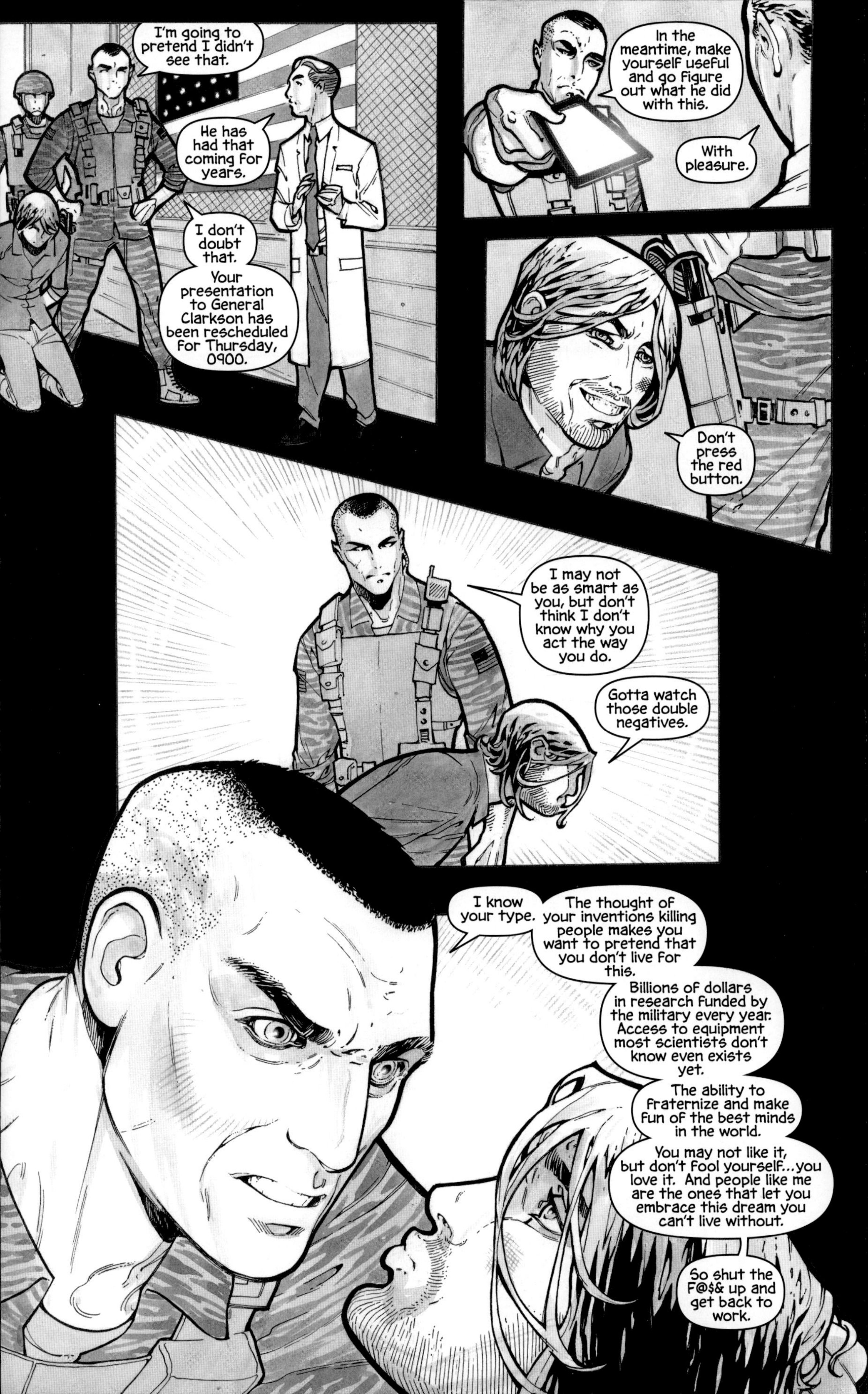
I'm going to pretend I didn't see that.
He has had that coming for years.
I don't doubt that.
Your presentation to General Clarkson has been rescheduled for Thursday, 0900.
In the meantime, make yourself useful and go figure out what he did with this.
With pleasure.
Don't press the red button.
I may not be as smart as you, but don't think I don't know why you act the way you do.
Gotta watch those double negatives.
I know your type.
The thought of your inventions killing people makes you want to pretend that you don't live for this.
Billions of dollars in research funded by the military every year. Access to equipment most scientists don't know even exists yet.
The ability to fraternize and make fun of the best minds in the world.
You may not like it, but don't fool yourself...you love it. And people like me are the ones that let you embrace this dream you can't live without.
So shut the F@$& up and get back to work.

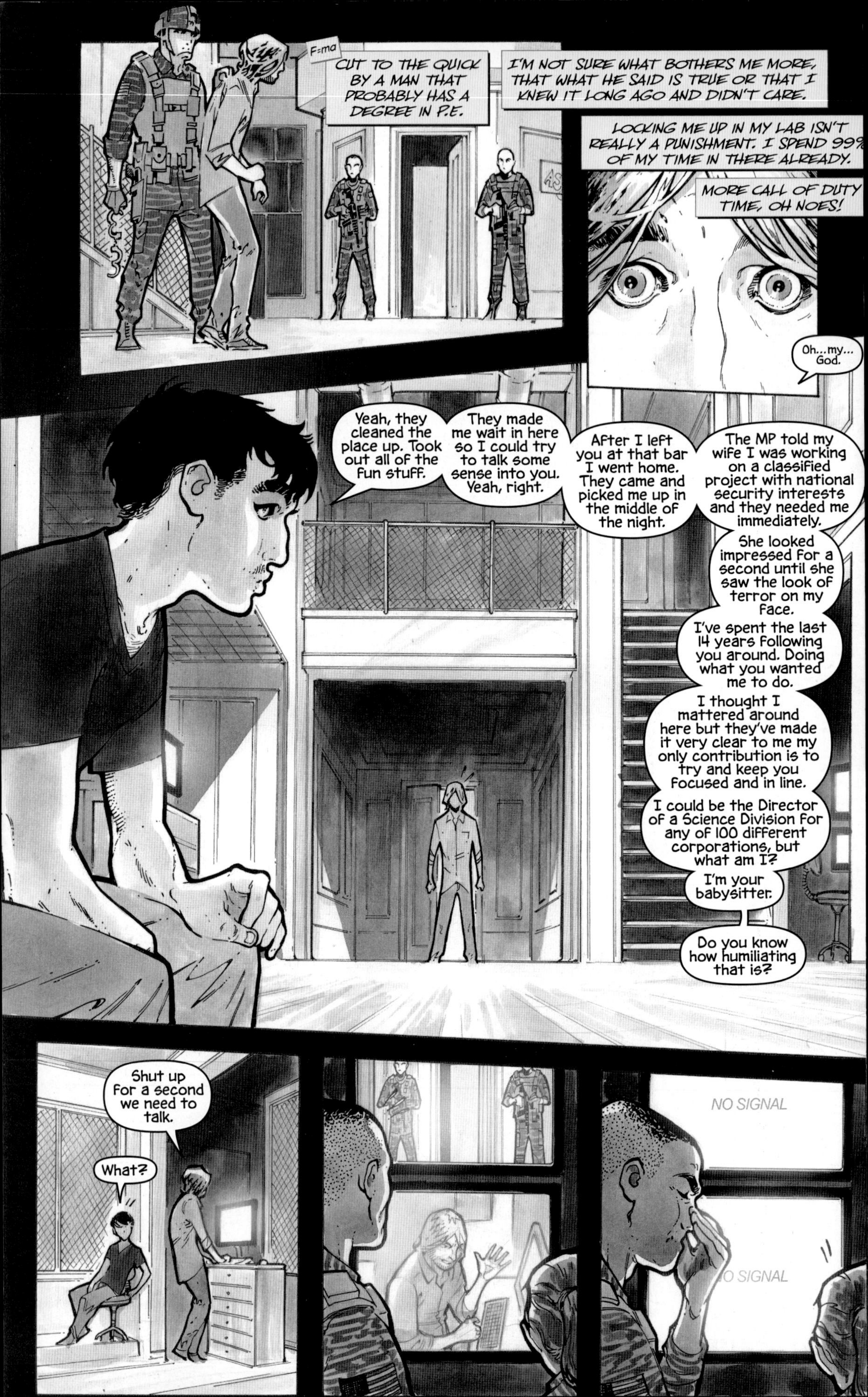

F=ma
CUT TO THE QUICK BY A MAN THAT PROBABLY HAS A DEGREE IN P.E.
I'M NOT SURE WHAT BOTHERS ME MORE, THAT WHAT HE SAID IS TRUE OR THAT I KNEW IT LONG AGO AND DIDN'T CARE.
LOCKING ME UP IN MY LAB ISN'T REALLY A PUNISHMENT. I SPEND 99% OF MY TIME IN THERE ALREADY.
MORE CALL OF DUTY TIME, OH NOES!
Oh...my... God.
Yeah, they cleaned the place up. Took out all of the fun stuff.
They made me wait in here so I could try to talk some sense into you. Yeah, right.
After I left you at that bar I went home. They came and picked me up in the middle of the night.
The MP told my wife I was working on a classified project with national security interests and they needed me immediately.
She looked impressed for a second until she saw the look of terror on my face.
I've spent the last 14 years following you around. Doing what you wanted me to do.
I thought I mattered around here but they've made it very clear to me my only contribution is to try and keep you focused and in line.
I could be the Director of a Science Division for any of 100 different corporations, but what am I?
I'm your babysitter.
Do you know how humiliating that is?
Shut up for a second we need to talk.
What?
NO SIGNAL

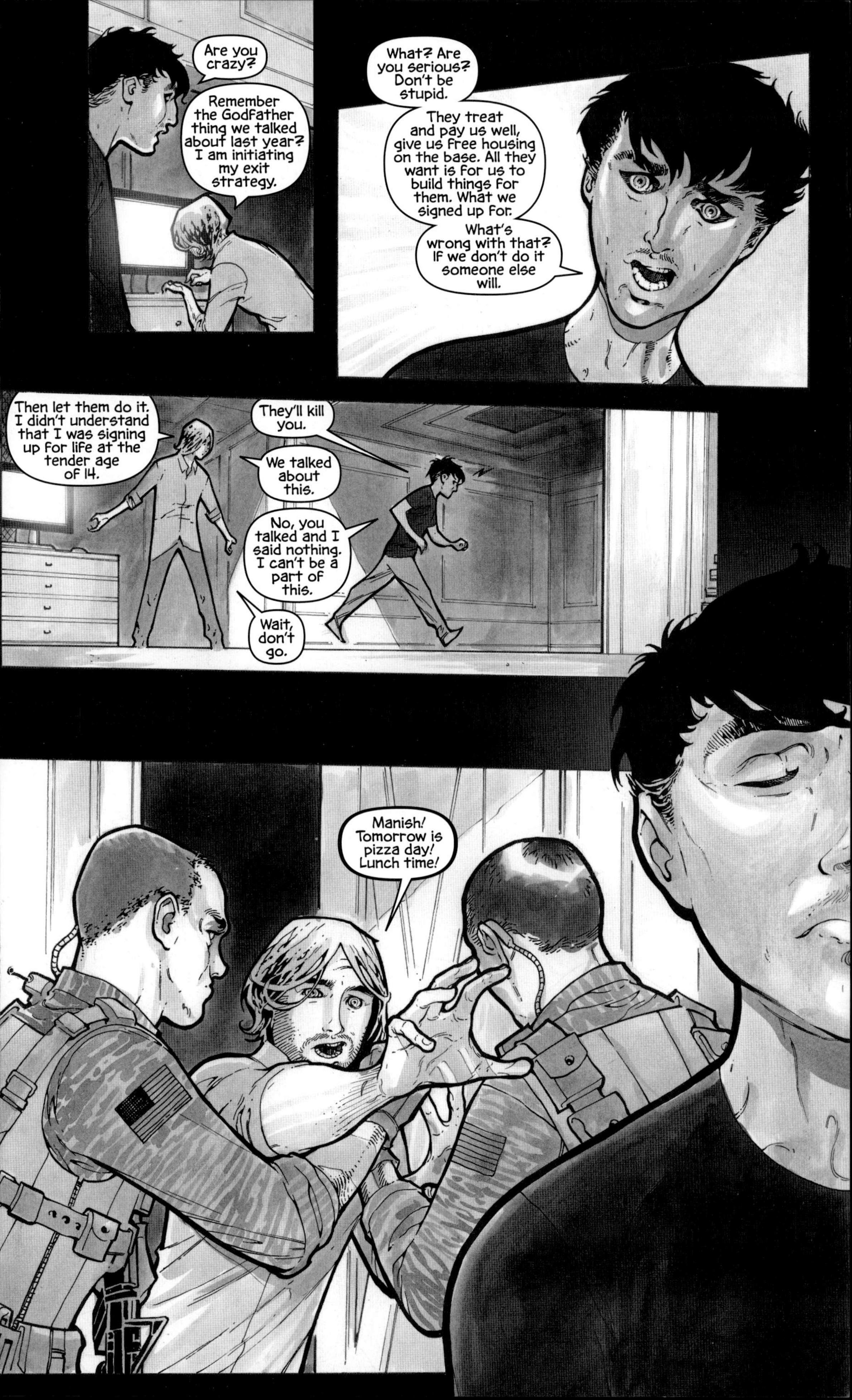

Are you crazy?
Remember the Godfather thing we talked about last year? I am initiating my exit strategy.
What? Are you serious? Don't be stupid.
They treat and pay us well, give us free housing on the base. All they want is for us to build things for them. What we signed up for.
What's wrong with that? If we don't do it someone else will.
Then let them do it. I didn't understand that I was signing up for life at the tender age of 14.
They'll kill you.
We talked about this.
No, you talked and I said nothing. I can't be a part of this.
Wait, don't go.
Manish! Tomorrow is pizza day! Lunch time!

F=ma

AND SO IT BEGINS.

8AM TUESDAY.

I HAVE 30 HOURS TO ESCAPE THE MOST SECURE FACILITY EVER BUILT, NESTLED AT THE HEART OF FORT GEORGE MEADE, ONE OF THE MOST HEAVILY FORTIFIED MILITARY BASES IN THE WORLD AND THEN VANISH FROM THE FARSEEING EYES OF THE U.S. GOVERNMENT AND ITS ALLIES.

EASY PEASY, EH?

WHAT DO THEY HAVE?

SECURITY GUARDS.

MILITARY WORKING DOGS.

PHYSICAL BARRIERS.

BADGING SYSTEMS.

LOCKING DEVICES.

INTRUSION DETECTION SYSTEMS.

SECURITY LIGHTING.

SURVEILLANCE SYSTEMS.

ACCESS CONTROL DEVICES.

FACILITY HARDENING.

IF THAT SOUNDS LIKE IT CAME OUT OF A HANDBOOK IT DID.

IF THERE'S ONE THING THE MILITARY CAN BE COUNTED ON, IT'S TO FOLLOW PROTOCOL.

AND THAT'S WHERE THEY'RE WEAK.

I COULD HAVE DISAPPEARED LAST NIGHT, BUT THIS DAVID WANTS TO TEACH GOLIATH A LESSON.

AND I'VE BEEN PLANNING THIS FOR YEARS.

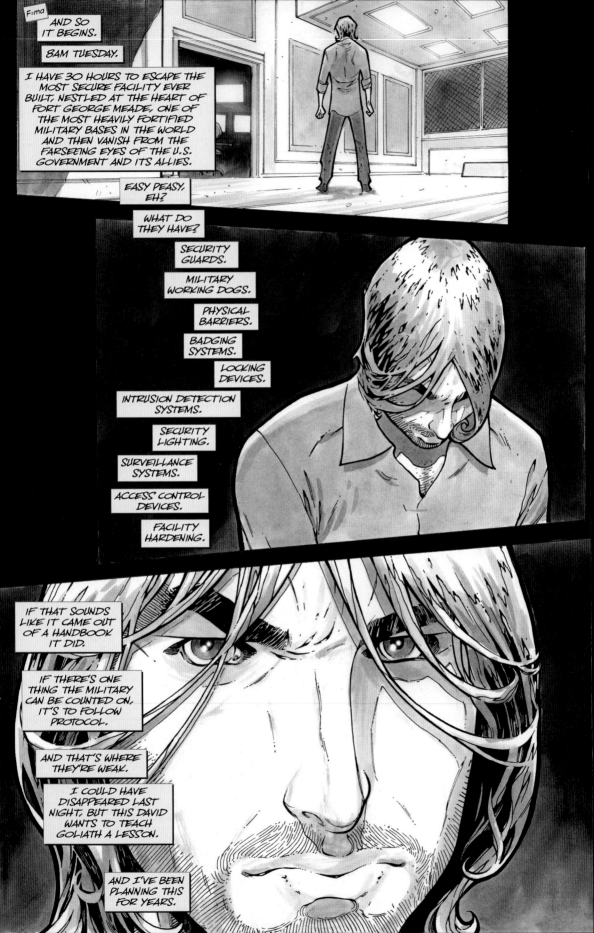

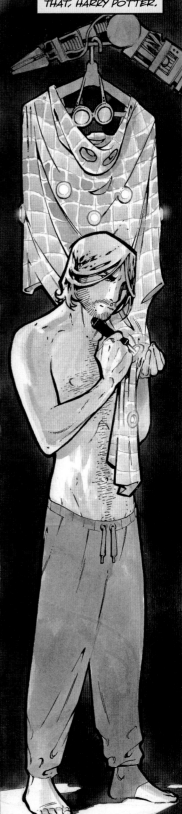

LIKE THE EMPEROR, OVERCONFIDENCE IS DEFINITELY MY WEAKNESS.

I'VE NEVER FAILED ON A PROJECT.

PART OF THAT IS A SELECTIVE CHOICE IN ENGAGING IN THINGS I KNOW I CAN DO.

BUT ANOTHER BIG PART IS AN OBSTINATE REFUSAL TO CONCEDE DEFEAT...EVER.

"ALL OF MY "FAILED" PROJECTS WORK, OF COURSE, AND THEY WILL ALL PLAY A KEY ROLE IN MY ESCAPE.

AN ELECTROMAGNETIC PULSE GRENADE, 5 METER RADIUS.

A SUGGESTION GAS THAT WILL ENSURE THAT THESE AREN'T THE DROIDS THEY'RE LOOKING FOR.

AND MY CHAMELEON CLOAK THAT TAKES MILLIONS OF PHOTOGRAPHS EVERY SECOND OF THE AREA RIGHT BEHIND IT AND PROJECTS IT TO THE FRONT GIVING AN ILLUSORY LIGHT-BENDING EFFECT.

FANCY LANGUAGE FOR BEING INVISIBLE. EAT THAT, HARRY POTTER.

F=ma

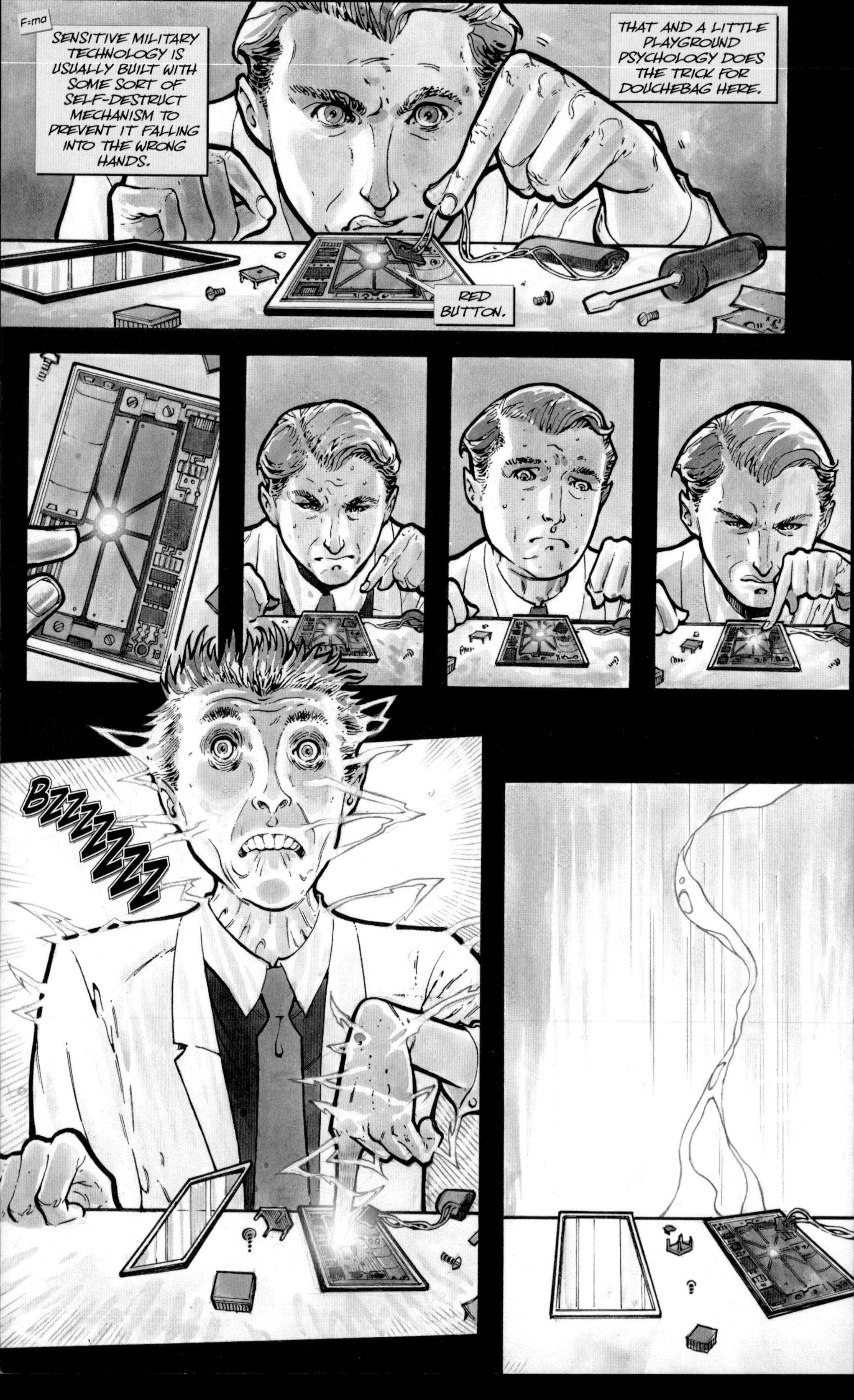
F=ma
SENSITIVE MILITARY TECHNOLOGY IS USUALLY BUILT WITH SOME SORT OF SELF-DESTRUCT MECHANISM TO PREVENT IT FALLING INTO THE WRONG HANDS.
THAT AND A LITTLE PLAYGROUND PSYCHOLOGY DOES THE TRICK FOR DOUCHEBAG HERE.
RED BUTTON.
BZZZZZZZ

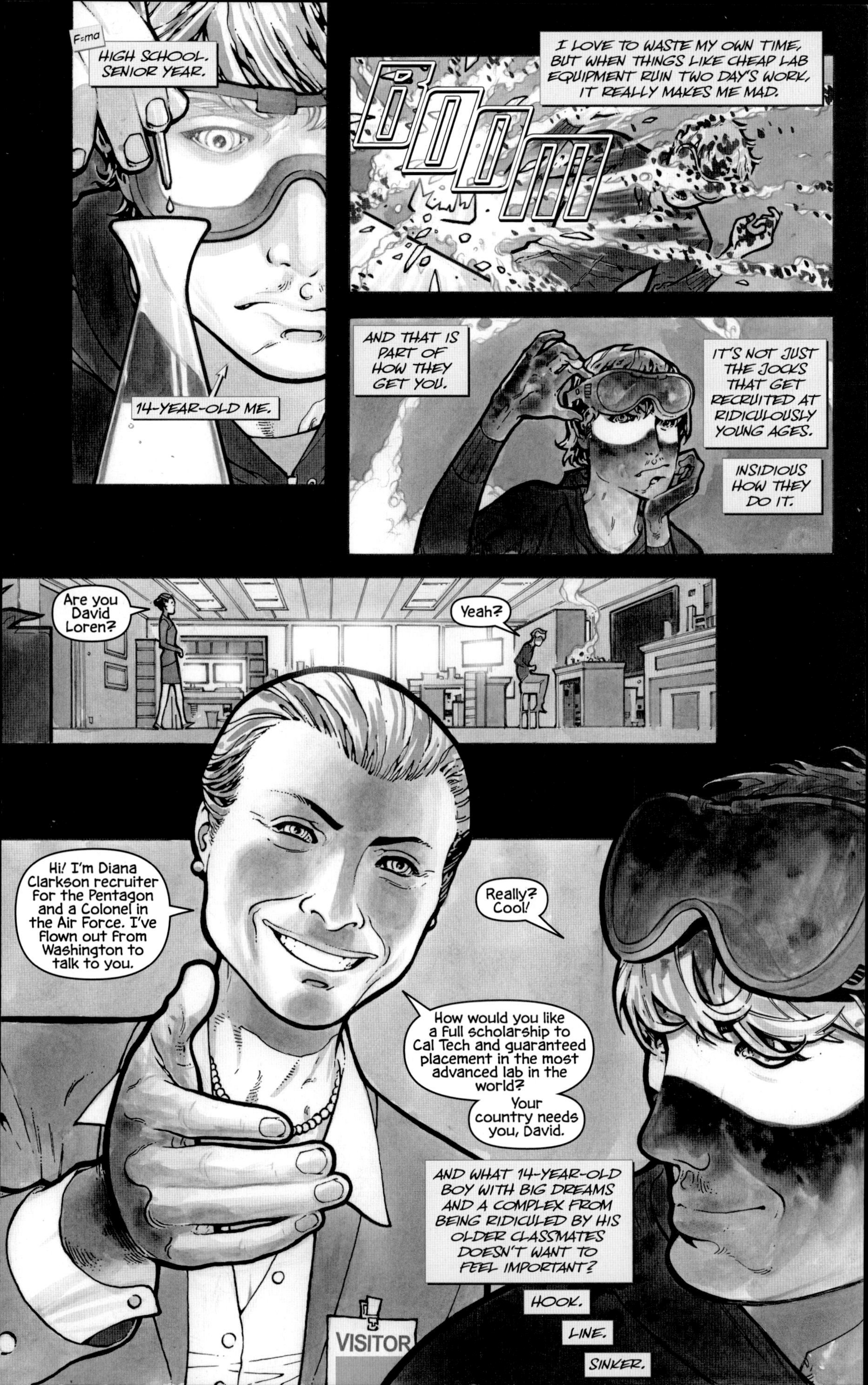
F=ma
HIGH SCHOOL. SENIOR YEAR.
14-YEAR-OLD ME.
I LOVE TO WASTE MY OWN TIME, BUT WHEN THINGS LIKE CHEAP LAB EQUIPMENT RUIN TWO DAY'S WORK, IT REALLY MAKES ME MAD.
BOOOM
AND THAT IS PART OF HOW THEY GET YOU.
IT'S NOT JUST THE JOCKS THAT GET RECRUITED AT RIDICULOUSLY YOUNG AGES.
INSIDIOUS HOW THEY DO IT.
Are you David Loren?
Yeah?
Hi! I'm Diana Clarkson recruiter for the Pentagon and a Colonel in the Air Force. I've flown out from Washington to talk to you.
Really? Cool!
How would you like a full scholarship to Cal Tech and guaranteed placement in the most advanced lab in the world?
Your country needs you, David.
AND WHAT 14-YEAR-OLD BOY WITH BIG DREAMS AND A COMPLEX FROM BEING RIDICULED BY HIS OLDER CLASSMATES DOESN'T WANT TO FEEL IMPORTANT?
HOOK.
LINE.
SINKER.
VISITOR

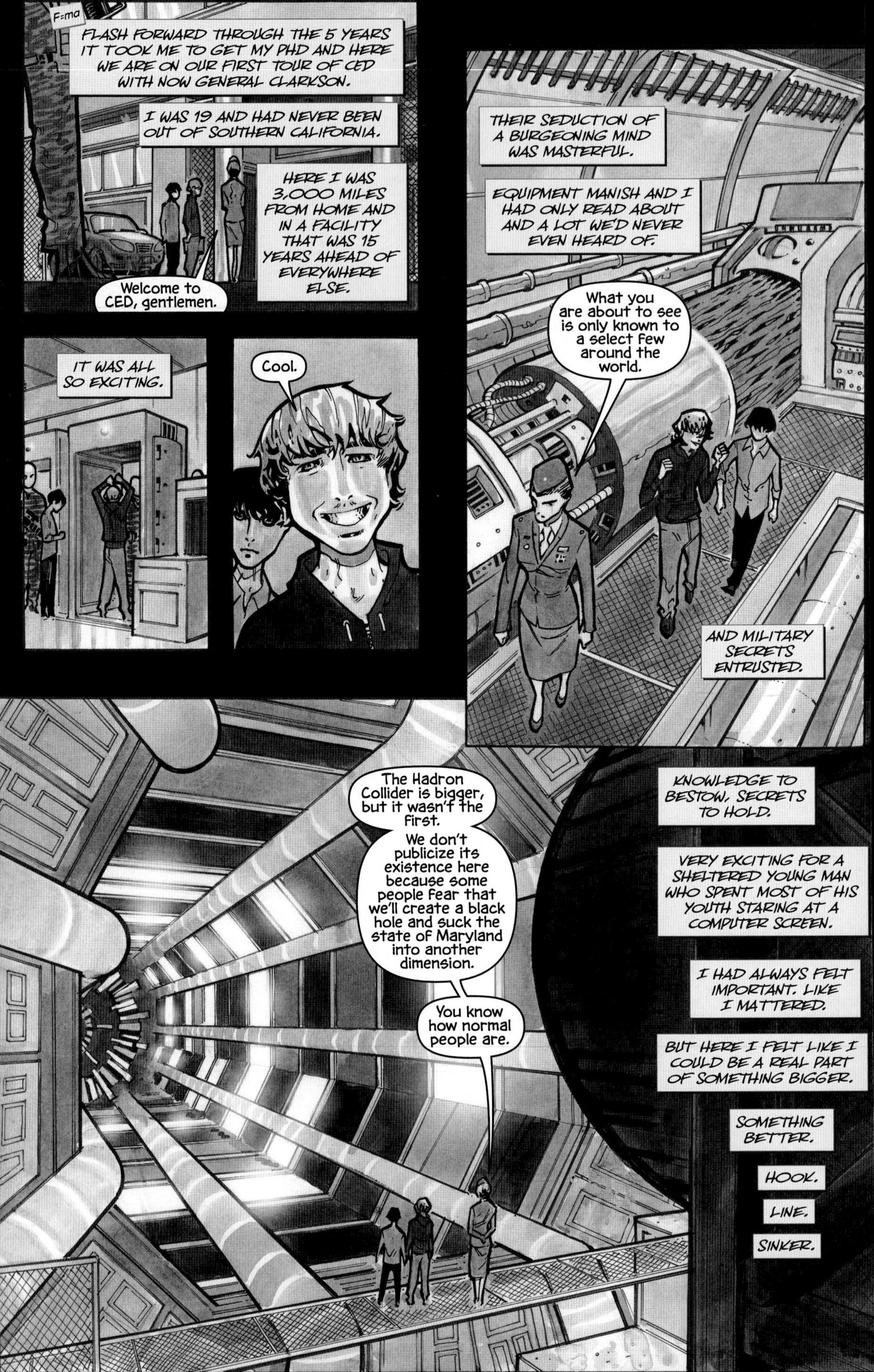
F=ma
FLASH FORWARD THROUGH THE 5 YEARS IT TOOK ME TO GET MY PHD AND HERE WE ARE ON OUR FIRST TOUR OF CED WITH NOW GENERAL CLARKSON.
I WAS 19 AND HAD NEVER BEEN OUT OF SOUTHERN CALIFORNIA.
HERE I WAS 3,000 MILES FROM HOME AND IN A FACILITY THAT WAS 15 YEARS AHEAD OF EVERYWHERE ELSE.
Welcome to CED, gentlemen.
THEIR SEDUCTION OF A BURGEONING MIND WAS MASTERFUL.
EQUIPMENT MANISH AND I HAD ONLY READ ABOUT AND A LOT WE'D NEVER EVEN HEARD OF.
What you are about to see is only known to a select few around the world.
AND MILITARY SECRETS ENTRUSTED.
IT WAS ALL SO EXCITING.
Cool.
The Hadron Collider is bigger, but it wasn't the first.
We don't publicize its existence here because some people fear that we'll create a black hole and suck the state of Maryland into another dimension.
You know how normal people are.
KNOWLEDGE TO BESTOW, SECRETS TO HOLD.
VERY EXCITING FOR A SHELTERED YOUNG MAN WHO SPENT MOST OF HIS YOUTH STARING AT A COMPUTER SCREEN.
I HAD ALWAYS FELT IMPORTANT. LIKE I MATTERED.
BUT HERE I FELT LIKE I COULD BE A REAL PART OF SOMETHING BIGGER.
SOMETHING BETTER.
HOOK.
LINE.
SINKER.

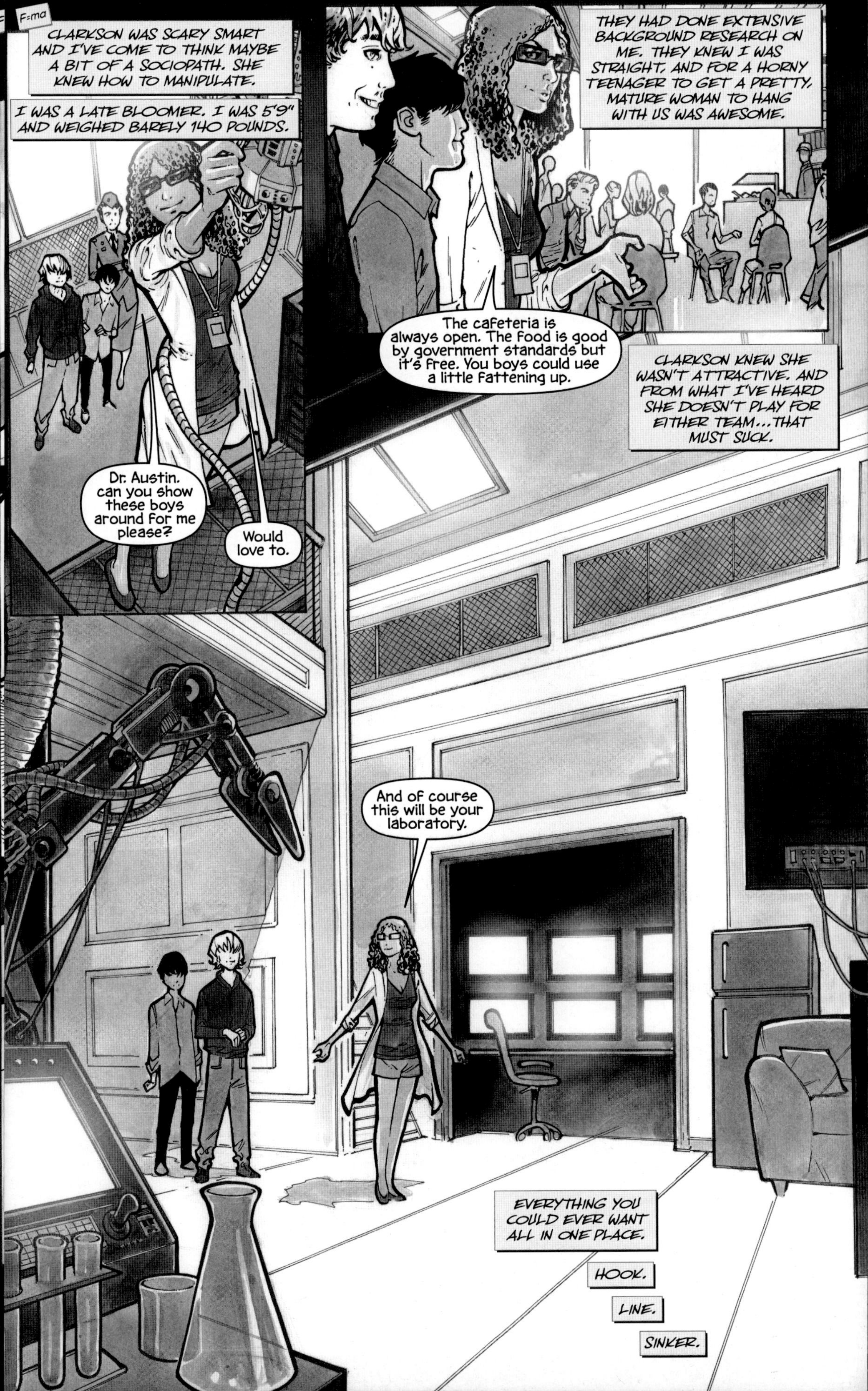
F=ma
CLARKSON WAS SCARY SMART AND I'VE COME TO THINK MAYBE A BIT OF A SOCIOPATH. SHE KNEW HOW TO MANIPULATE.
I WAS A LATE BLOOMER. I WAS 5'9" AND WEIGHED BARELY 140 POUNDS.
Dr. Austin. can you show these boys around for me please?
Would love to.
THEY HAD DONE EXTENSIVE BACKGROUND RESEARCH ON ME. THEY KNEW I WAS STRAIGHT, AND FOR A HORNY TEENAGER TO GET A PRETTY, MATURE WOMAN TO HANG WITH US WAS AWESOME.
The cafeteria is always open. The food is good by government standards but it's free. You boys could use a little fattening up.
CLARKSON KNEW SHE WASN'T ATTRACTIVE. AND FROM WHAT I'VE HEARD SHE DOESN'T PLAY FOR EITHER TEAM...THAT MUST SUCK.
And of course this will be your laboratory.
EVERYTHING YOU COULD EVER WANT ALL IN ONE PLACE.
HOOK.
LINE.
SINKER.

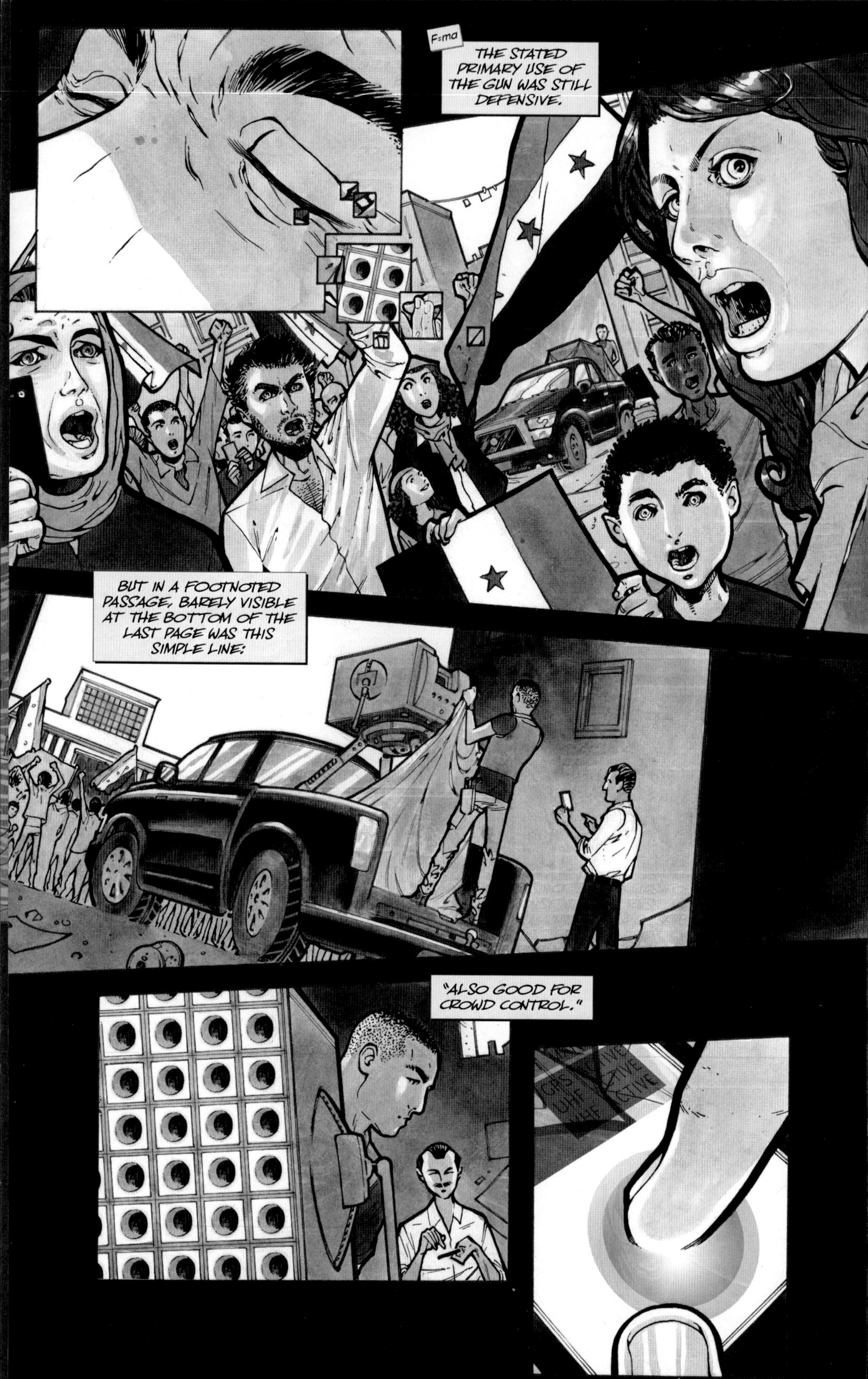
F=ma
THE STATED PRIMARY USE OF THE GUN WAS STILL DEFENSIVE.
BUT IN A FOOTNOTED PASSAGE, BARELY VISIBLE AT THE BOTTOM OF THE LAST PAGE WAS THIS SIMPLE LINE:
"ALSO GOOD FOR CROWD CONTROL."

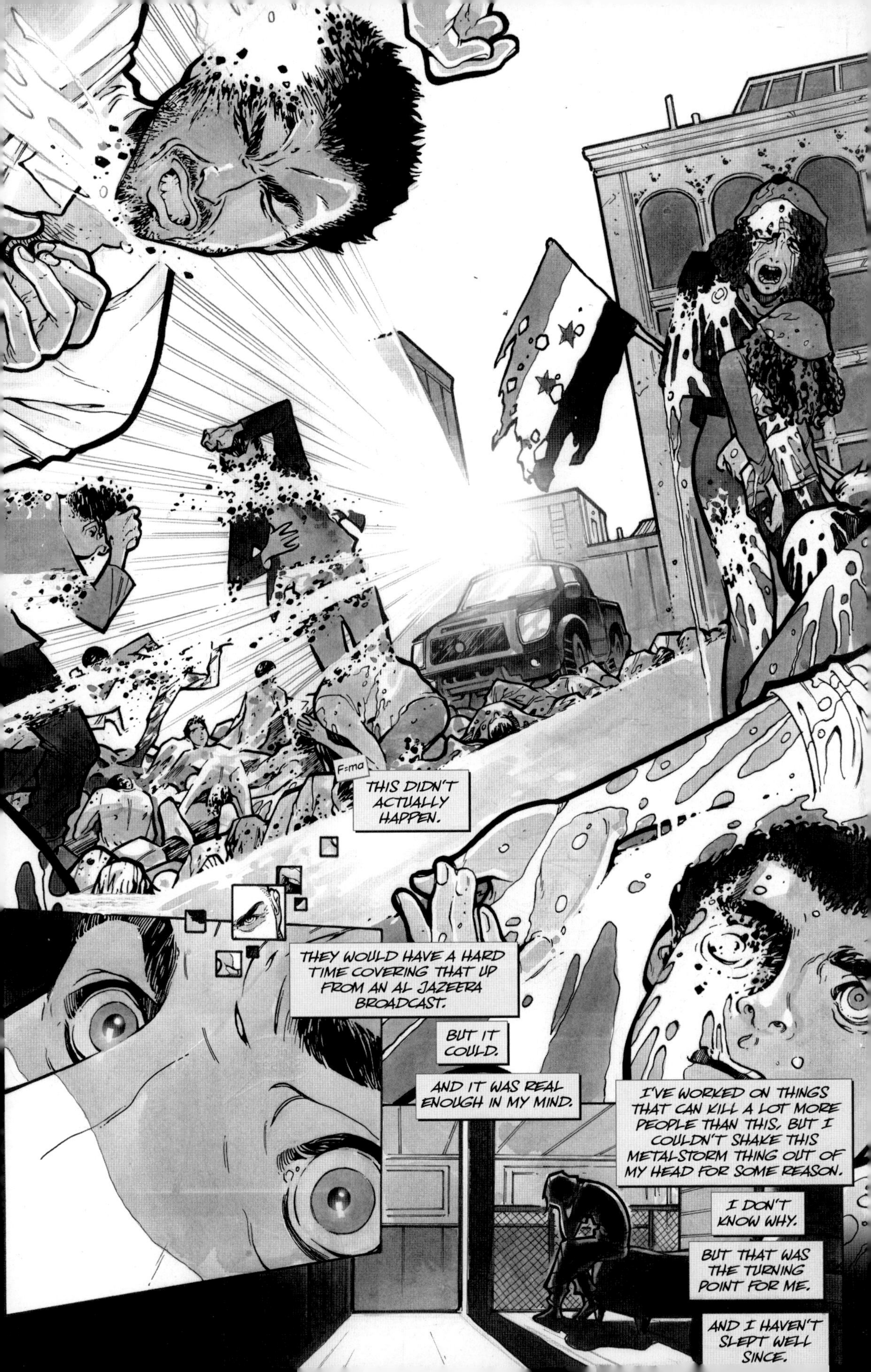
F=ma
THIS DIDN'T ACTUALLY HAPPEN.
THEY WOULD HAVE A HARD TIME COVERING THAT UP FROM AN AL JAZEERA BROADCAST.
BUT IT COULD.
AND IT WAS REAL ENOUGH IN MY MIND.
I'VE WORKED ON THINGS THAT CAN KILL A LOT MORE PEOPLE THAN THIS, BUT I COULDN'T SHAKE THIS METALSTORM THING OUT OF MY HEAD FOR SOME REASON.
I DON'T KNOW WHY.
BUT THAT WAS THE TURNING POINT FOR ME.
AND I HAVEN'T SLEPT WELL SINCE.

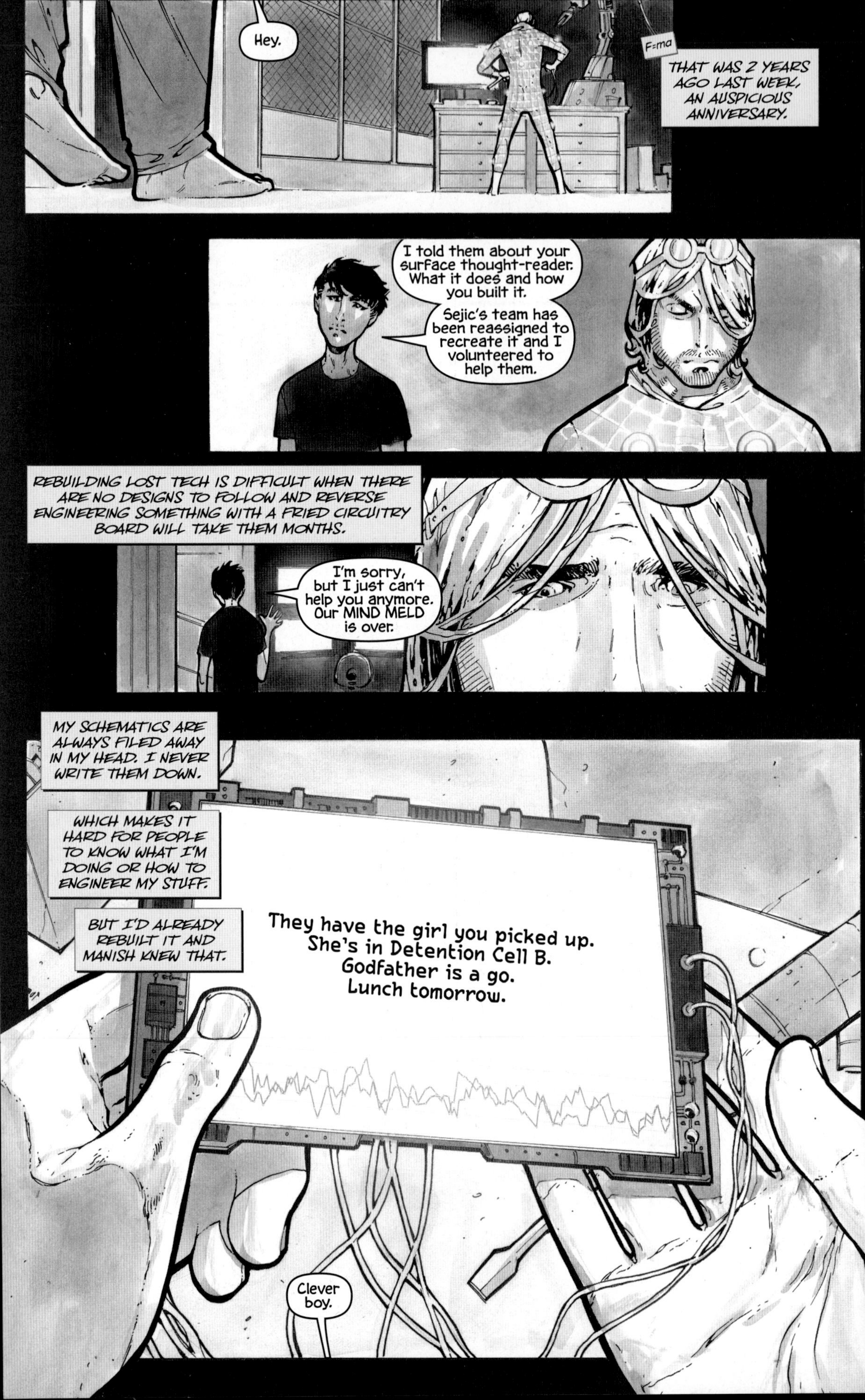
Hey.
F=ma
THAT WAS 2 YEARS AGO LAST WEEK, AN AUSPICIOUS ANNIVERSARY.
I told them about your surface thought-reader. What it does and how you built it.
Sejic's team has been reassigned to recreate it and I volunteered to help them.
REBUILDING LOST TECH IS DIFFICULT WHEN THERE ARE NO DESIGNS TO FOLLOW AND REVERSE ENGINEERING SOMETHING WITH A FRIED CIRCUITRY BOARD WILL TAKE THEM MONTHS.
I'm sorry, but I just can't help you anymore. Our MIND MELD is over.
MY SCHEMATICS ARE ALWAYS FILED AWAY IN MY HEAD. I NEVER WRITE THEM DOWN.
WHICH MAKES IT HARD FOR PEOPLE TO KNOW WHAT I'M DOING OR HOW TO ENGINEER MY STUFF.
BUT I'D ALREADY REBUILT IT AND MANISH KNEW THAT.
They have the girl you picked up.
She's in Detention Cell B.
Godfather is a go.
Lunch tomorrow.
Clever boy.

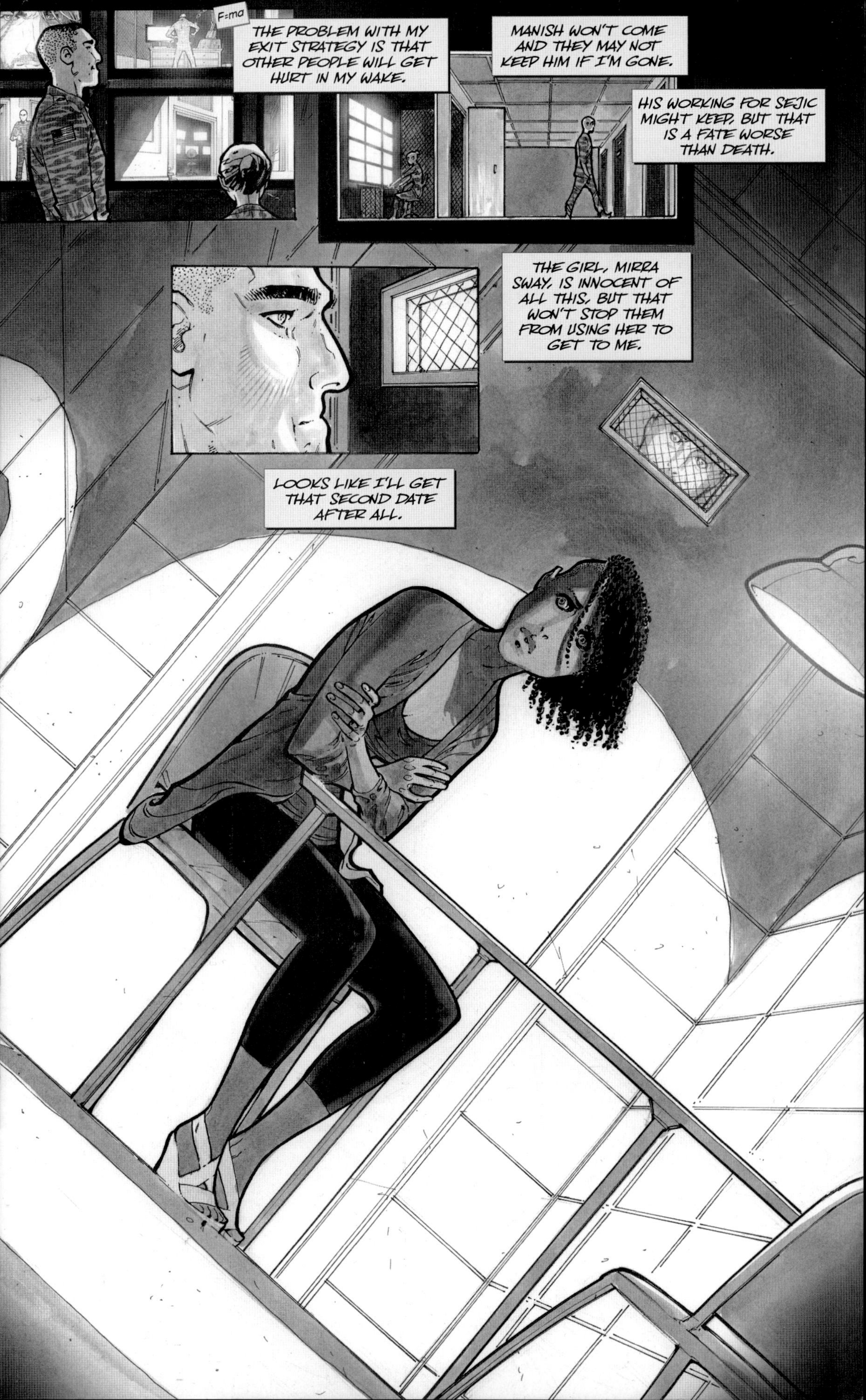
F=ma
THE PROBLEM WITH MY EXIT STRATEGY IS THAT OTHER PEOPLE WILL GET HURT IN MY WAKE.
MANISH WON'T COME AND THEY MAY NOT KEEP HIM IF I'M GONE.
HIS WORKING FOR SEJIC MIGHT KEEP, BUT THAT IS A FATE WORSE THAN DEATH.
THE GIRL, MIRRA SWAY, IS INNOCENT OF ALL THIS, BUT THAT WON'T STOP THEM FROM USING HER TO GET TO ME.
LOOKS LIKE I'LL GET THAT SECOND DATE AFTER ALL.

CHAPTER 3

THINK TANK

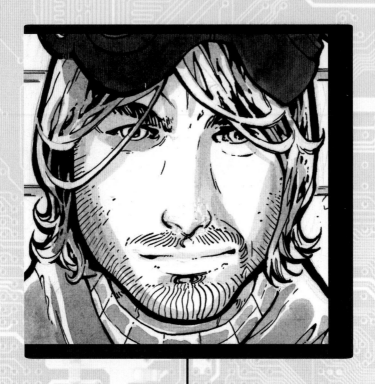

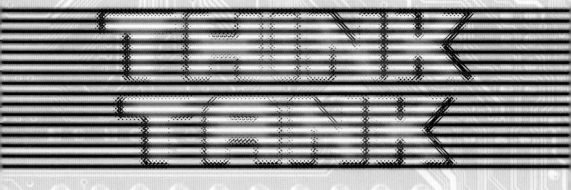

$$\oint \vec{E} \; d\vec{A} = \frac{1}{\varepsilon_0} q_{in} \qquad \oint \vec{B} \; d\vec{A} = 0 \qquad \oint E \; d\vec{x} = -\frac{d}{dt} \int B \; d\vec{A}$$

$$\oint \vec{B} \; d\vec{l} = \mu_0 I_{in} \qquad\qquad \vec{F} = q(\vec{v} \times \vec{B} + \vec{E}) \qquad i = \frac{dq}{dt}$$

nt charge $\qquad E = \frac{1}{4\pi \varepsilon_0} \frac{q}{r^2} \qquad V = \frac{1}{4\pi \varepsilon_0} \frac{q}{r} \qquad\qquad p = qd$

$$V_f - V_i = -\int_i^f \vec{E} \; d\vec{s} \qquad E_x = -\frac{\partial V}{\partial x} \qquad\qquad \vec{\tau} = \vec{p} \times \vec{E}$$

$$C = \frac{Q}{V} \qquad U_E = \frac{1}{2} QV = \frac{1}{2} CV^2 = \frac{1}{2} \frac{Q^2}{C} \qquad\qquad C = \varepsilon_0 \frac{A}{d}$$

$$R = \frac{V}{i} \qquad P = Vi \qquad P = i^2 R = \frac{V^2}{R} \qquad R = \rho \frac{L}{A}$$

$$R_{eq} = R_1 + R_2$$

"TECHNOLOGICAL PROGRESS IS LIKE AN AXE IN THE HANDS OF A PATHOLOGICAL CRIMINAL." ~ALBERT EINSTEIN

$$\frac{1}{R_{eq}} = \frac{1}{R_1} + \frac{1}{R_2}$$

$$d\vec{B} = \frac{\mu_0}{4\pi} \frac{i \; d\vec{s} \times \hat{r}}{r^2} \qquad B = \frac{\mu_0}{2\pi} \frac{i}{r} \qquad B = \mu_0 n i \qquad \vec{\tau} = \vec{\mu} \times \vec{B}$$

$$\mathcal{E} = -\frac{d\Phi}{dt} \qquad \mathcal{E} = -N \frac{d\Phi}{dt} \qquad L = \frac{|\mathcal{E}|}{\left|\frac{di}{dt}\right|} = \frac{N\Phi}{i}$$

$$u_E = \frac{1}{2} \varepsilon_0 E^2 \qquad u_B = \frac{1}{2} \frac{B^2}{\mu_0} \qquad U_B = \frac{1}{2} Li^2$$

$$q_0 e^{-t/\tau_c} \qquad q = C\mathcal{E}(1 - e^{-t/\tau_c}) \qquad i = i_0 e^{-t/\tau_L} \qquad i = \frac{\mathcal{E}}{R}(1 - e^{-t/\tau_L})$$

$$\frac{L}{R} \qquad \tau_c = RC \qquad \mu = NiA \qquad \frac{1}{4\pi\varepsilon_0} = 9 \times 10^9 \qquad \frac{\mu_0}{4\pi} = 10^{-7}$$

I means $10^6 \qquad \mu$ means 10^{-6}

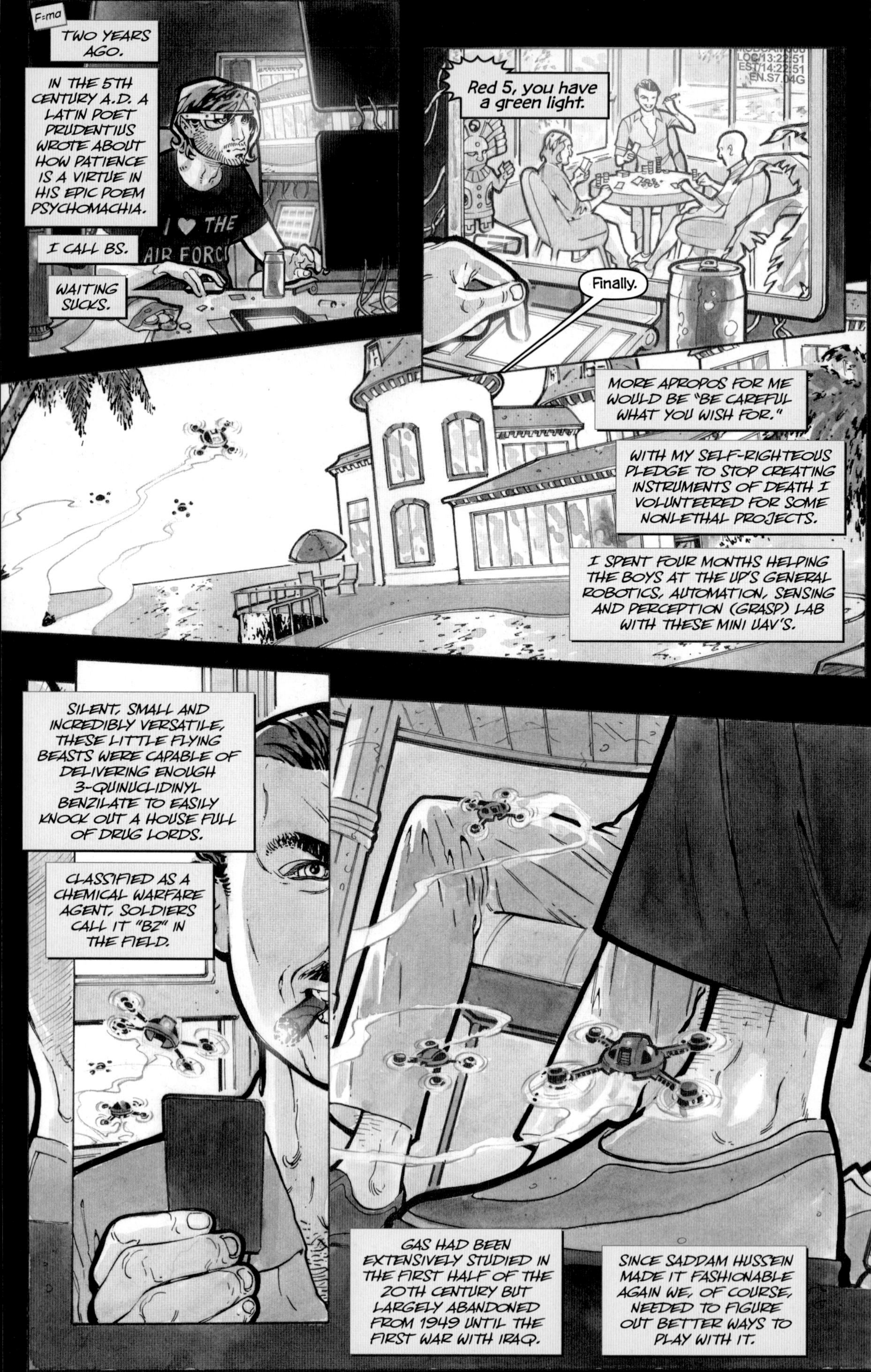
F=ma
TWO YEARS AGO.
IN THE 5TH CENTURY A.D. A LATIN POET PRUDENTIUS WROTE ABOUT HOW PATIENCE IS A VIRTUE IN HIS EPIC POEM PSYCHOMACHIA.
I ♥ THE AIR FORC
I CALL BS.
WAITING SUCKS.
LOC/13:22:51
EST/14:22:51
EN.S7.04G
Red 5, you have a green light.
Finally.
MORE APROPOS FOR ME WOULD BE "BE CAREFUL WHAT YOU WISH FOR."
WITH MY SELF-RIGHTEOUS PLEDGE TO STOP CREATING INSTRUMENTS OF DEATH I VOLUNTEERED FOR SOME NONLETHAL PROJECTS.
I SPENT FOUR MONTHS HELPING THE BOYS AT THE UP'S GENERAL ROBOTICS, AUTOMATION, SENSING AND PERCEPTION (GRASP) LAB WITH THESE MINI UAV'S.
SILENT, SMALL AND INCREDIBLY VERSATILE, THESE LITTLE FLYING BEASTS WERE CAPABLE OF DELIVERING ENOUGH 3-QUINUCLIDINYL BENZILATE TO EASILY KNOCK OUT A HOUSE FULL OF DRUG LORDS.
CLASSIFIED AS A CHEMICAL WARFARE AGENT, SOLDIERS CALL IT "BZ" IN THE FIELD.
GAS HAD BEEN EXTENSIVELY STUDIED IN THE FIRST HALF OF THE 20TH CENTURY BUT LARGELY ABANDONED FROM 1949 UNTIL THE FIRST WAR WITH IRAQ.
SINCE SADDAM HUSSEIN MADE IT FASHIONABLE AGAIN WE, OF COURSE, NEEDED TO FIGURE OUT BETTER WAYS TO PLAY WITH IT.

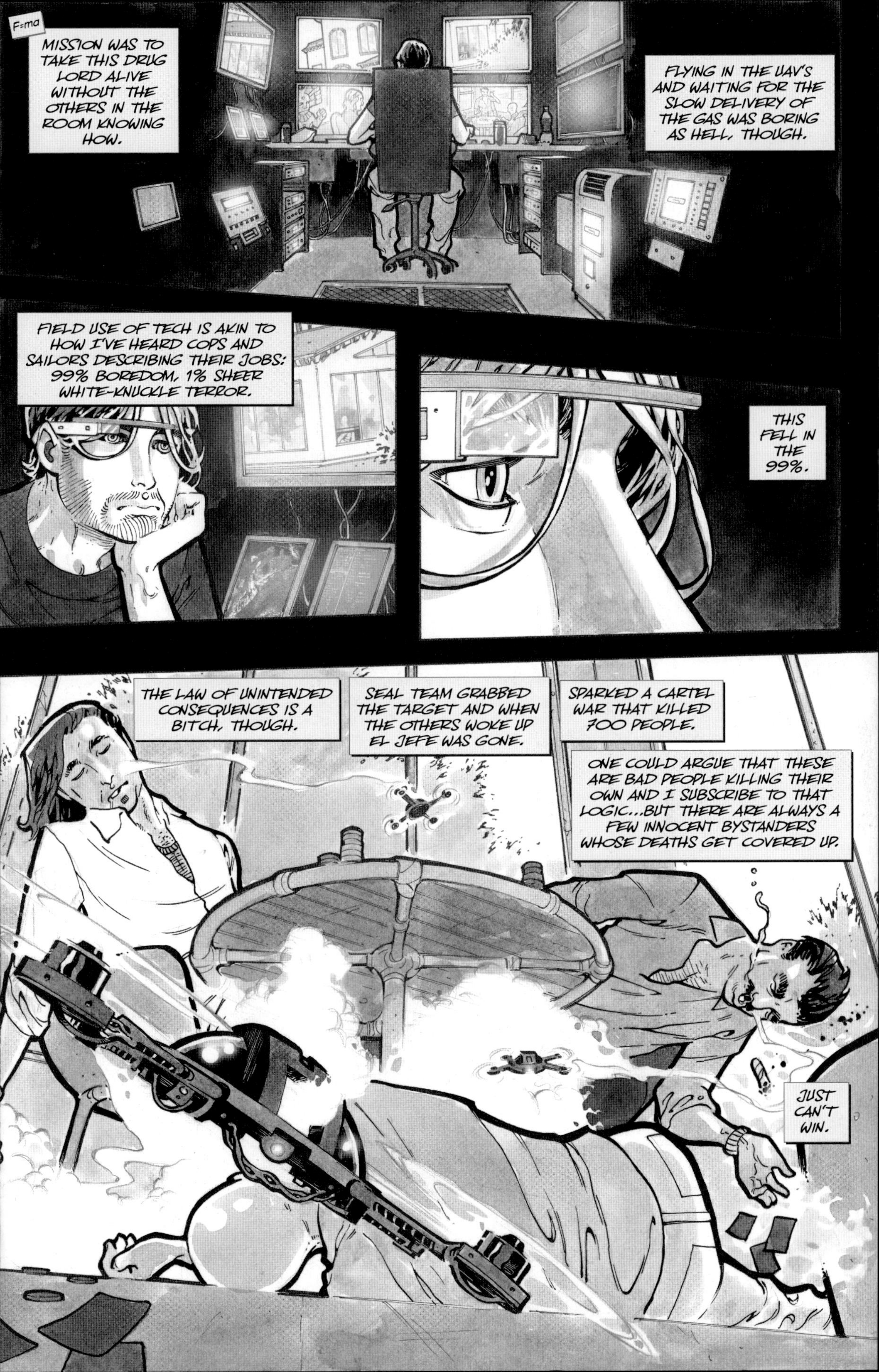
F=ma
MISSION WAS TO TAKE THIS DRUG LORD ALIVE WITHOUT THE OTHERS IN THE ROOM KNOWING HOW.
FLYING IN THE UAV'S AND WAITING FOR THE SLOW DELIVERY OF THE GAS WAS BORING AS HELL, THOUGH.
FIELD USE OF TECH IS AKIN TO HOW I'VE HEARD COPS AND SAILORS DESCRIBING THEIR JOBS: 99% BOREDOM, 1% SHEER WHITE-KNUCKLE TERROR.
THIS FELL IN THE 99%.
THE LAW OF UNINTENDED CONSEQUENCES IS A BITCH, THOUGH.
SEAL TEAM GRABBED THE TARGET AND WHEN THE OTHERS WOKE UP EL JEFE WAS GONE.
SPARKED A CARTEL WAR THAT KILLED 700 PEOPLE.
ONE COULD ARGUE THAT THESE ARE BAD PEOPLE KILLING THEIR OWN AND I SUBSCRIBE TO THAT LOGIC...BUT THERE ARE ALWAYS A FEW INNOCENT BYSTANDERS WHOSE DEATHS GET COVERED UP.
JUST CAN'T WIN.

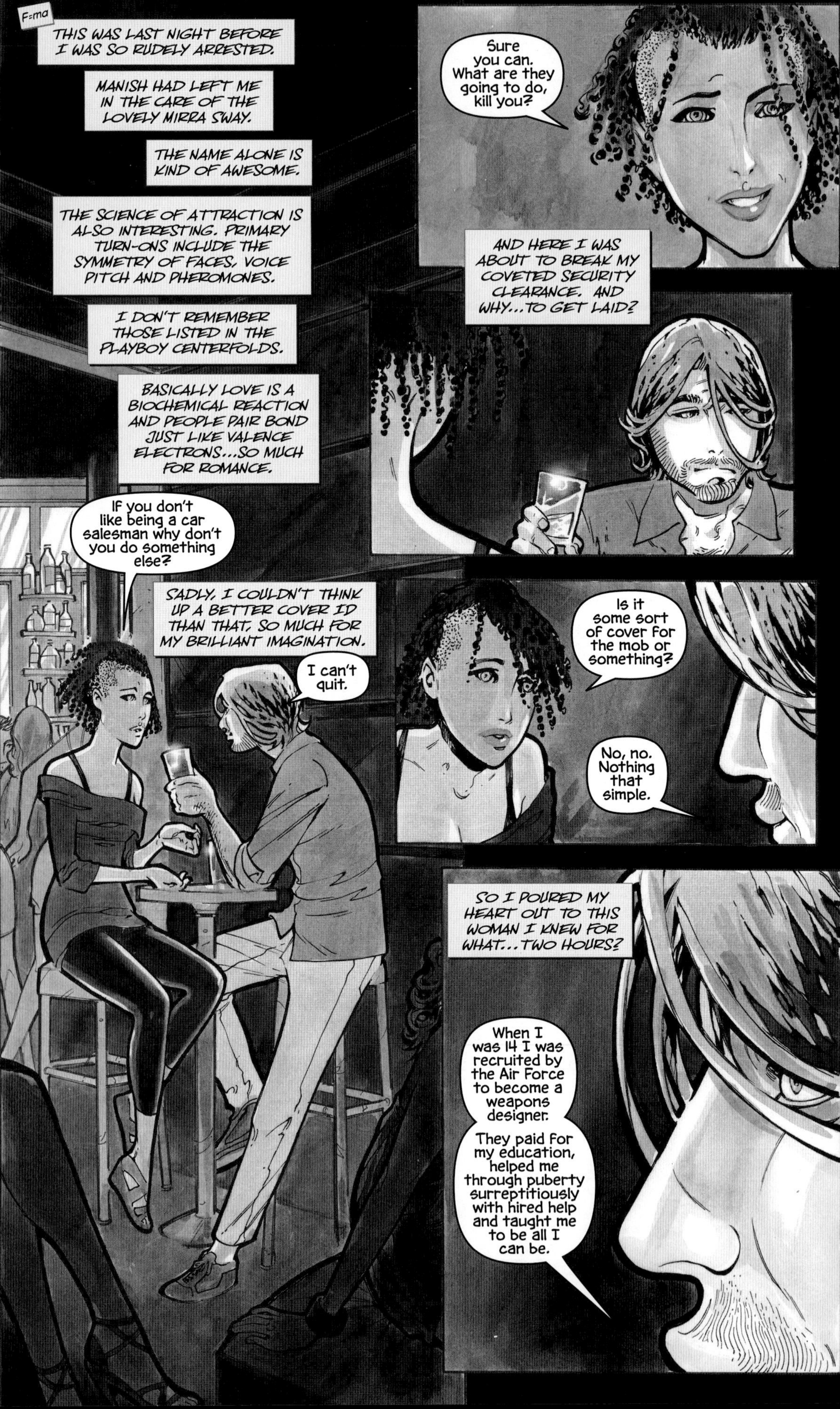
F=ma
THIS WAS LAST NIGHT BEFORE I WAS SO RUDELY ARRESTED.
MANISH HAD LEFT ME IN THE CARE OF THE LOVELY MIRRA SWAY.
THE NAME ALONE IS KIND OF AWESOME.
THE SCIENCE OF ATTRACTION IS ALSO INTERESTING. PRIMARY TURN-ONS INCLUDE THE SYMMETRY OF FACES, VOICE PITCH AND PHEROMONES.
I DON'T REMEMBER THOSE LISTED IN THE PLAYBOY CENTERFOLDS.
BASICALLY LOVE IS A BIOCHEMICAL REACTION AND PEOPLE PAIR BOND JUST LIKE VALENCE ELECTRONS...SO MUCH FOR ROMANCE.
If you don't like being a car salesman why don't you do something else?
SADLY, I COULDN'T THINK UP A BETTER COVER ID THAN THAT, SO MUCH FOR MY BRILLIANT IMAGINATION.
I can't quit.
Sure you can. What are they going to do, kill you?
AND HERE I WAS ABOUT TO BREAK MY COVETED SECURITY CLEARANCE. AND WHY...TO GET LAID?
Is it some sort of cover for the mob or something?
No, no. Nothing that simple.
SO I POURED MY HEART OUT TO THIS WOMAN I KNEW FOR WHAT...TWO HOURS?
When I was 14 I was recruited by the Air Force to become a weapons designer.
They paid for my education, helped me through puberty surreptitiously with hired help and taught me to be all I can be.

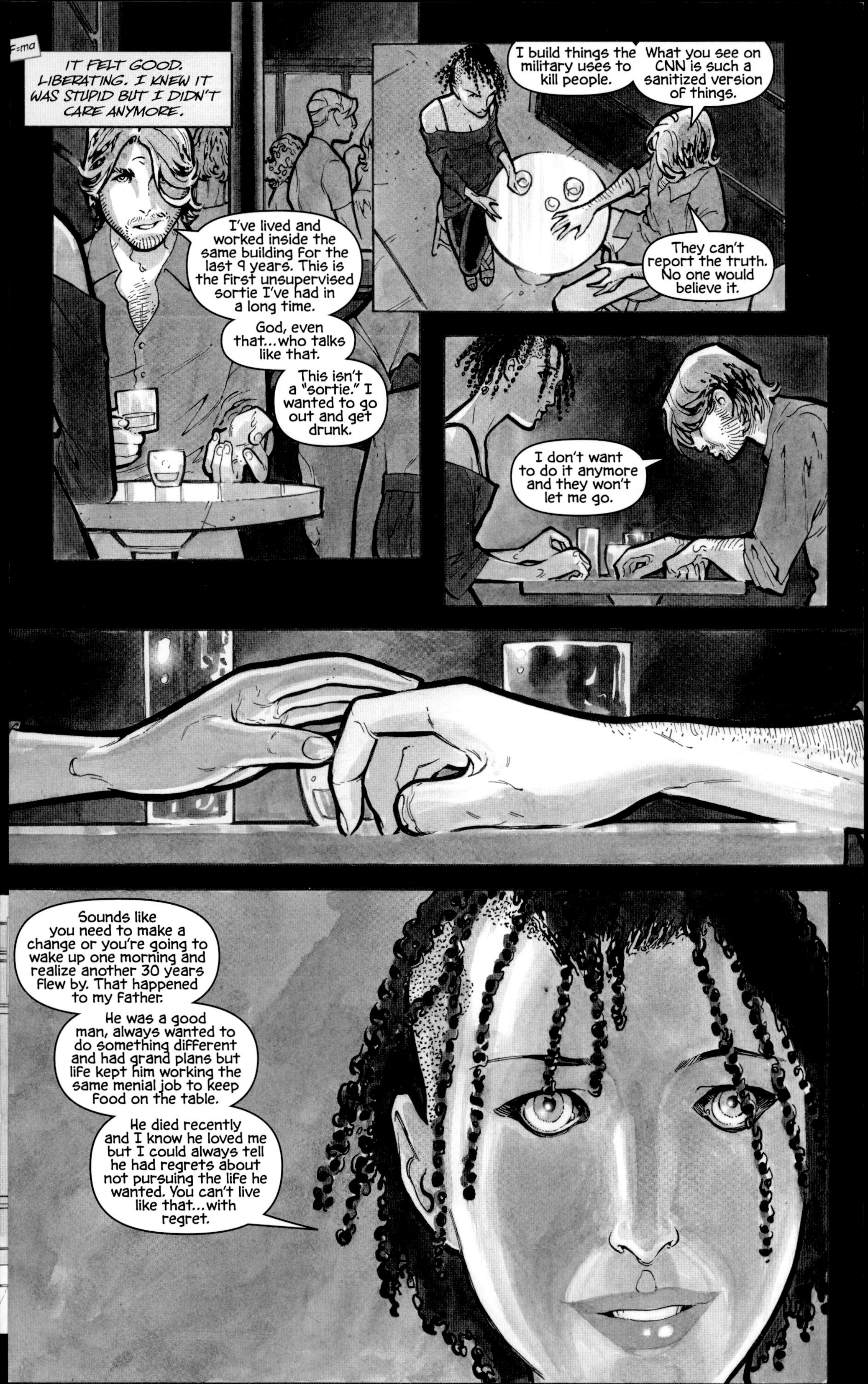
F=ma
IT FELT GOOD. LIBERATING. I KNEW IT WAS STUPID BUT I DIDN'T CARE ANYMORE.
I've lived and worked inside the same building for the last 9 years. This is the first unsupervised sortie I've had in a long time.
God, even that...who talks like that.
This isn't a "sortie." I wanted to go out and get drunk.
I build things the military uses to kill people.
What you see on CNN is such a sanitized version of things.
They can't report the truth. No one would believe it.
I don't want to do it anymore and they won't let me go.
Sounds like you need to make a change or you're going to wake up one morning and realize another 30 years flew by. That happened to my father.
He was a good man, always wanted to do something different and had grand plans but life kept him working the same menial job to keep food on the table.
He died recently and I know he loved me but I could always tell he had regrets about not pursuing the life he wanted. You can't live like that...with regret.

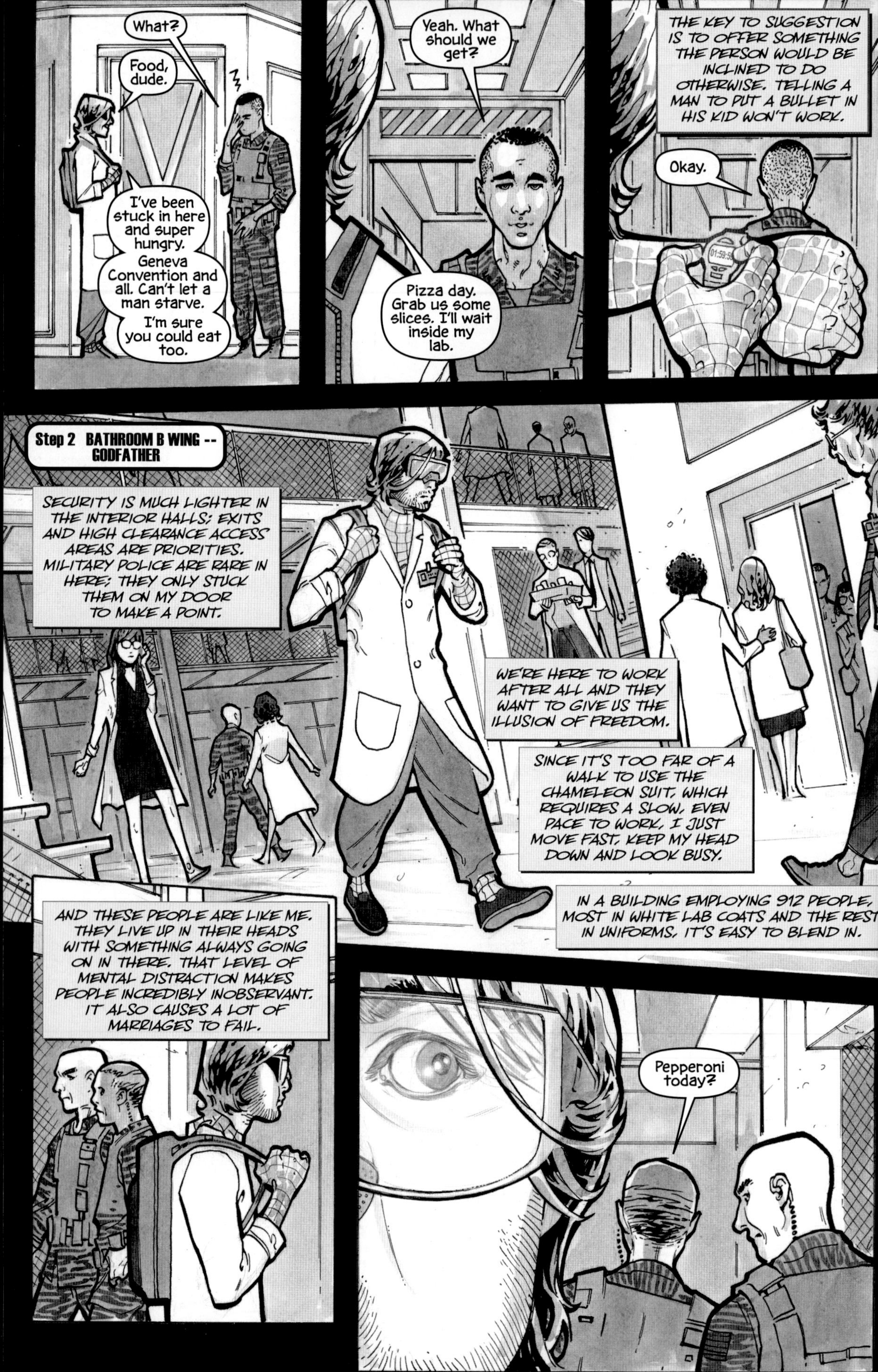
What?
Food, dude.
I've been stuck in here and super hungry.
Geneva Convention and all. Can't let a man starve.
I'm sure you could eat too.
Yeah. What should we get?
Pizza day. Grab us some slices. I'll wait inside my lab.
THE KEY TO SUGGESTION IS TO OFFER SOMETHING THE PERSON WOULD BE INCLINED TO DO OTHERWISE. TELLING A MAN TO PUT A BULLET IN HIS KID WON'T WORK.
Okay.
01:59:58
Step 2 BATHROOM B WING -- GODFATHER
SECURITY IS MUCH LIGHTER IN THE INTERIOR HALLS; EXITS AND HIGH CLEARANCE ACCESS AREAS ARE PRIORITIES. MILITARY POLICE ARE RARE IN HERE; THEY ONLY STUCK THEM ON MY DOOR TO MAKE A POINT.
WE'RE HERE TO WORK AFTER ALL AND THEY WANT TO GIVE US THE ILLUSION OF FREEDOM.
SINCE IT'S TOO FAR OF A WALK TO USE THE CHAMELEON SUIT, WHICH REQUIRES A SLOW, EVEN PACE TO WORK, I JUST MOVE FAST, KEEP MY HEAD DOWN AND LOOK BUSY.
IN A BUILDING EMPLOYING 912 PEOPLE, MOST IN WHITE LAB COATS AND THE REST IN UNIFORMS, IT'S EASY TO BLEND IN.
AND THESE PEOPLE ARE LIKE ME. THEY LIVE UP IN THEIR HEADS WITH SOMETHING ALWAYS GOING ON IN THERE. THAT LEVEL OF MENTAL DISTRACTION MAKES PEOPLE INCREDIBLY INOBSERVANT. IT ALSO CAUSES A LOT OF MARRIAGES TO FAIL.
Pepperoni today?

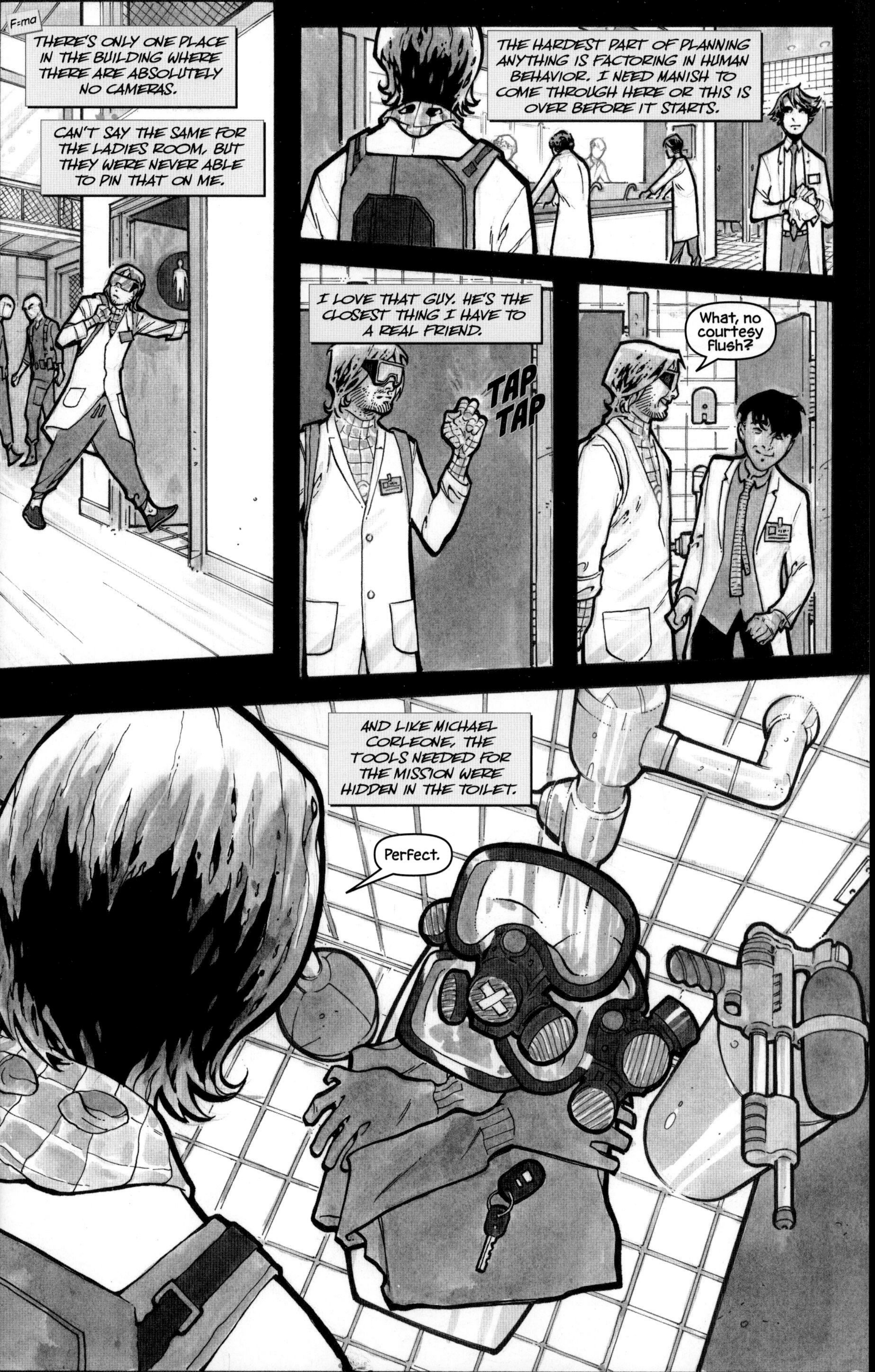
F=ma
THERE'S ONLY ONE PLACE IN THE BUILDING WHERE THERE ARE ABSOLUTELY NO CAMERAS.
CAN'T SAY THE SAME FOR THE LADIES ROOM, BUT THEY WERE NEVER ABLE TO PIN THAT ON ME.
THE HARDEST PART OF PLANNING ANYTHING IS FACTORING IN HUMAN BEHAVIOR. I NEED MANISH TO COME THROUGH HERE OR THIS IS OVER BEFORE IT STARTS.
I LOVE THAT GUY. HE'S THE CLOSEST THING I HAVE TO A REAL FRIEND.
TAP TAP
What, no courtesy flush?
AND LIKE MICHAEL CORLEONE, THE TOOLS NEEDED FOR THE MISSION WERE HIDDEN IN THE TOILET.
Perfect.

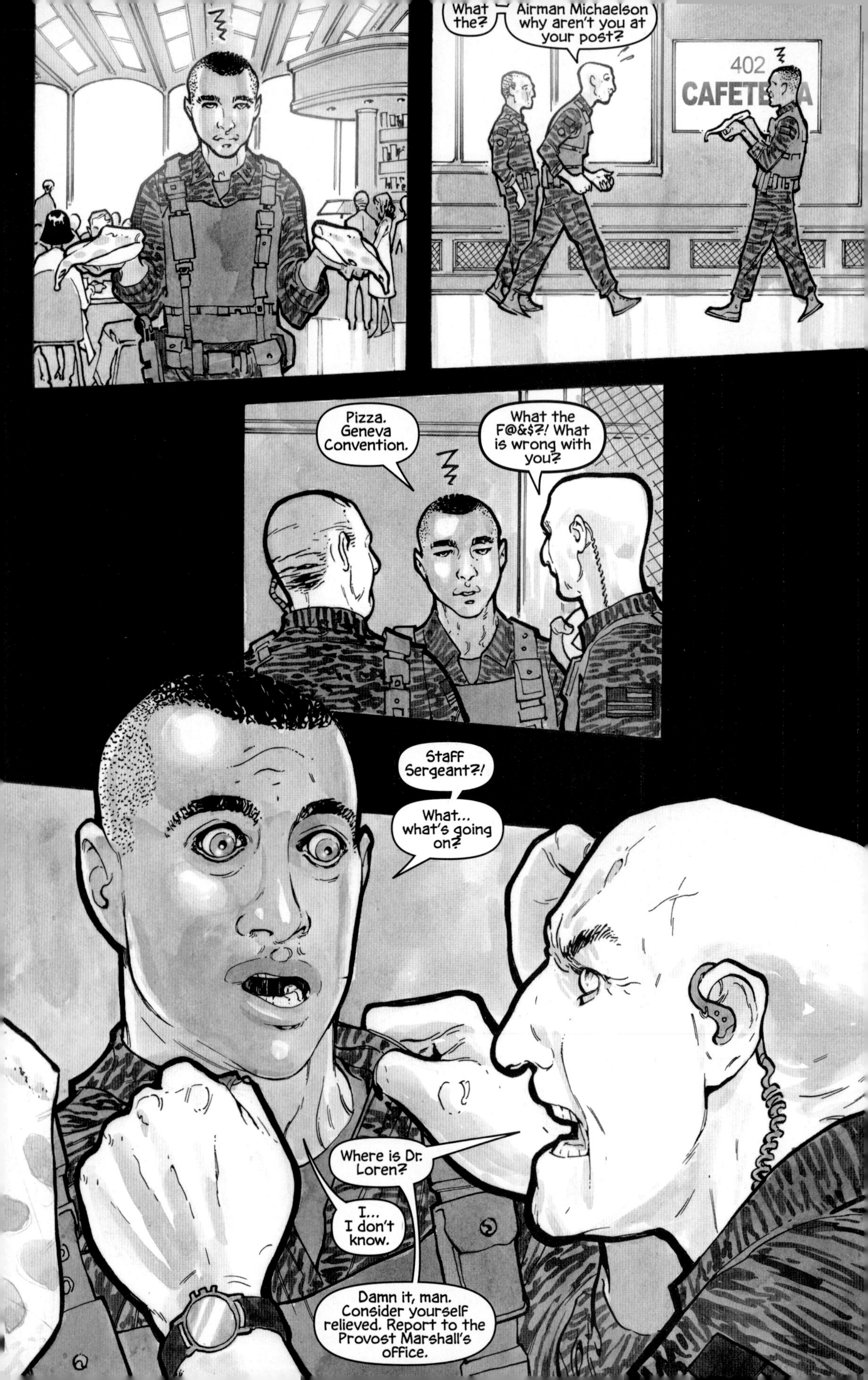
What the?
Airman Michaelson why aren't you at your post?
402
CAFETE
A
Pizza. Geneva Convention.
What the F@&$?! What is wrong with you?
Staff Sergeant?!
What... what's going on?
Where is Dr. Loren?
I... I don't know.
Damn it, man. Consider yourself relieved. Report to the Provost Marshall's office.

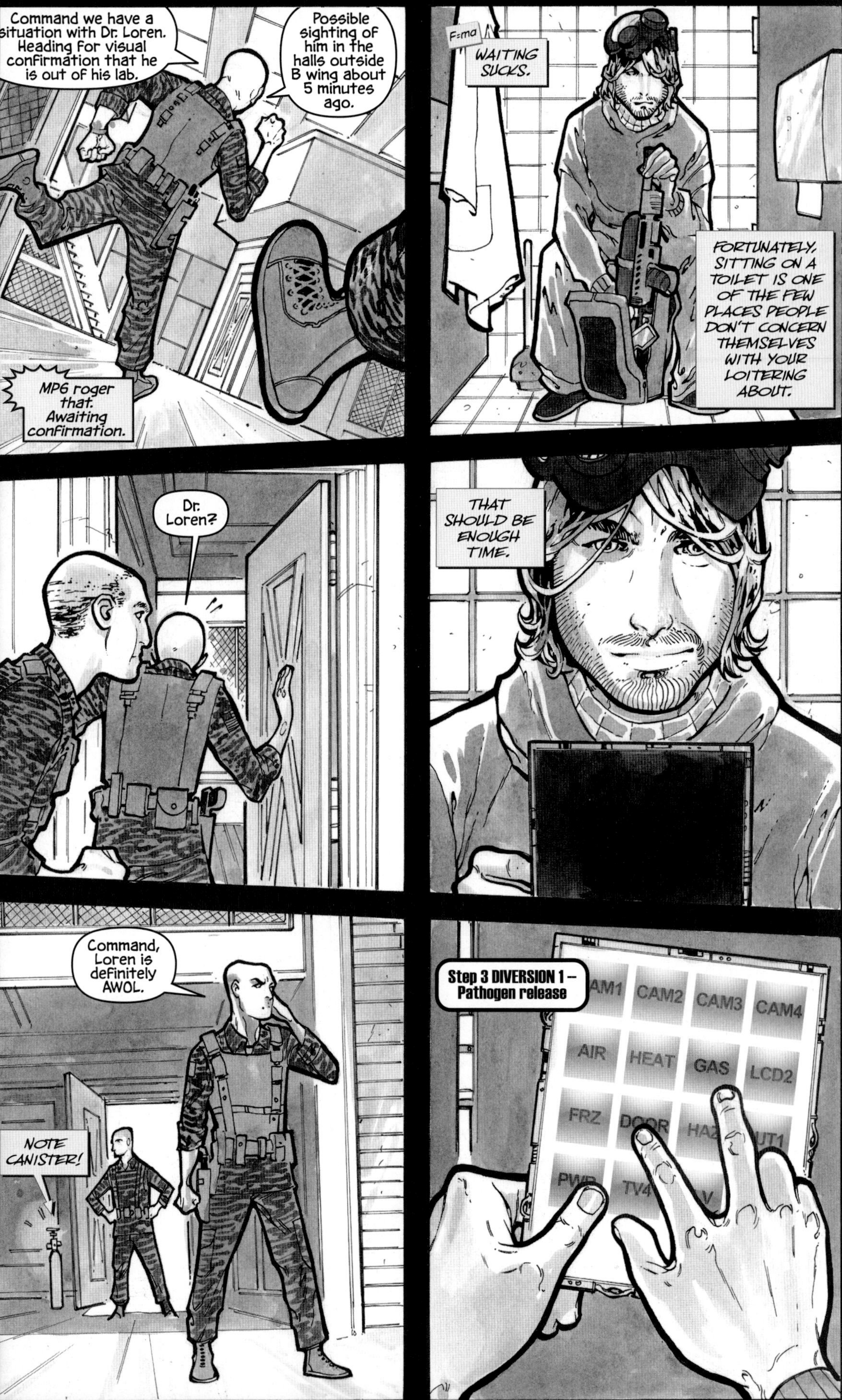
Command we have a situation with Dr. Loren. Heading for visual confirmation that he is out of his lab.
Possible sighting of him in the halls outside B wing about 5 minutes ago.
MP6 roger that. Awaiting confirmation.
F=ma
WAITING SUCKS.
FORTUNATELY, SITTING ON A TOILET IS ONE OF THE FEW PLACES PEOPLE DON'T CONCERN THEMSELVES WITH YOUR LOITERING ABOUT.
Dr. Loren?
THAT SHOULD BE ENOUGH TIME.
Command, Loren is definitely AWOL.
NOTE CANISTER!
Step 3 DIVERSION 1 – Pathogen release
CAM2
CAM3
CAM4
AIR
HEAT
GAS
LCD2
FRZ
TV4

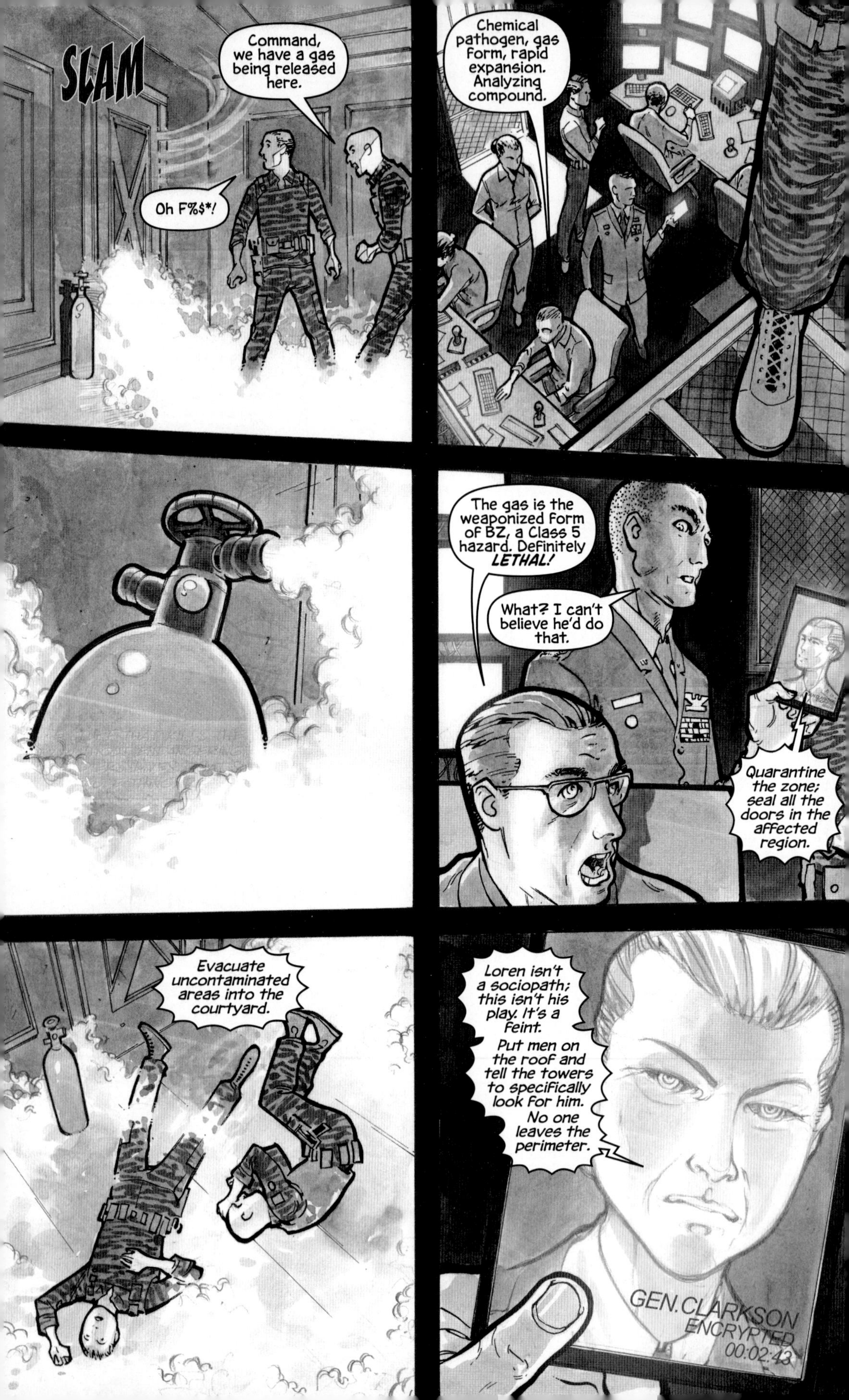

SLAM
Command, we have a gas being released here.
Oh F%$*!
Chemical pathogen, gas form, rapid expansion. Analyzing compound.
The gas is the weaponized form of BZ, a Class 5 hazard. Definitely LETHAL!
What? I can't believe he'd do that.
Quarantine the zone; seal all the doors in the affected region.
Evacuate uncontaminated areas into the courtyard.
Loren isn't a sociopath; this isn't his play. It's a feint.
Put men on the roof and tell the towers to specifically look for him.
No one leaves the perimeter.
GEN. CLARKSON
ENCRYPTED
00:02:43

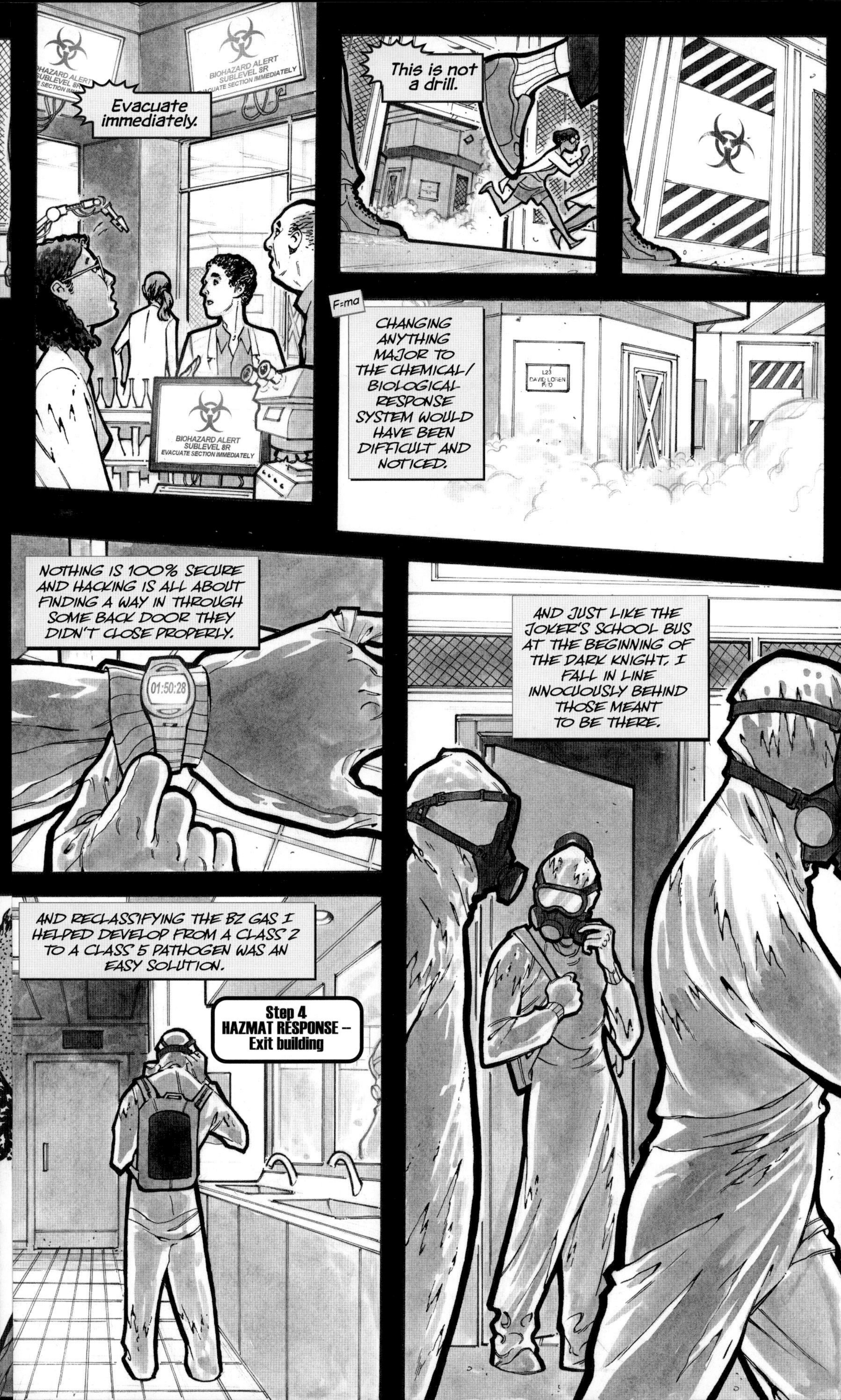
BIOHAZARD ALERT
SUBLEVEL 8R
EVACUATE SECTION IMMEDIATELY
Evacuate immediately.
BIOHAZARD ALERT
SUBLEVEL 8R
EVACUATE SECTION IMMEDIATELY
This is not a drill.
F=ma
CHANGING ANYTHING MAJOR TO THE CHEMICAL/ BIOLOGICAL RESPONSE SYSTEM WOULD HAVE BEEN DIFFICULT AND NOTICED.
L23
DAVID LOREN
PhD
NOTHING IS 100% SECURE AND HACKING IS ALL ABOUT FINDING A WAY IN THROUGH SOME BACK DOOR THEY DIDN'T CLOSE PROPERLY.
01:50:28
AND JUST LIKE THE JOKER'S SCHOOL BUS AT THE BEGINNING OF THE DARK KNIGHT, I FALL IN LINE INNOCUOUSLY BEHIND THOSE MEANT TO BE THERE.
AND RECLASSIFYING THE BZ GAS I HELPED DEVELOP FROM A CLASS 2 TO A CLASS 5 PATHOGEN WAS AN EASY SOLUTION.
Step 4
HAZMAT RESPONSE –
Exit building

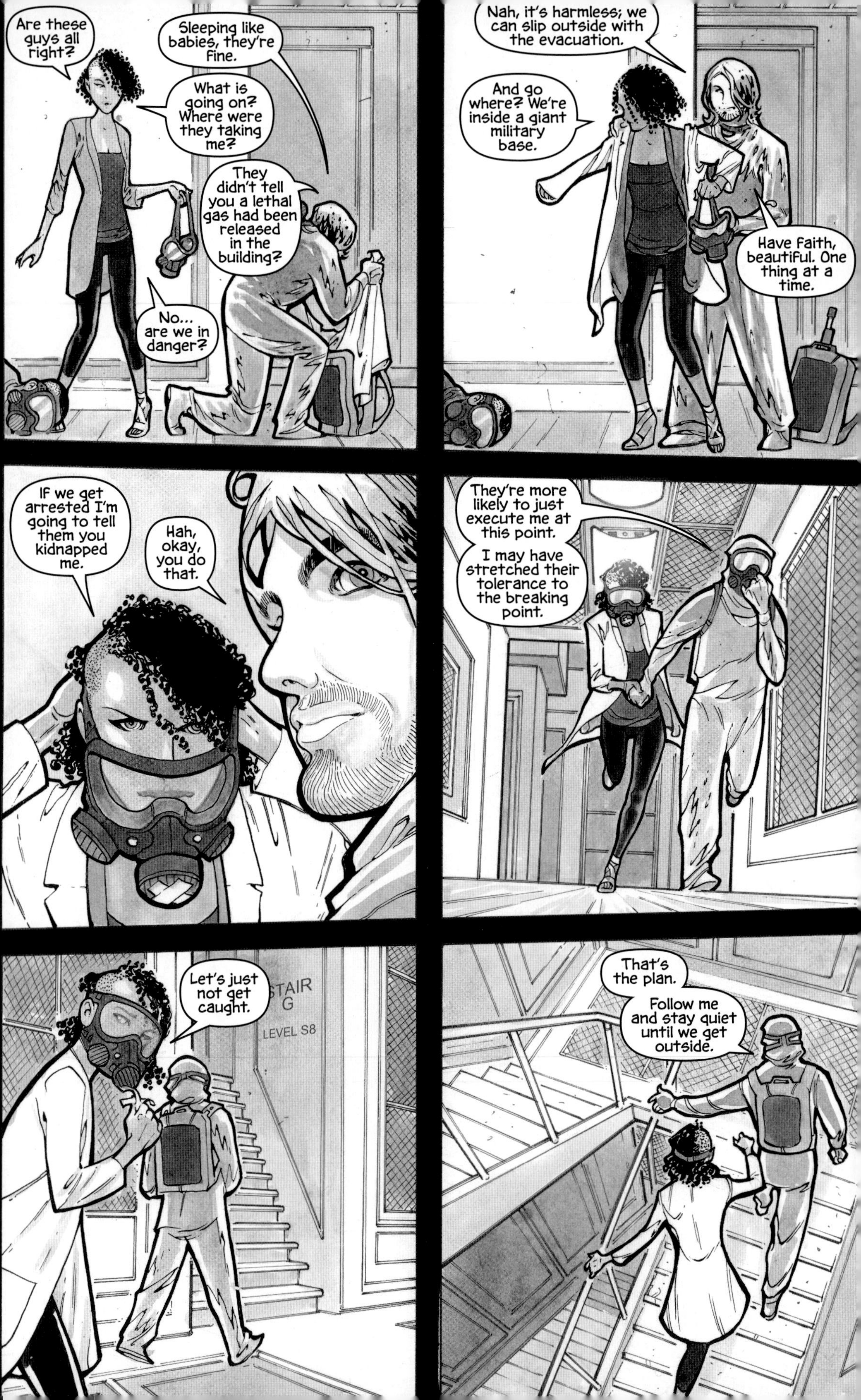
Are these guys all right?
Sleeping like babies, they're fine.
What is going on? Where were they taking me?
They didn't tell you a lethal gas had been released in the building?
No... are we in danger?
Nah, it's harmless; we can slip outside with the evacuation.
And go where? We're inside a giant military base.
Have faith, beautiful. One thing at a time.
If we get arrested I'm going to tell them you kidnapped me.
Hah, okay, you do that.
They're more likely to just execute me at this point.
I may have stretched their tolerance to the breaking point.
Let's just not get caught.
STAIR G
LEVEL S8
That's the plan.
Follow me and stay quiet until we get outside.

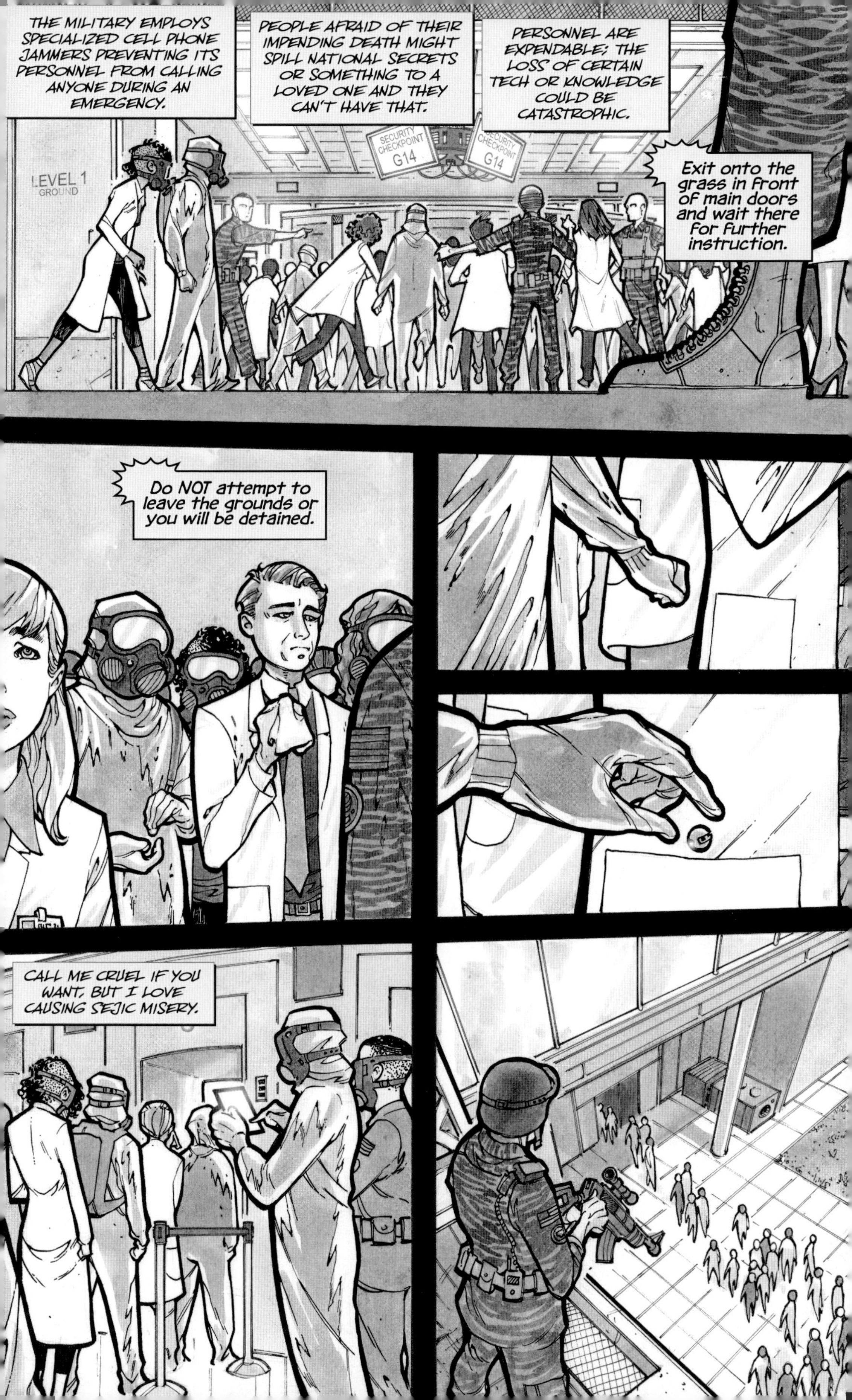
THE MILITARY EMPLOYS SPECIALIZED CELL PHONE JAMMERS PREVENTING ITS PERSONNEL FROM CALLING ANYONE DURING AN EMERGENCY.
PEOPLE AFRAID OF THEIR IMPENDING DEATH MIGHT SPILL NATIONAL SECRETS OR SOMETHING TO A LOVED ONE AND THEY CAN'T HAVE THAT.
PERSONNEL ARE EXPENDABLE; THE LOSS OF CERTAIN TECH OR KNOWLEDGE COULD BE CATASTROPHIC.
SECURITY CHECKPOINT G14
SECURITY CHECKPOINT G14
LEVEL 1 GROUND
Exit onto the grass in front of main doors and wait there for further instruction.
Do NOT attempt to leave the grounds or you will be detained.
CALL ME CRUEL IF YOU WANT, BUT I LOVE CAUSING SEJIC MISERY.

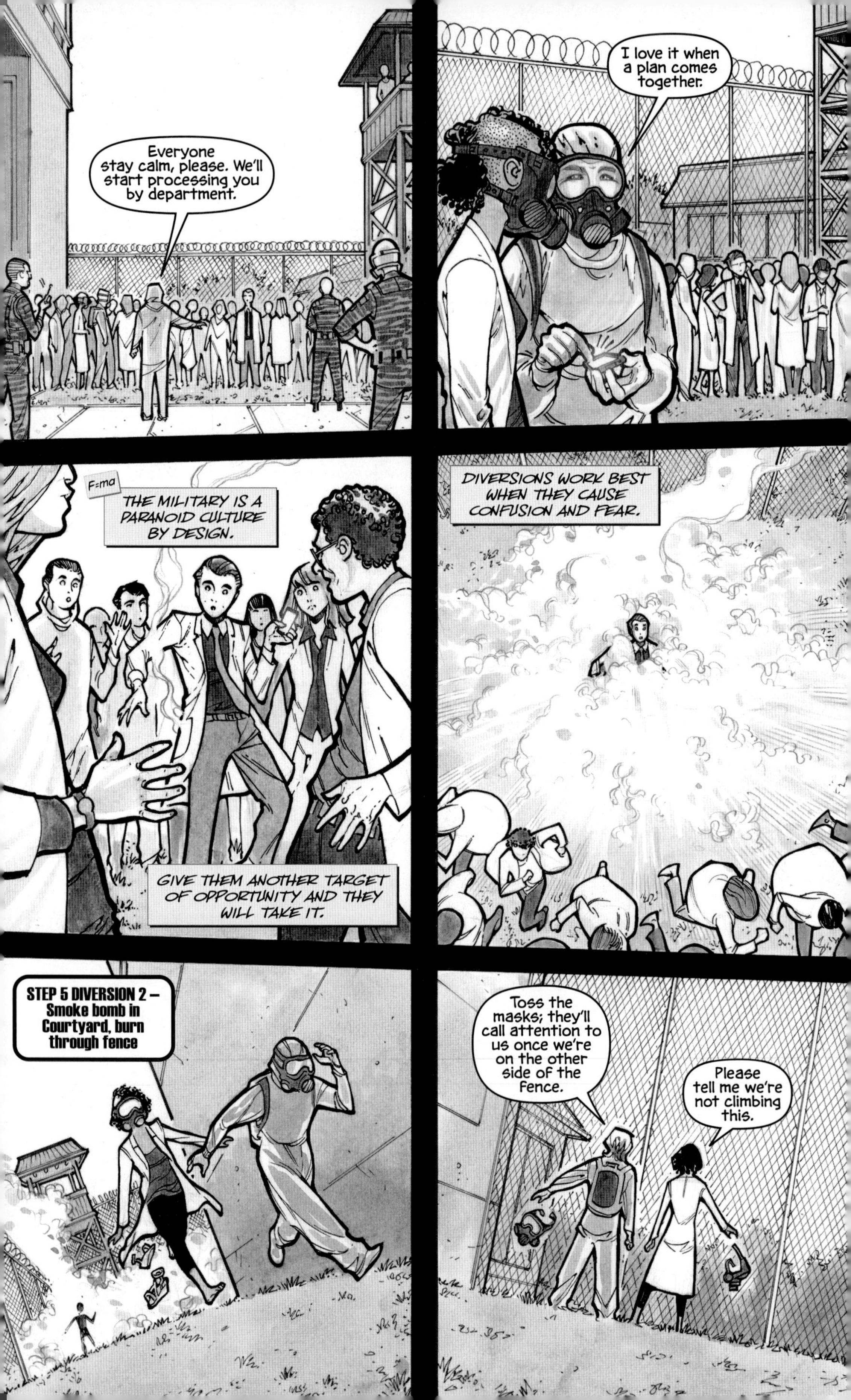
Everyone stay calm, please. We'll start processing you by department.
I love it when a plan comes together.
F=ma
THE MILITARY IS A PARANOID CULTURE BY DESIGN.
GIVE THEM ANOTHER TARGET OF OPPORTUNITY AND THEY WILL TAKE IT.
DIVERSIONS WORK BEST WHEN THEY CAUSE CONFUSION AND FEAR.
STEP 5 DIVERSION 2 – Smoke bomb in Courtyard, burn through fence
Toss the masks; they'll call attention to us once we're on the other side of the fence.
Please tell me we're not climbing this.

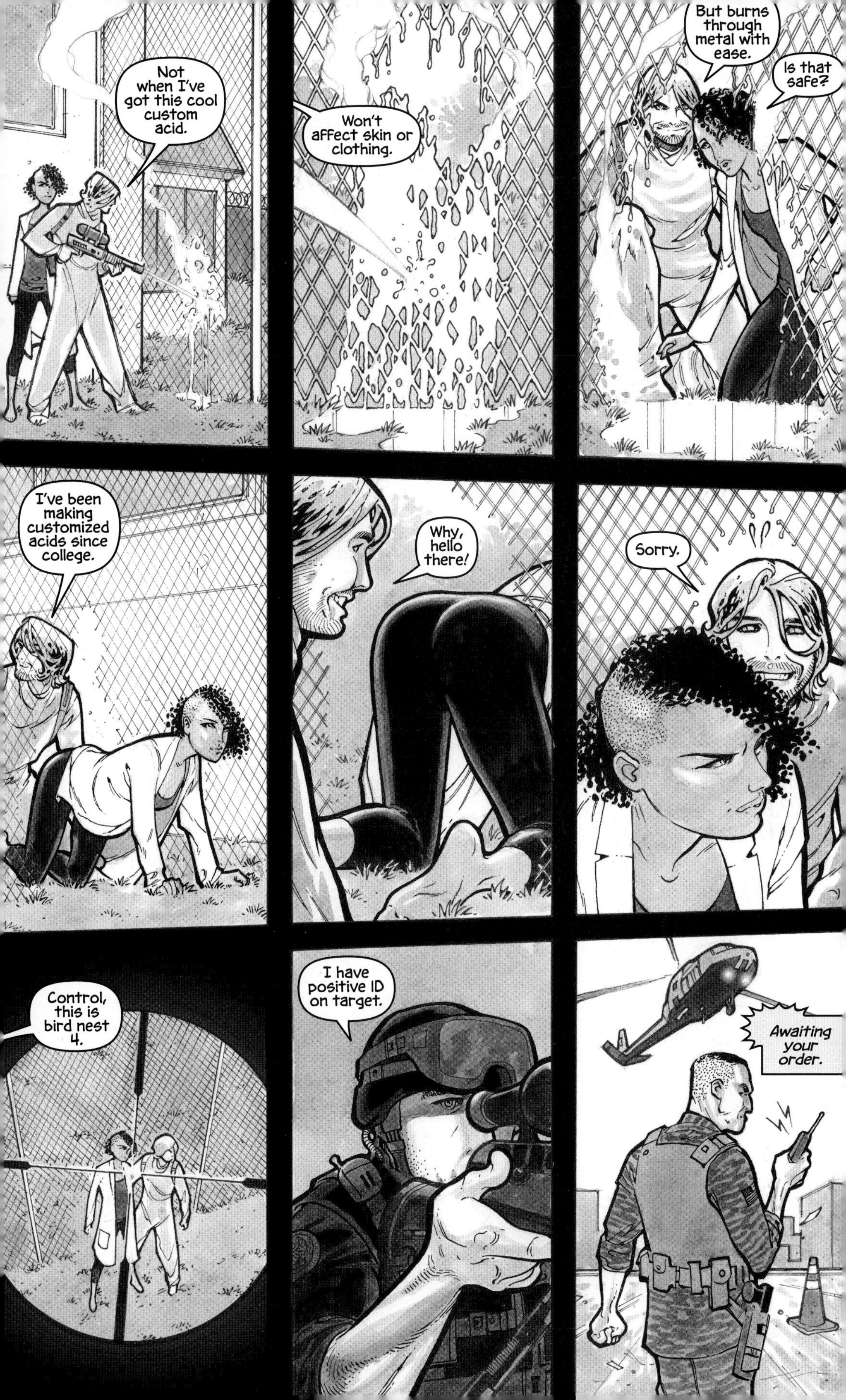
Not when I've got this cool custom acid.
Won't affect skin or clothing.
But burns through metal with ease.
Is that safe?
I've been making customized acids since college.
Why, hello there!
Sorry.
Control, this is bird nest 4.
I have positive ID on target.
Awaiting your order.

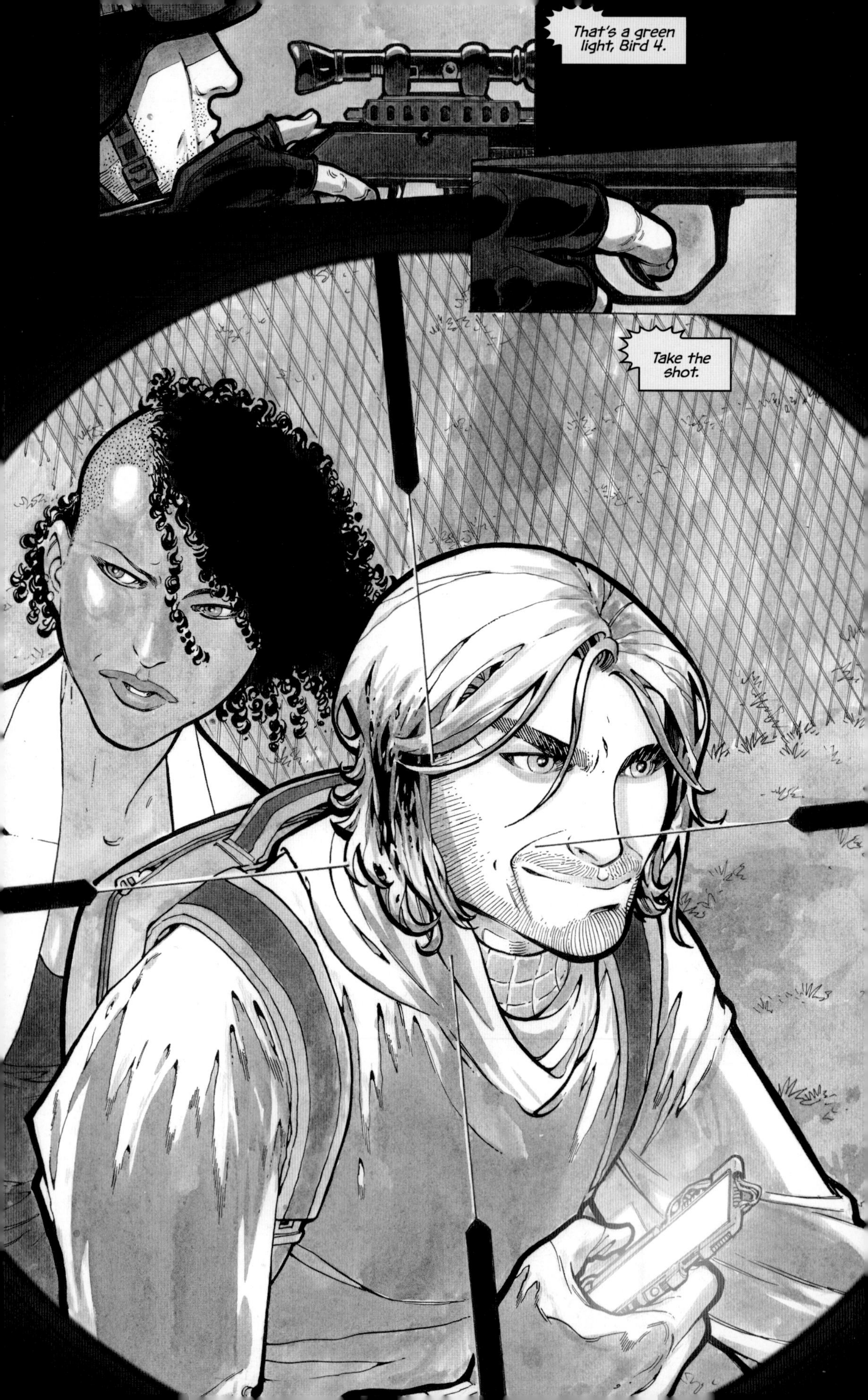
That's a green light, Bird 4.
Take the shot.

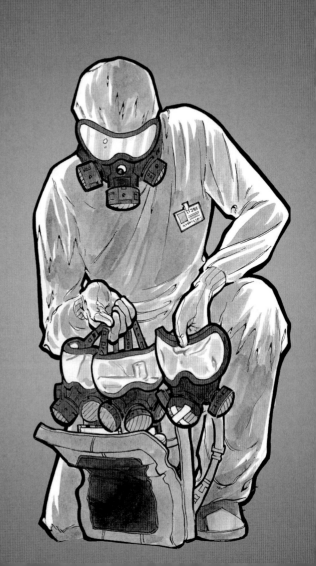

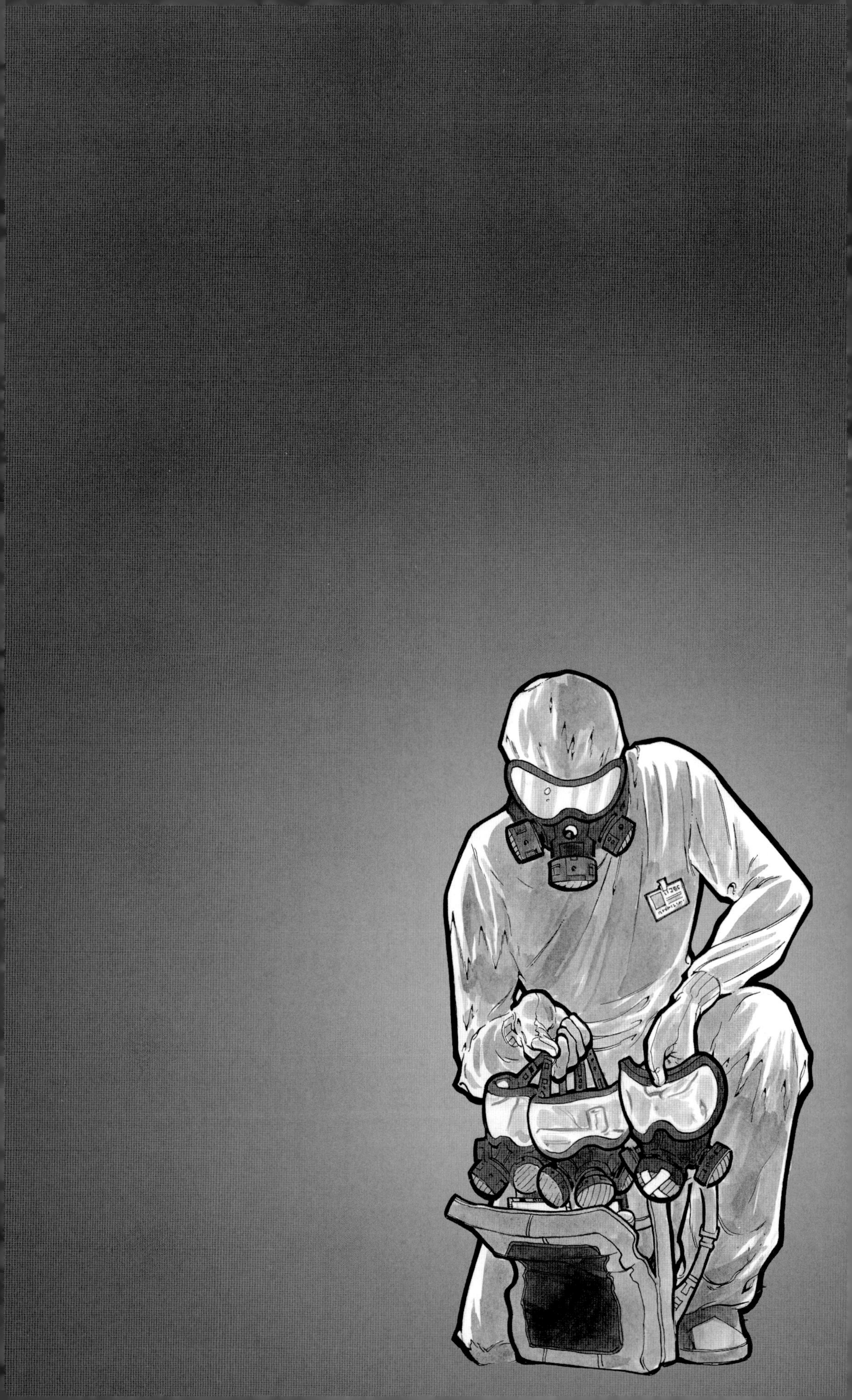

CHAPTER 4

THINK TANK

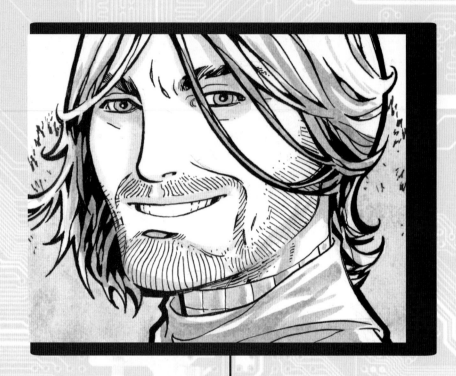

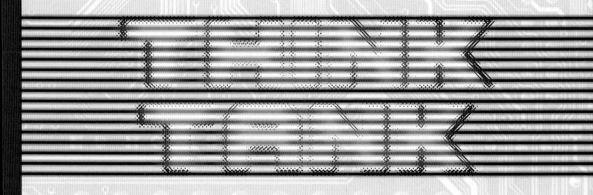

$$\oint \vec{E} \ d\vec{A} = \frac{1}{\varepsilon_0} q_{in} \qquad \oint \vec{B} \ d\vec{A} = 0 \qquad \oint \vec{E} \ d\ell = -\frac{d}{dt} \int B \ dA$$

$$\oint \vec{B} \ d\vec{\ell} = \mu_0 I_{in} \qquad \vec{F} = q(\vec{v} \times \vec{B} + \vec{E}) \qquad i = \frac{dq}{dt}$$

nt charge $\quad E = \frac{1}{4\pi \varepsilon_0} \frac{q}{r^2} \qquad V = \frac{1}{4\pi \varepsilon_0} \frac{q}{r} \qquad p = qd$

$$V_f - V_i = -\int_i^f \vec{E} \ d\vec{s} \qquad E_x = -\frac{\partial V}{\partial x} \qquad \vec{\tau} = \vec{p} \times \vec{E}$$

$$C = \frac{Q}{V} \qquad U_E = \frac{1}{2} QV = \frac{1}{2} CV^2 = \frac{1}{2} \frac{Q^2}{C} \qquad C = \varepsilon_0 \frac{A}{d}$$

$$R = \frac{V}{i} \qquad P = Vi \qquad P = i^2 R = \frac{V^2}{R} \qquad R = \rho \frac{L}{A}$$

$$R_{eq} = R_1 + R_2$$

"THE DIFFERENCE BETWEEN
STUPIDITY AND GENIUS IS THAT
GENIUS HAS ITS LIMITS."
~ALBERT EINSTEIN

$$\frac{1}{R_{eq}} = \frac{1}{R_1} + \frac{1}{R_2}$$

$$d\vec{B} = \frac{\mu_0}{4\pi} \frac{i \ d\vec{s} \times \hat{r}}{r^2} \qquad B = \frac{\mu_0}{2\pi} \frac{i}{r} \qquad B = \mu_0 n i \qquad \vec{\tau} = \vec{\mu} \times \vec{B}$$

$$\mathcal{E} = -\frac{d\Phi}{dt} \qquad \mathcal{E} = -N \frac{d\Phi}{dt} \qquad L = \frac{|\mathcal{E}|}{|\frac{di}{dt}|} = \frac{N\Phi}{i}$$

$$u_E = \frac{1}{2} \varepsilon_0 E^2 \qquad u_B = \frac{1}{2} \frac{B^2}{\mu_0} \qquad U_B = \frac{1}{2} L i^2$$

$$q_o e^{-t/\tau_c} \qquad q = C\mathcal{E}(1 - e^{-t/\tau_c}) \qquad i = i_o e^{-t/\tau_L} \qquad i = \frac{\mathcal{E}}{R}(1 - e^{-t/\tau_L})$$

$$\frac{L}{R} \qquad \tau_c = RC \qquad \mu = NiA \qquad \frac{1}{4\pi \varepsilon_0} = 9 \times 10^9 \qquad \frac{\mu_0}{4\pi} = 10^{-7}$$

means $10^6 \qquad \mu$ means 10^{-6}

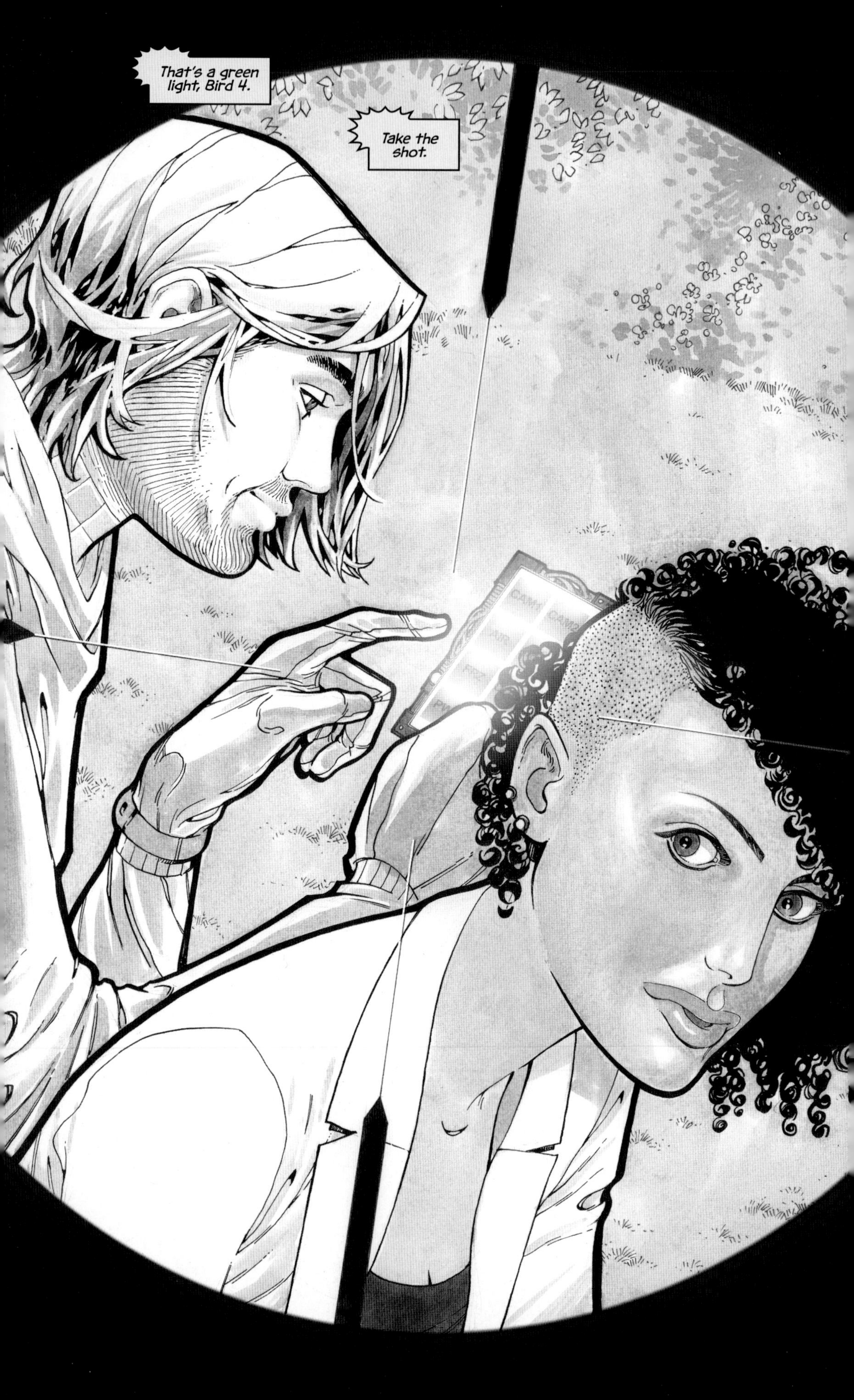
That's a green light, Bird 4.
Take the shot.

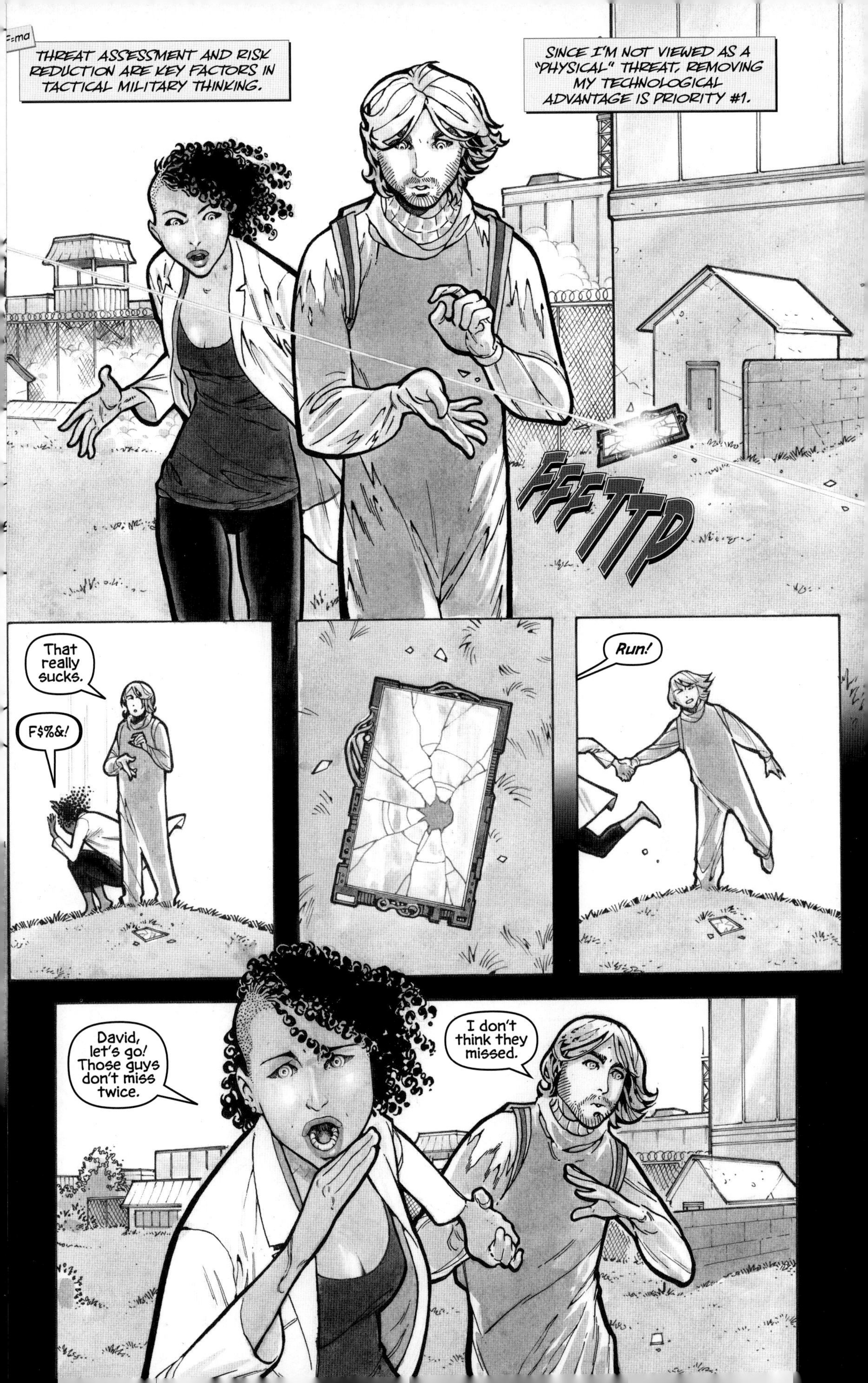
THREAT ASSESSMENT AND RISK REDUCTION ARE KEY FACTORS IN TACTICAL MILITARY THINKING.
SINCE I'M NOT VIEWED AS A "PHYSICAL" THREAT, REMOVING MY TECHNOLOGICAL ADVANTAGE IS PRIORITY #1.
FFFTTP
That really sucks.
F$%&!
Run!
David, let's go! Those guys don't miss twice.
I don't think they missed.

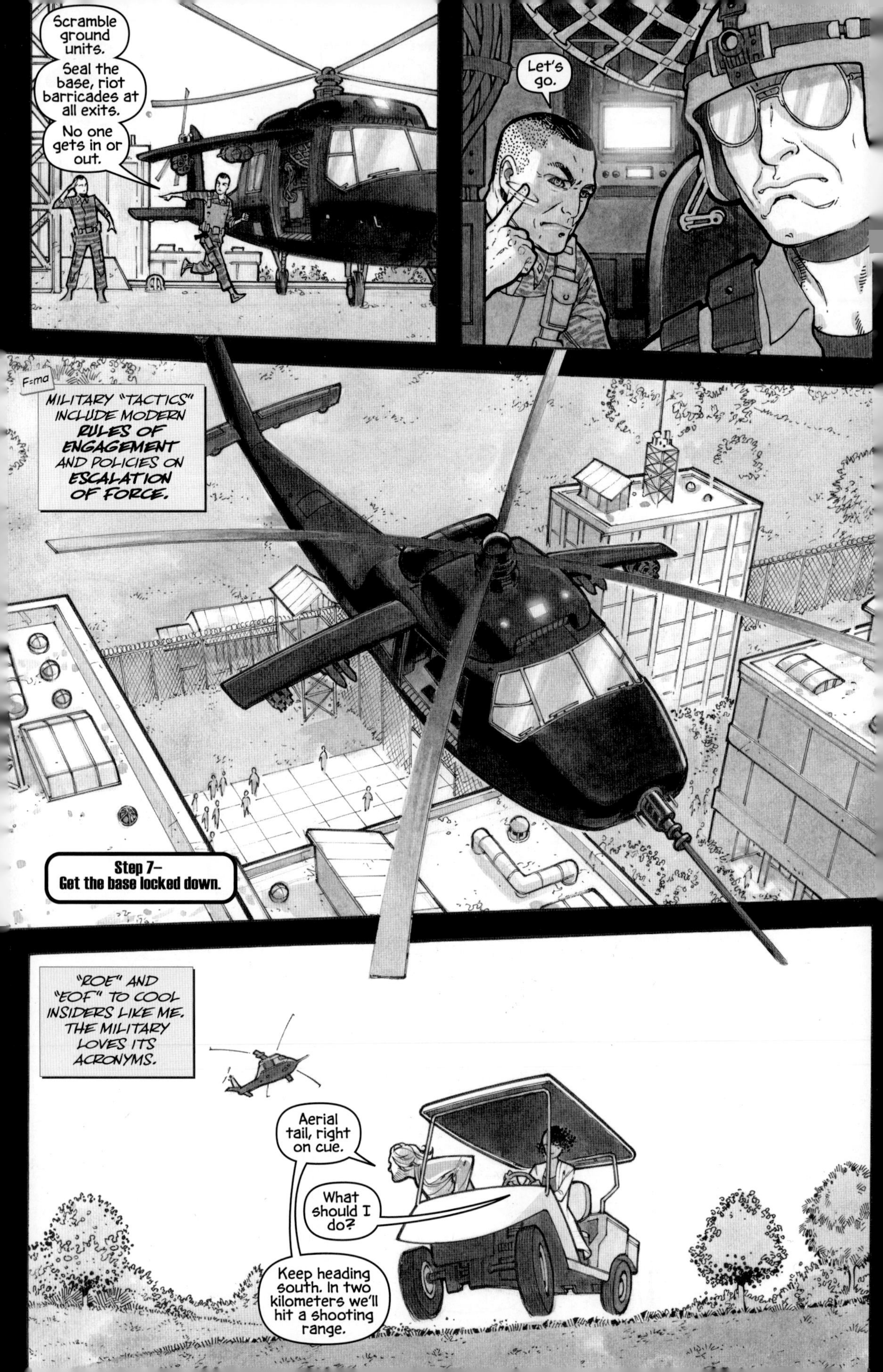
Scramble ground units.
Seal the base, riot barricades at all exits.
No one gets in or out.
Let's go.
F=ma
MILITARY "TACTICS" INCLUDE MODERN RULES OF ENGAGEMENT AND POLICIES ON ESCALATION OF FORCE.
Step 7– Get the base locked down.
"ROE" AND "EOF" TO COOL INSIDERS LIKE ME. THE MILITARY LOVES ITS ACRONYMS.
Aerial tail, right on cue.
What should I do?
Keep heading south. In two kilometers we'll hit a shooting range.

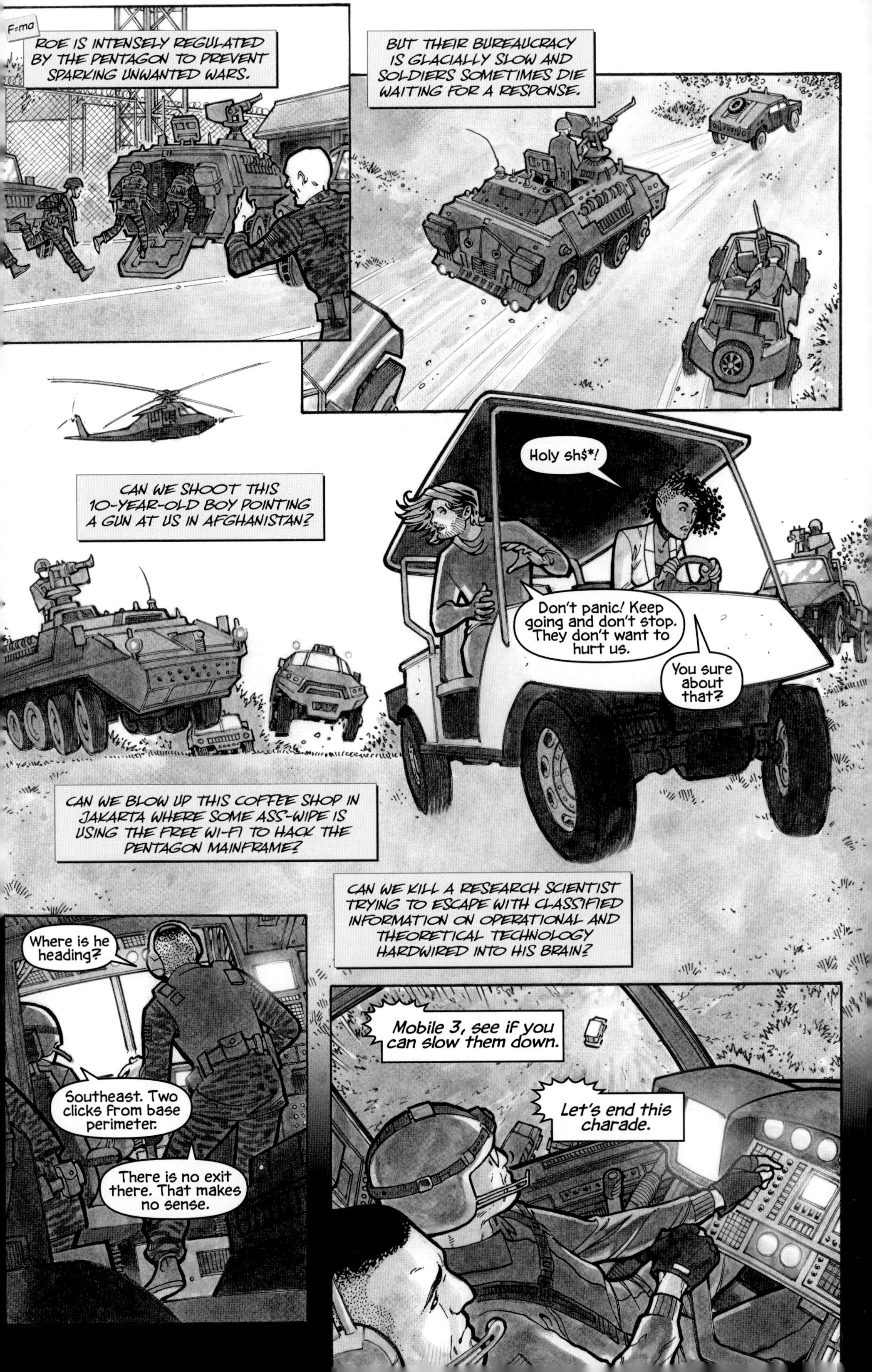
F=ma
ROE IS INTENSELY REGULATED BY THE PENTAGON TO PREVENT SPARKING UNWANTED WARS.
BUT THEIR BUREAUCRACY IS GLACIALLY SLOW AND SOLDIERS SOMETIMES DIE WAITING FOR A RESPONSE.
CAN WE SHOOT THIS 10-YEAR-OLD BOY POINTING A GUN AT US IN AFGHANISTAN?
Holy sh$*!
Don't panic! Keep going and don't stop. They don't want to hurt us.
You sure about that?
CAN WE BLOW UP THIS COFFEE SHOP IN JAKARTA WHERE SOME ASS-WIPE IS USING THE FREE WI-FI TO HACK THE PENTAGON MAINFRAME?
CAN WE KILL A RESEARCH SCIENTIST TRYING TO ESCAPE WITH CLASSIFIED INFORMATION ON OPERATIONAL AND THEORETICAL TECHNOLOGY HARDWIRED INTO HIS BRAIN?
Where is he heading?
Southeast. Two clicks from base perimeter.
There is no exit there. That makes no sense.
Mobile 3, see if you can slow them down.
Let's end this charade.

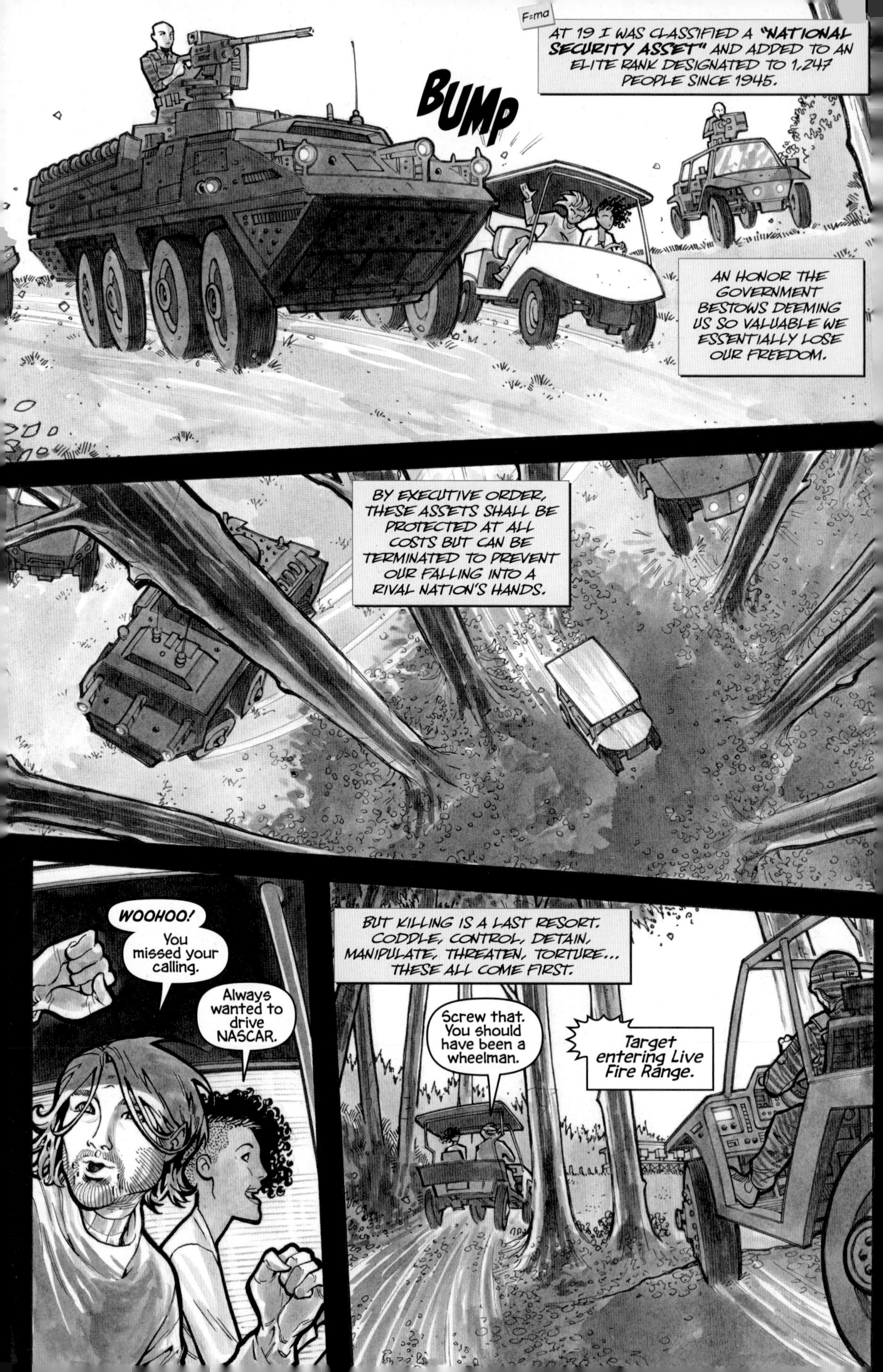
F=ma
AT 19 I WAS CLASSIFIED A "NATIONAL SECURITY ASSET" AND ADDED TO AN ELITE RANK DESIGNATED TO 1,247 PEOPLE SINCE 1945.
BUMP
AN HONOR THE GOVERNMENT BESTOWS DEEMING US SO VALUABLE WE ESSENTIALLY LOSE OUR FREEDOM.
BY EXECUTIVE ORDER, THESE ASSETS SHALL BE PROTECTED AT ALL COSTS BUT CAN BE TERMINATED TO PREVENT OUR FALLING INTO A RIVAL NATION'S HANDS.
WOOHOO! You missed your calling.
Always wanted to drive NASCAR.
BUT KILLING IS A LAST RESORT. CODDLE, CONTROL, DETAIN, MANIPULATE, THREATEN, TORTURE... THESE ALL COME FIRST.
Screw that. You should have been a wheelman.
Target entering Live Fire Range.

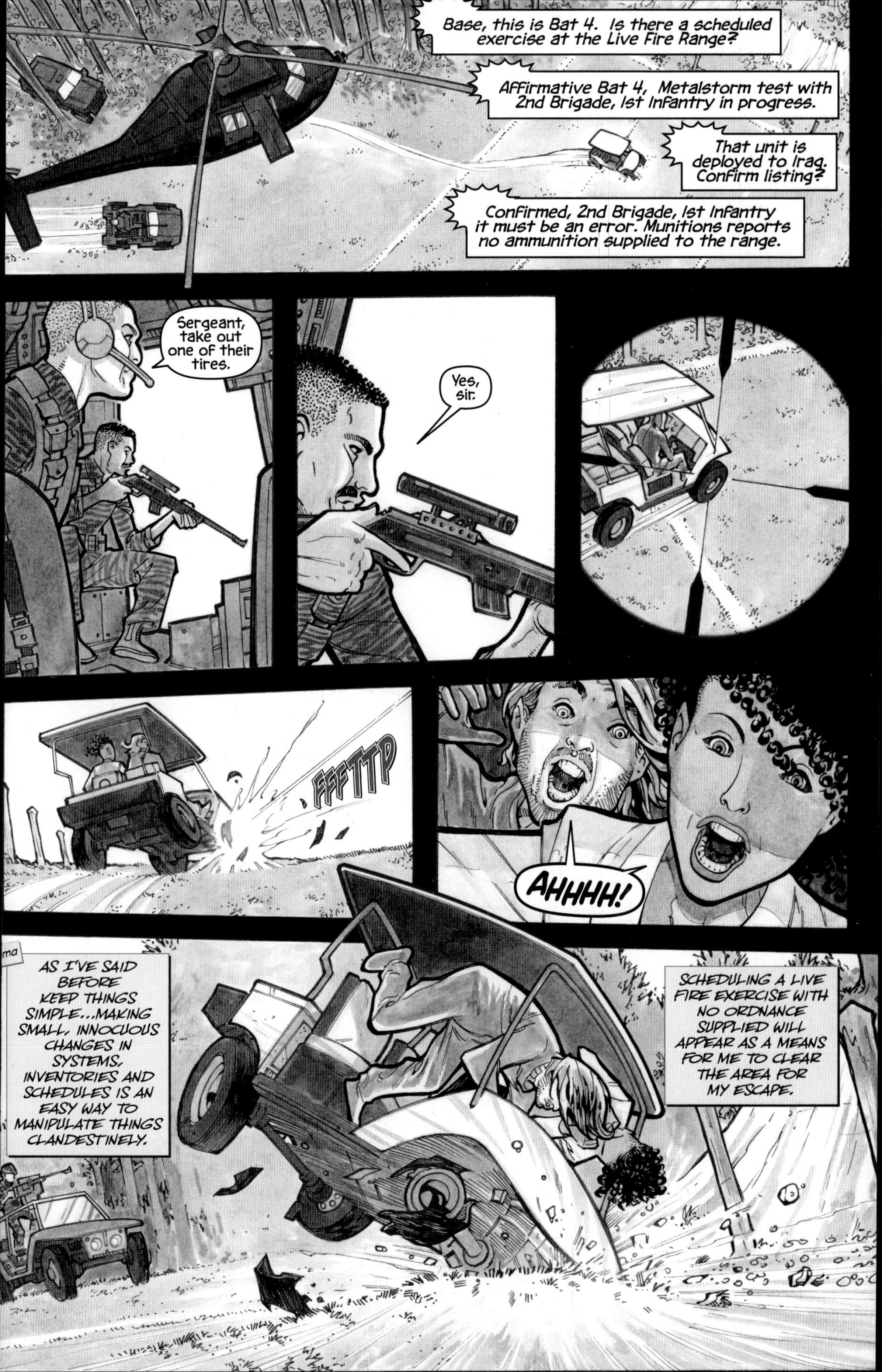
Base, this is Bat 4. Is there a scheduled exercise at the Live Fire Range?
Affirmative Bat 4, Metalstorm test with 2nd Brigade, 1st Infantry in progress.
That unit is deployed to Iraq. Confirm listing?
Confirmed, 2nd Brigade, 1st Infantry it must be an error. Munitions reports no ammunition supplied to the range.
Sergeant, take out one of their tires.
Yes, sir.
FFFTTP
AHHHH!
AS I'VE SAID BEFORE KEEP THINGS SIMPLE...MAKING SMALL, INNOCUOUS CHANGES IN SYSTEMS, INVENTORIES AND SCHEDULES IS AN EASY WAY TO MANIPULATE THINGS CLANDESTINELY.
SCHEDULING A LIVE FIRE EXERCISE WITH NO ORDNANCE SUPPLIED WILL APPEAR AS A MEANS FOR ME TO CLEAR THE AREA FOR MY ESCAPE.

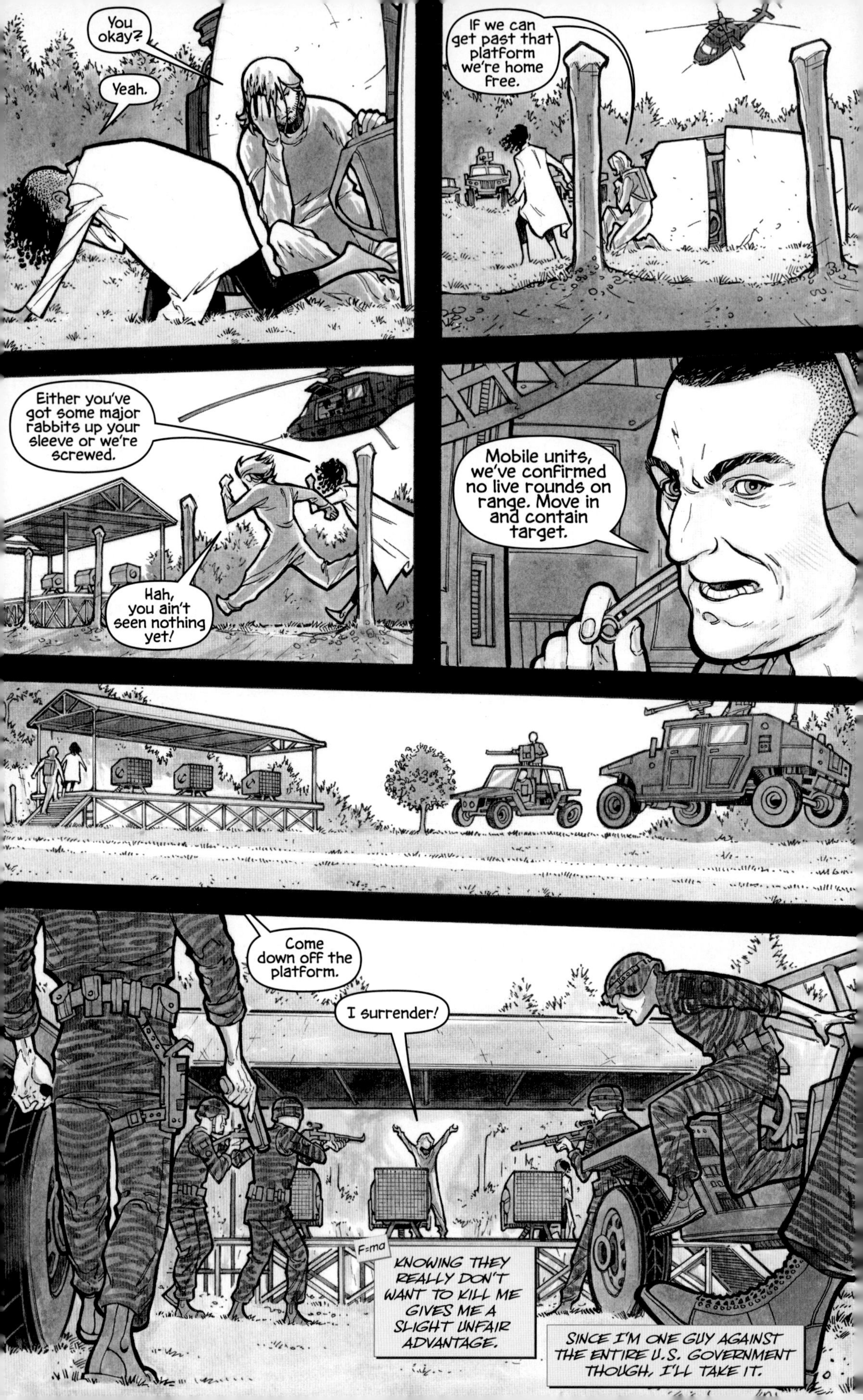
You okay?
Yeah.
If we can get past that platform we're home free.
Either you've got some major rabbits up your sleeve or we're screwed.
Hah, you ain't seen nothing yet!
Mobile units, we've confirmed no live rounds on range. Move in and contain target.
Come down off the platform.
I surrender!
F=ma
KNOWING THEY REALLY DON'T WANT TO KILL ME GIVES ME A SLIGHT UNFAIR ADVANTAGE.
SINCE I'M ONE GUY AGAINST THE ENTIRE U.S. GOVERNMENT THOUGH, I'LL TAKE IT.

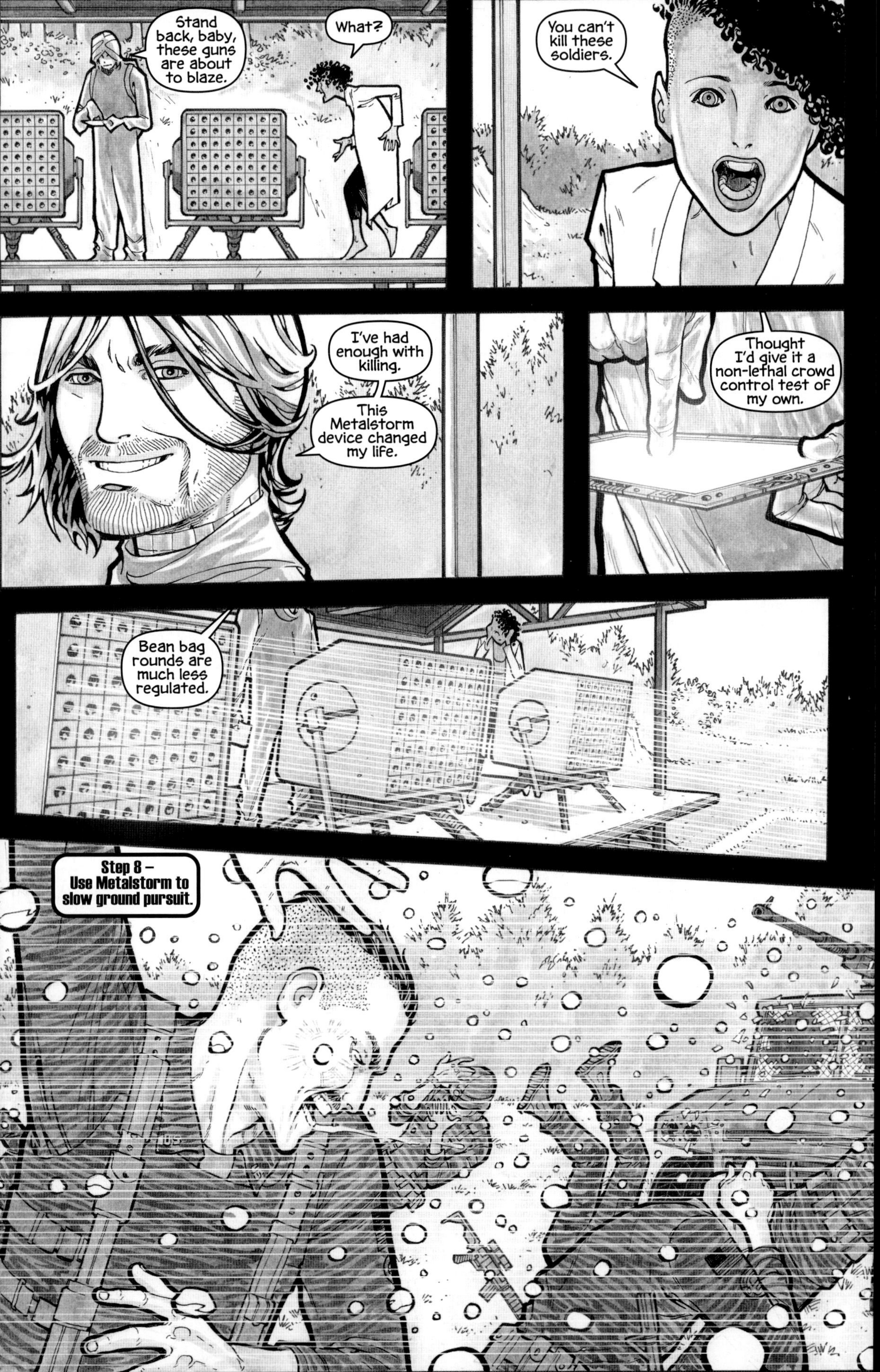
Stand back, baby, these guns are about to blaze.
What?
You can't kill these soldiers.
I've had enough with killing.
This Metalstorm device changed my life.
Thought I'd give it a non-lethal crowd control test of my own.
Bean bag rounds are much less regulated.
Step 8 – Use Metalstorm to slow ground pursuit.

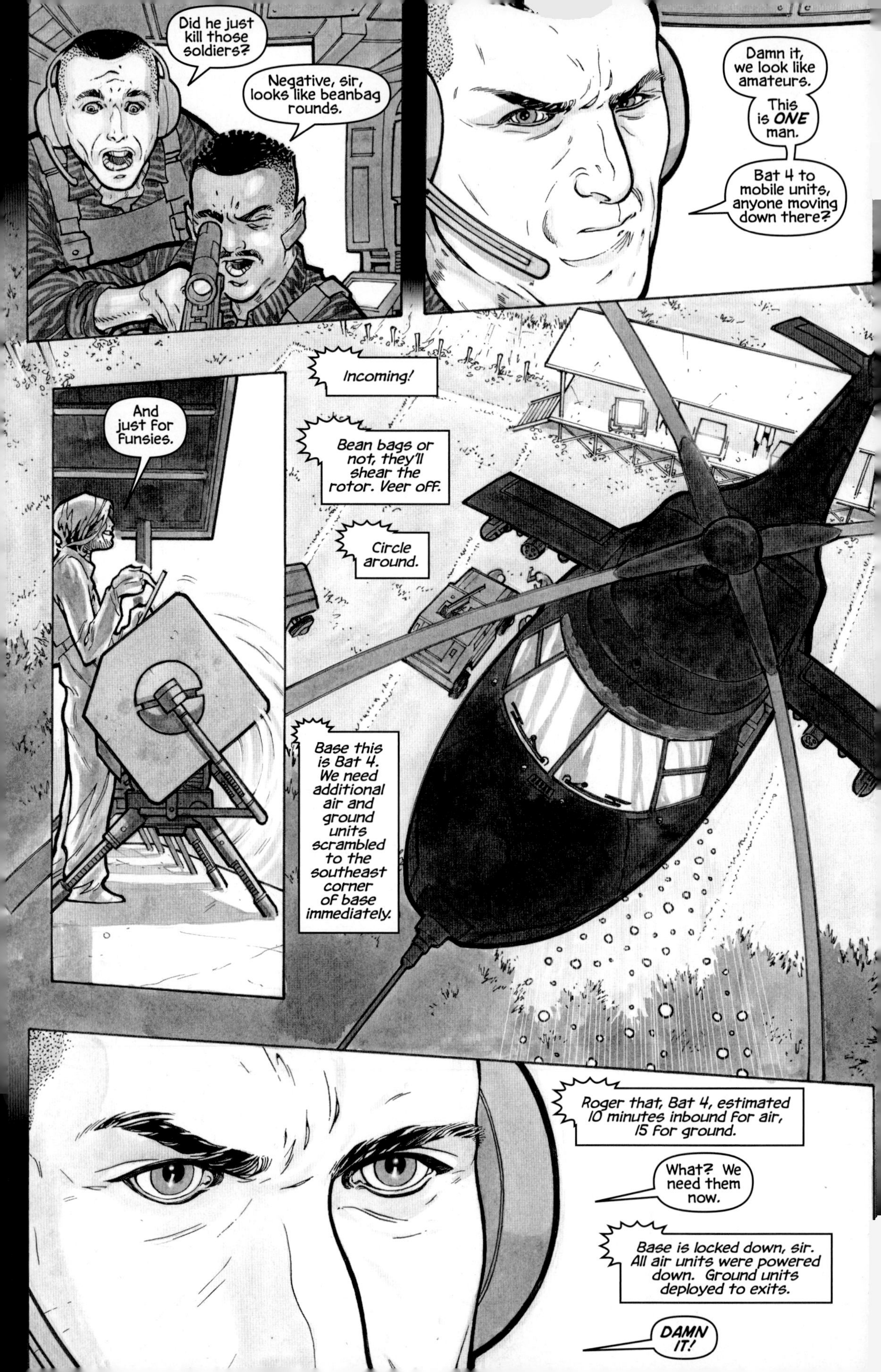
Did he just kill those soldiers?
Negative, sir, looks like beanbag rounds.
Damn it, we look like amateurs.
This is ONE man.
Bat 4 to mobile units, anyone moving down there?
Incoming!
And just for funsies.
Bean bags or not, they'll shear the rotor. Veer off.
Circle around.
Base this is Bat 4. We need additional air and ground units scrambled to the southeast corner of base immediately.
Roger that, Bat 4, estimated 10 minutes inbound for air, 15 for ground.
What? We need them now.
Base is locked down, sir. All air units were powered down. Ground units deployed to exits.
DAMN IT!

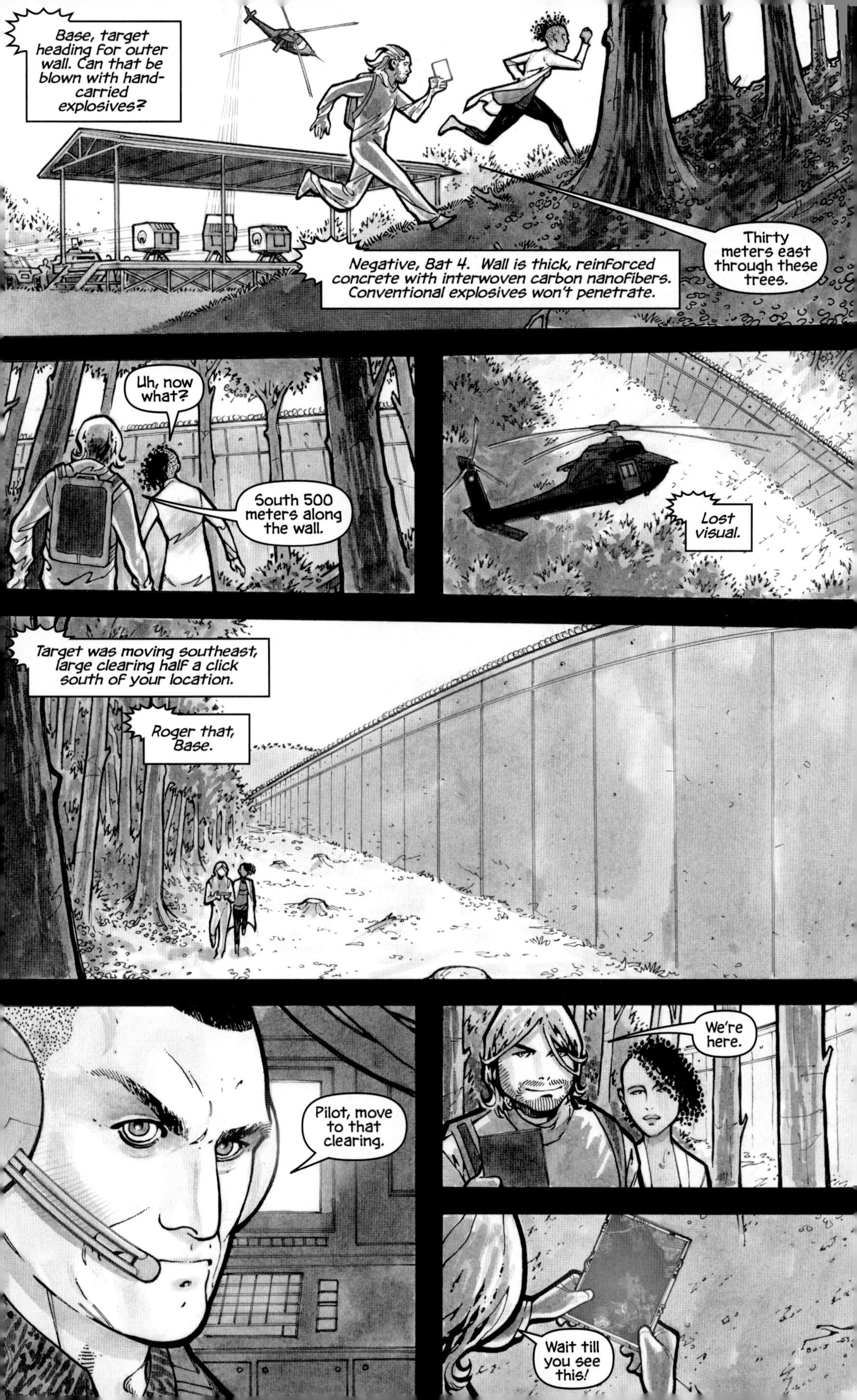
Base, target heading for outer wall. Can that be blown with hand-carried explosives?
Thirty meters east through these trees.
Negative, Bat 4. Wall is thick, reinforced concrete with interwoven carbon nanofibers. Conventional explosives won't penetrate.
Uh, now what?
South 500 meters along the wall.
Lost visual.
Target was moving southeast, large clearing half a click south of your location.
Roger that, Base.
Pilot, move to that clearing.
We're here.
Wait till you see this!

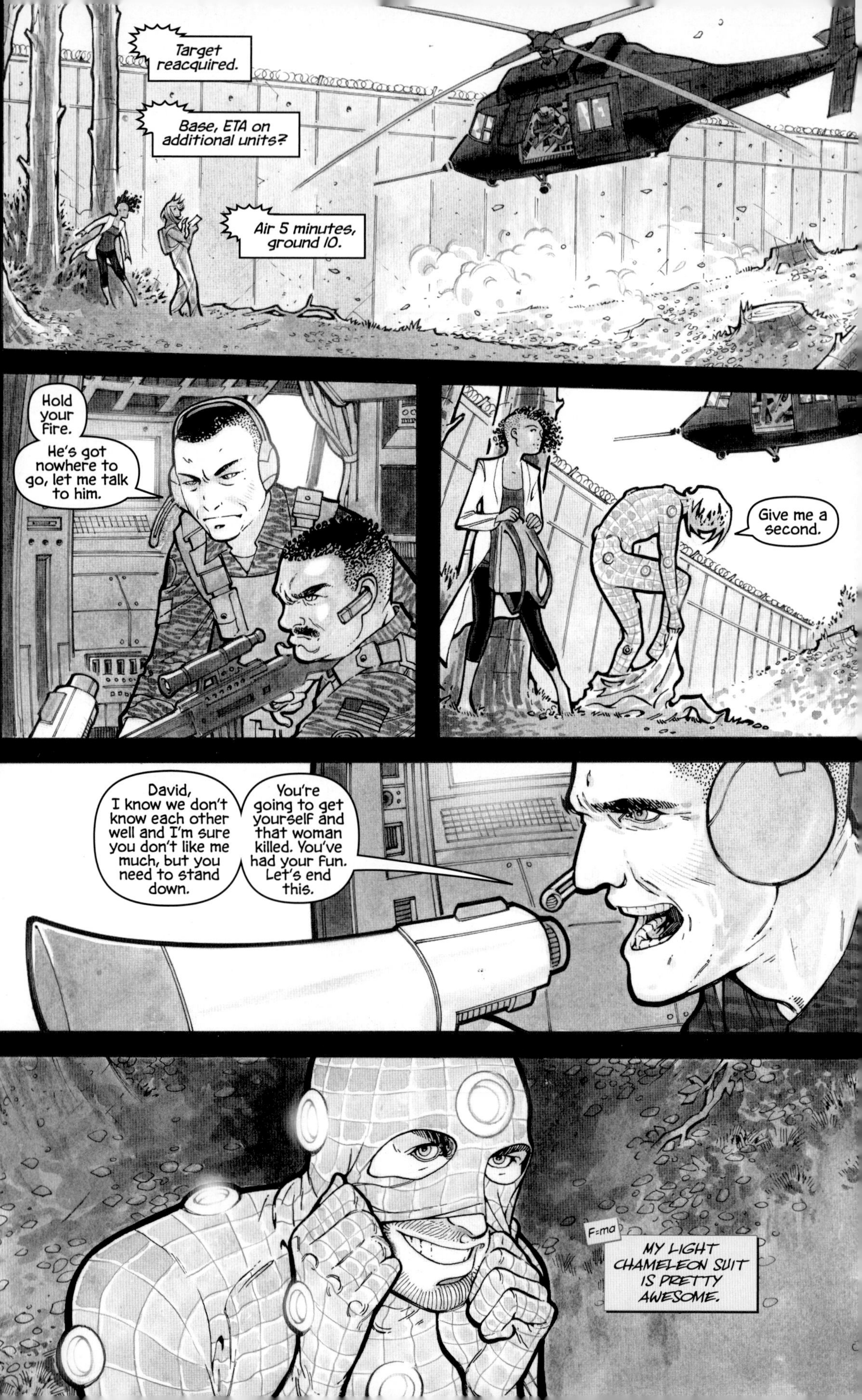
Target reacquired.
Base, ETA on additional units?
Air 5 minutes, ground 10.
Hold your Fire.
He's got nowhere to go, let me talk to him.
Give me a second.
David, I know we don't know each other well and I'm sure you don't like me much, but you need to stand down.
You're going to get yourself and that woman killed. You've had your fun. Let's end this.
F=ma
MY LIGHT CHAMELEON SUIT IS PRETTY AWESOME.

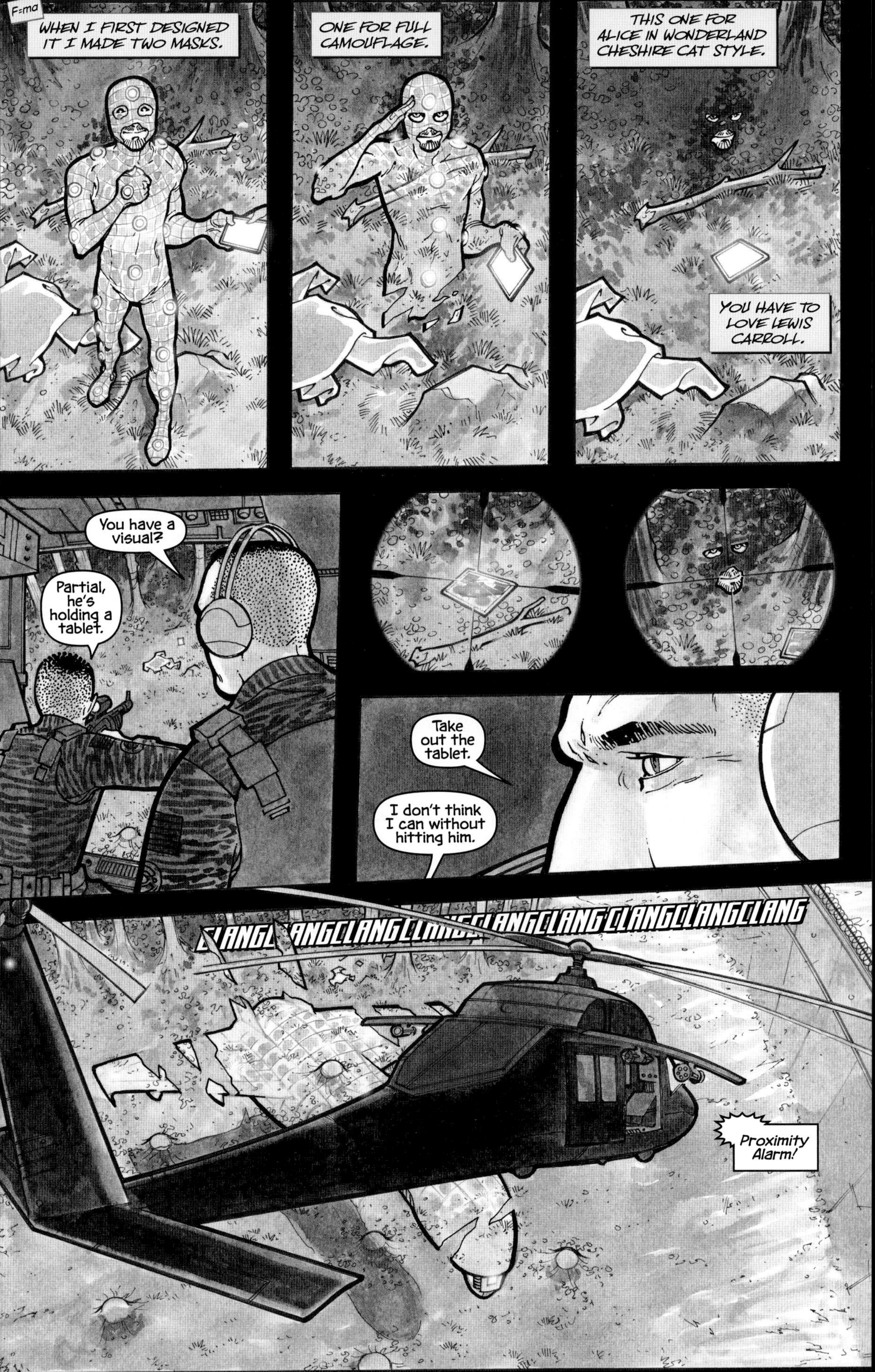
F=ma
WHEN I FIRST DESIGNED IT I MADE TWO MASKS.
ONE FOR FULL CAMOUFLAGE.
THIS ONE FOR ALICE IN WONDERLAND CHESHIRE CAT STYLE.
YOU HAVE TO LOVE LEWIS CARROLL.
You have a visual?
Partial, he's holding a tablet.
Take out the tablet.
I don't think I can without hitting him.
CLANGCLANGCLANGCLANGCLANGCLANGCLANGCLANGCLANG
Proximity Alarm!

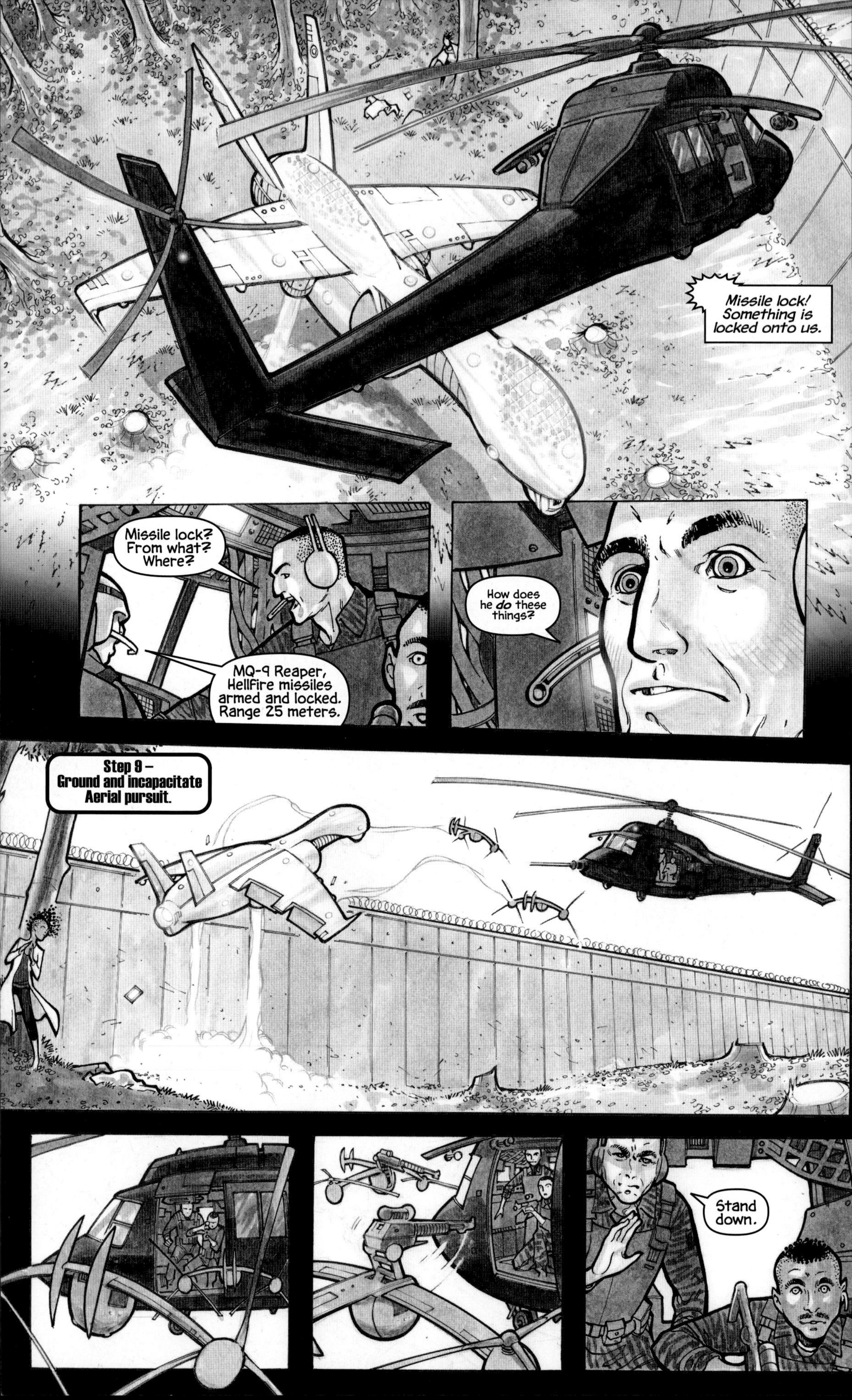
Missile lock! Something is locked onto us.
Missile lock? From what? Where?
MQ-9 Reaper, Hellfire missiles armed and locked. Range 25 meters.
How does he *do* these things?
Step 9 – Ground and incapacitate Aerial pursuit.
Stand down.

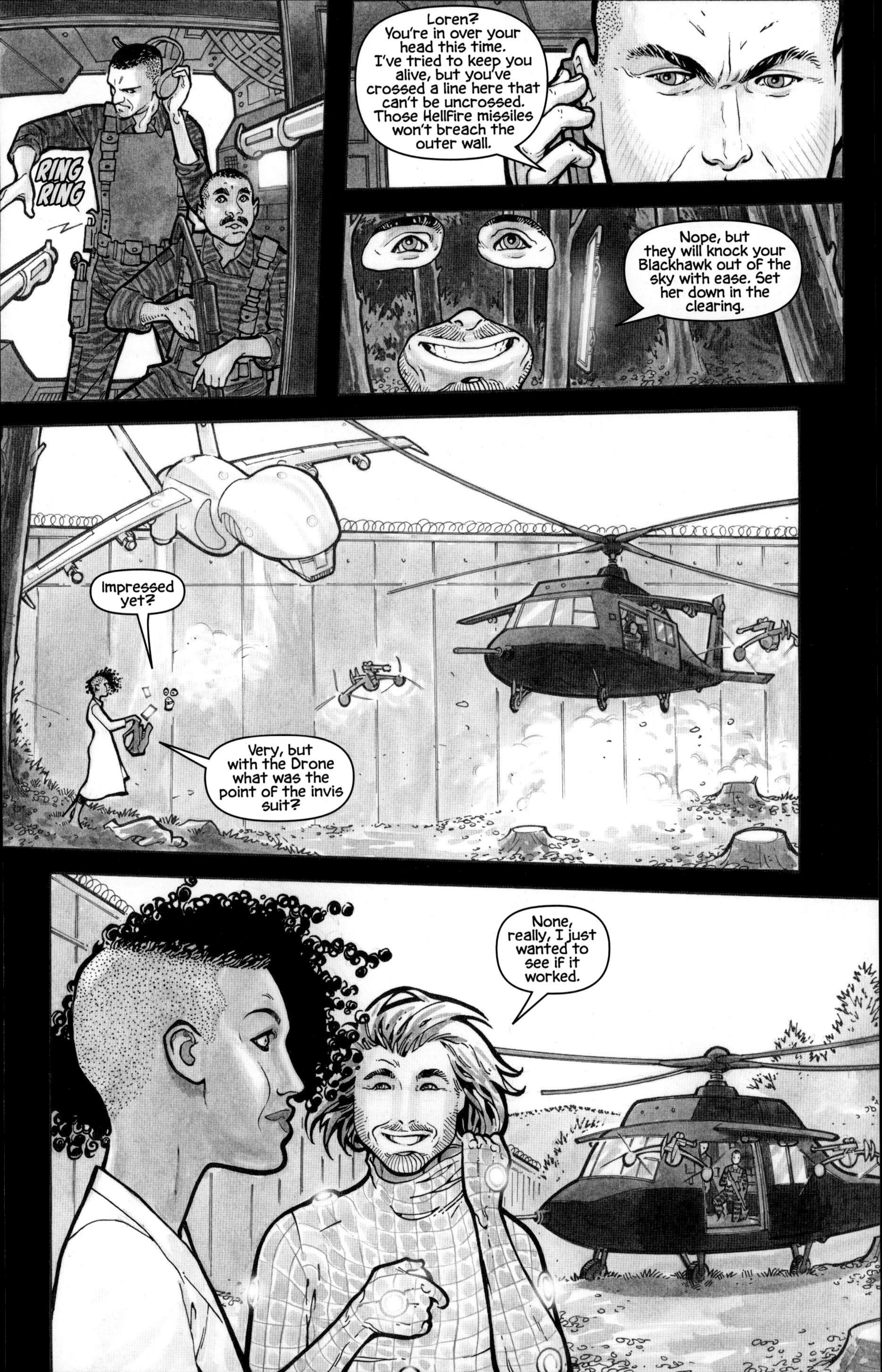
RING RING
Loren?
You're in over your head this time. I've tried to keep you alive, but you've crossed a line here that can't be uncrossed. Those HellFire missiles won't breach the outer wall.
Nope, but they will knock your Blackhawk out of the sky with ease. Set her down in the clearing.
Impressed yet?
Very, but with the Drone what was the point of the invis suit?
None, really, I just wanted to see if it worked.

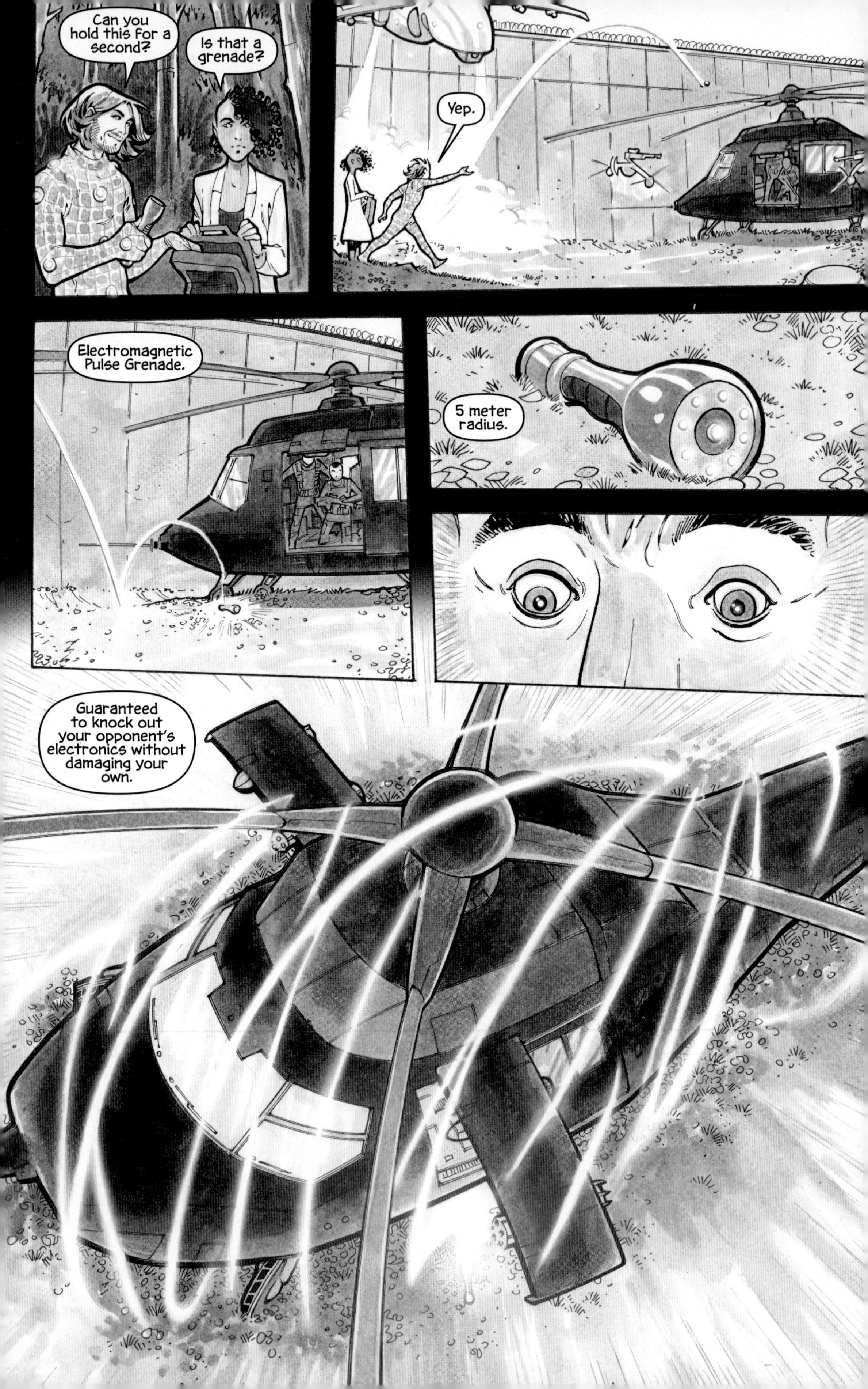
Can you hold this for a second?
Is that a grenade?
Yep.
Electromagnetic Pulse Grenade.
5 meter radius.
Guaranteed to knock out your opponent's electronics without damaging your own.

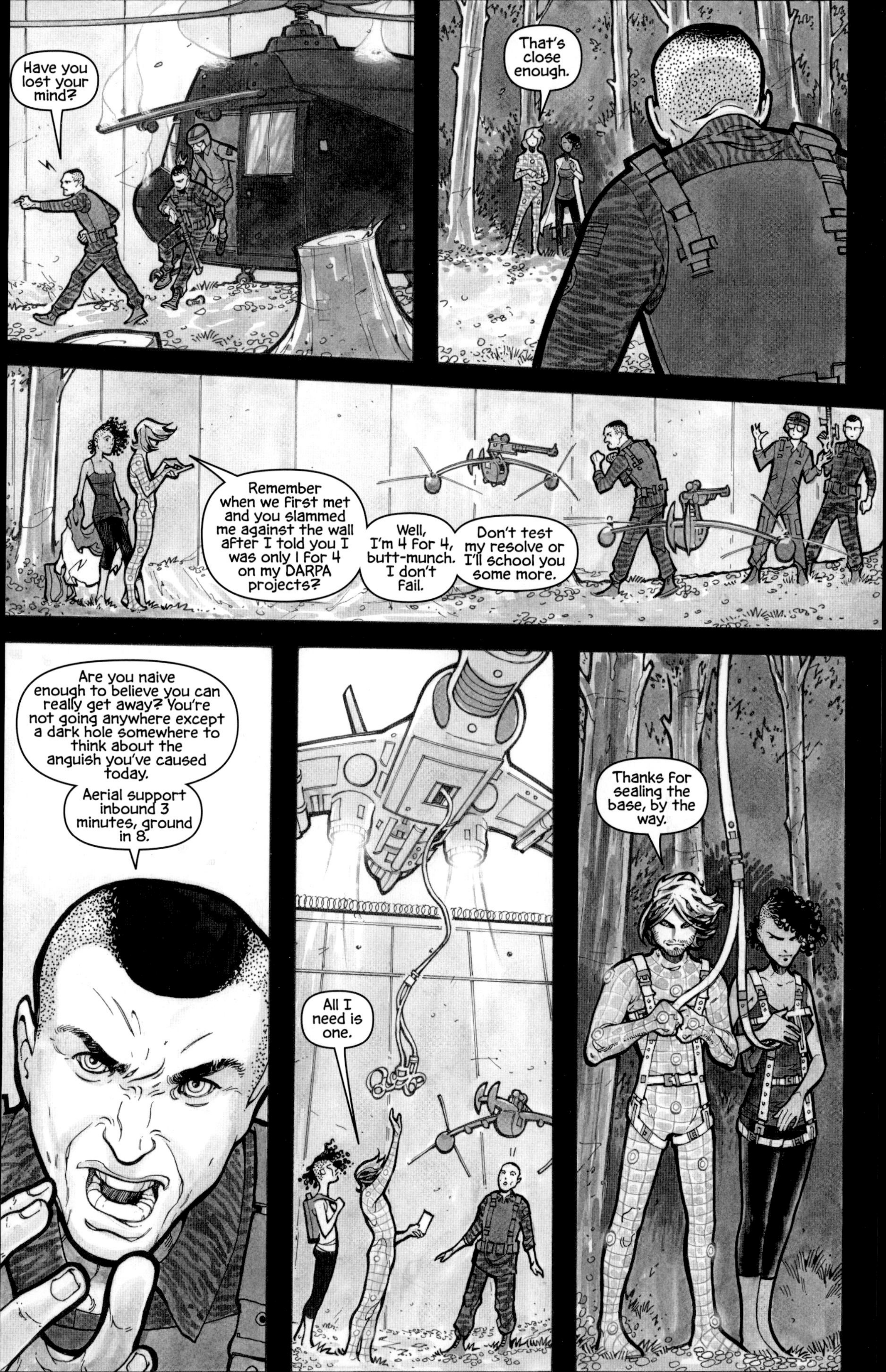
Have you lost your mind?
That's close enough.
Remember when we first met and you slammed me against the wall after I told you I was only 1 for 4 on my DARPA projects?
Well, I'm 4 for 4, butt-munch. I don't fail.
Don't test my resolve or I'll school you some more.
Are you naive enough to believe you can really get away? You're not going anywhere except a dark hole somewhere to think about the anguish you've caused today.
Aerial support inbound 3 minutes, ground in 8.
All I need is one.
Thanks for sealing the base, by the way.

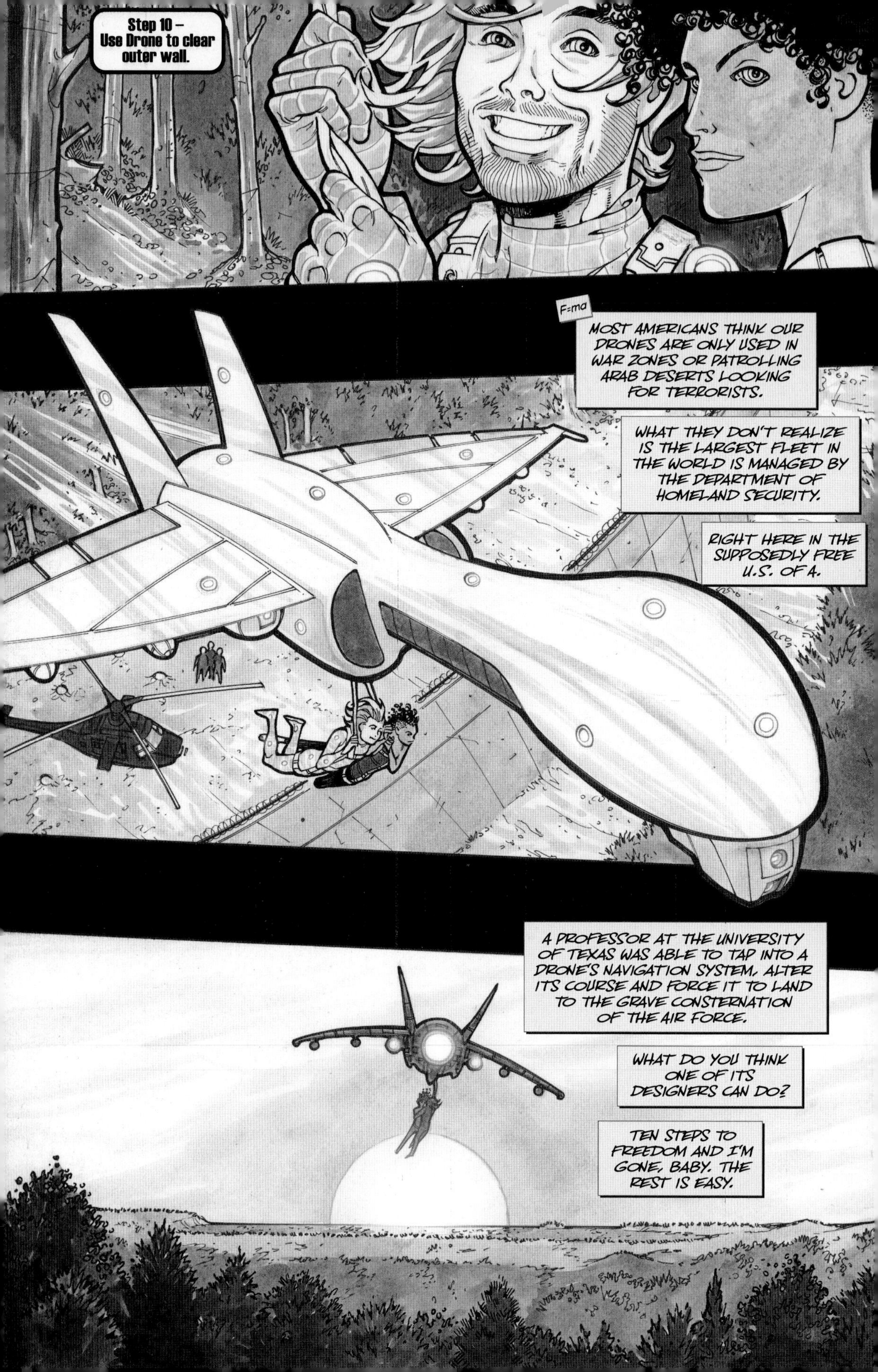

Step 10 –
Use Drone to clear outer wall.
F=ma
MOST AMERICANS THINK OUR DRONES ARE ONLY USED IN WAR ZONES OR PATROLLING ARAB DESERTS LOOKING FOR TERRORISTS.
WHAT THEY DON'T REALIZE IS THE LARGEST FLEET IN THE WORLD IS MANAGED BY THE DEPARTMENT OF HOMELAND SECURITY.
RIGHT HERE IN THE SUPPOSEDLY FREE U.S. OF A.
A PROFESSOR AT THE UNIVERSITY OF TEXAS WAS ABLE TO TAP INTO A DRONE'S NAVIGATION SYSTEM, ALTER ITS COURSE AND FORCE IT TO LAND TO THE GRAVE CONSTERNATION OF THE AIR FORCE.
WHAT DO YOU THINK ONE OF ITS DESIGNERS CAN DO?
TEN STEPS TO FREEDOM AND I'M GONE, BABY. THE REST IS EASY.

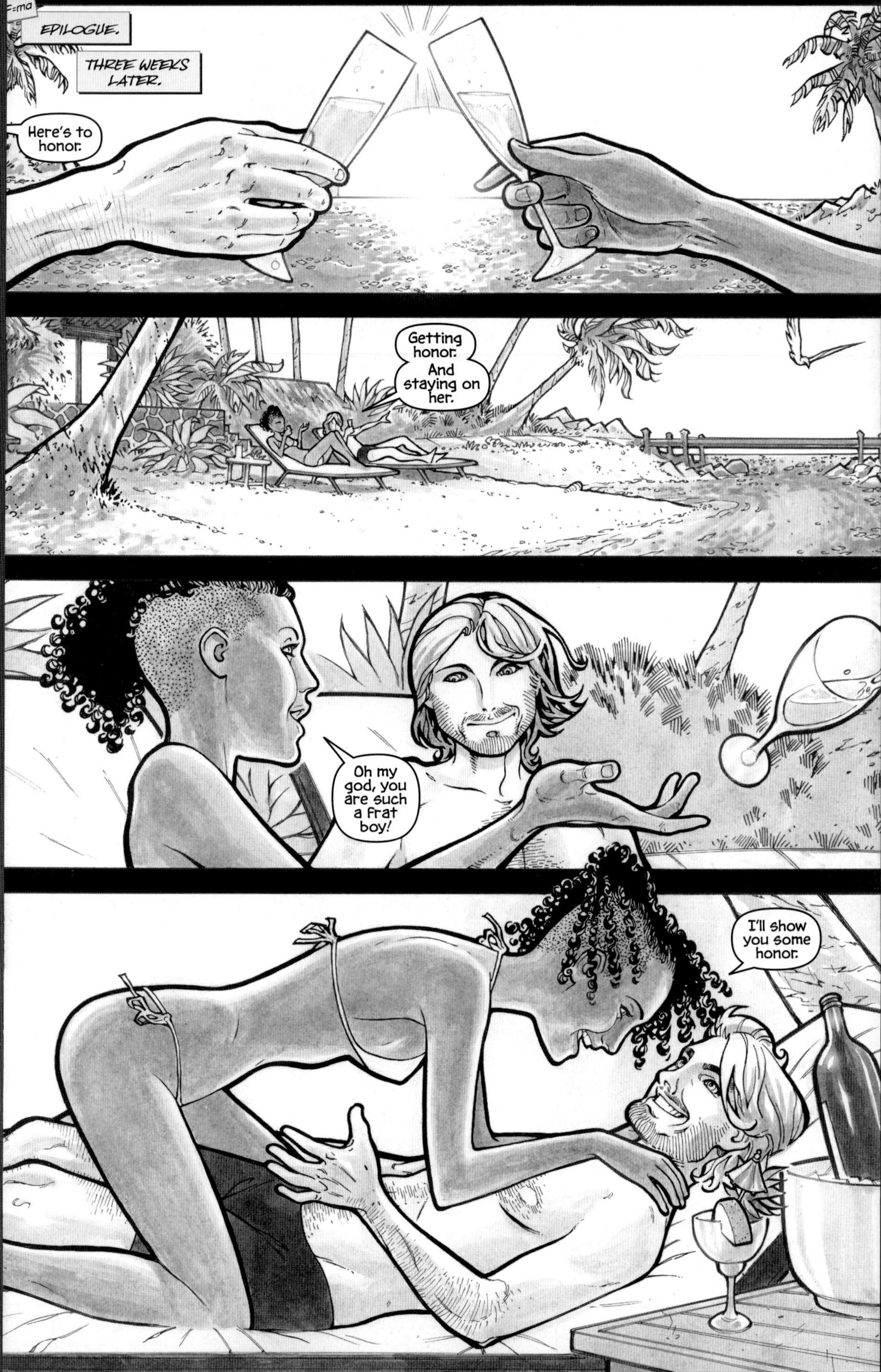
F=ma
EPILOGUE.
THREE WEEKS LATER.
Here's to honor.
Getting honor.
And staying on her.
Oh my god, you are such a frat boy!
I'll show you some honor.

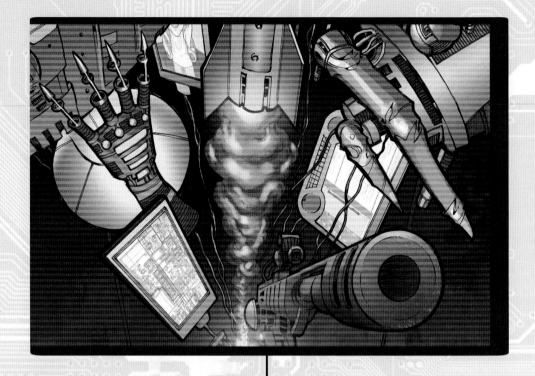

SCIENCE CLASS

THINK
TANK

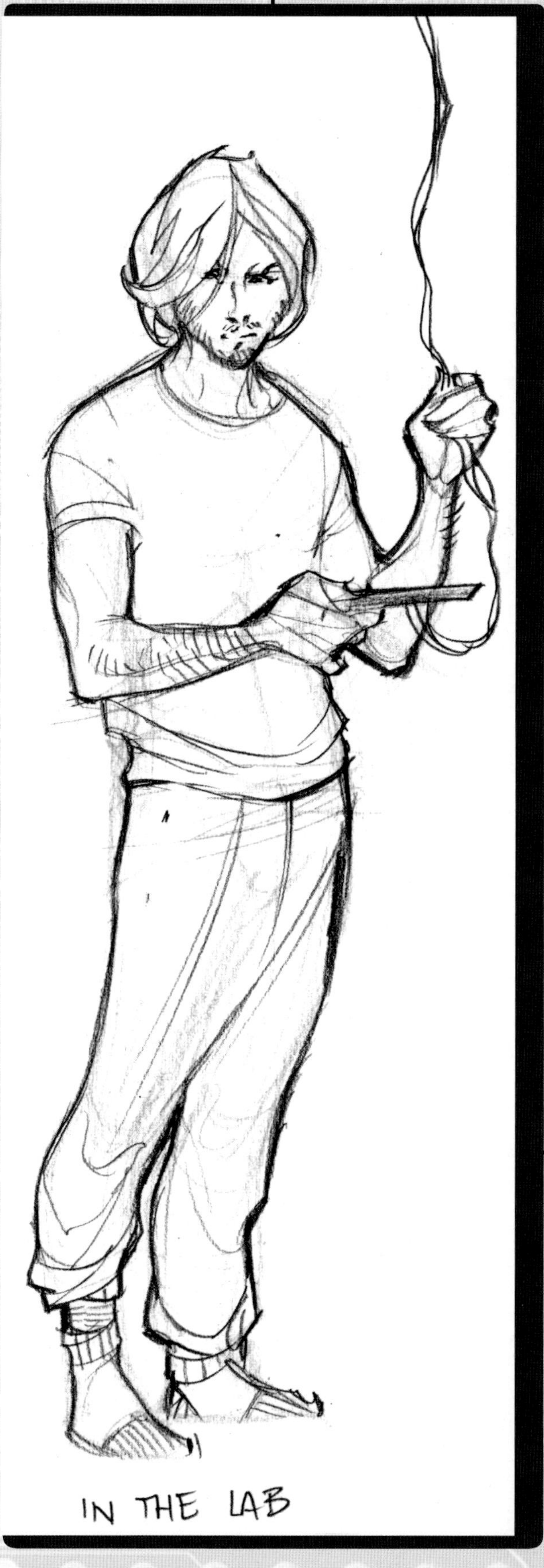
IN THE LAB

SCIENCE CLASS
by Matt Hawkins

Why *Think Tank*? I want people to like Science. It's awesome and fun and not boring like people think. The idea for *Think Tank* came to me when I started hanging with some friends from college who had stayed in the science field. I've visited several Think Tanks including RAND and DARPA and have seen only the declassified stuff, but even that is fascinating. Just walking into one of these you feel like you're stepping into the future. I studied science for many years in college and have a few degrees but have only learned to love it recently, many years after leaving academia far behind.

I'm not quite as smart as David Loren, but this character has a lot of me in it. I've always been interested in people who are conflicted and I feel that way myself all the time. With David we have a guy who loves what he does, but is troubled by how his creations are used. I would love to write about this character for 100+ issues but that all depends on whether I can find an audience for the book so if you like it please tell a friend! I love to hear from readers directly so feel free to pester me on:

Twitter @topcowmatt
Facebook Matt Hawkins (both actual and "likeable" author page)
Google + Matt Hawkins (for all you Google employees)

Warning; if you are easily offended you may want to pass, as I tend to speak my mind on these.

Anyway, wanted to give some thoughts and commentary on why I did some of what I did here and how a lot of it is based on real science. I'm happy to answer some questions in the back pages of future issues and trades, so hit me up!

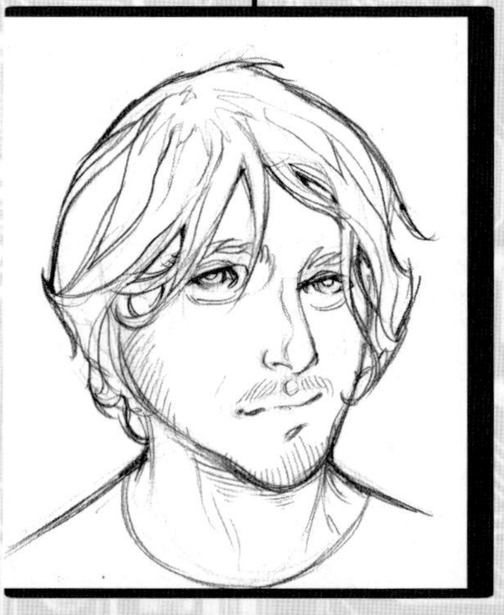

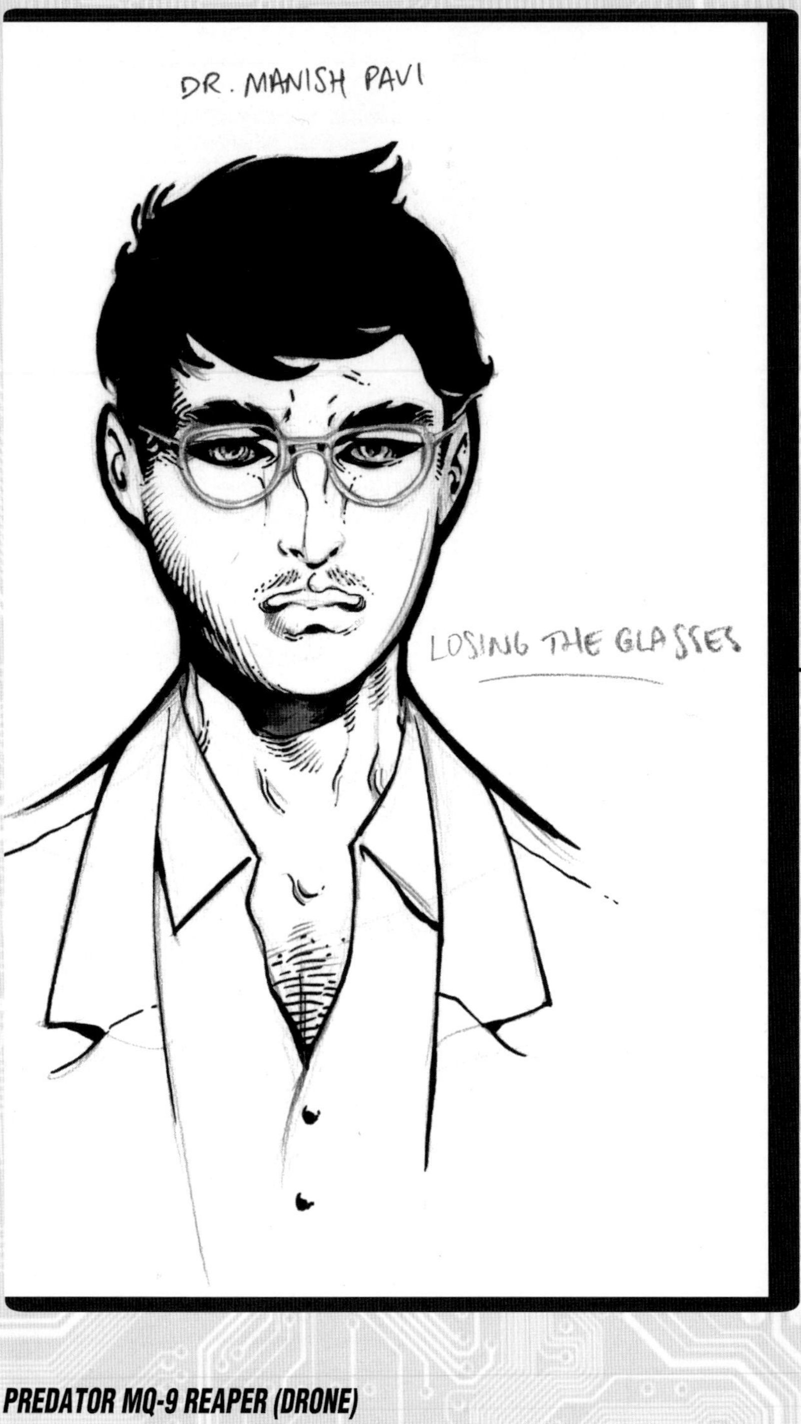

DR. MANISH PAVI
LOSING THE GLASSES

ALBERT EINSTEIN

Einstein's quotes are pretty fascinating considering what all he accomplished. He was not an atheist like myself and many other current scientists. "Science is a wonderful thing if one does not have to earn one's living at it," is my favorite quote and I've had many comic book writers/artists tell me that it is also applicable to working in comics as well.

F=ma

The F=ma on the first narrative balloon on each page is Force = mass times acceleration which is one of Physics core equations. If you note on David's shirt in the first chapter, it says Fun = Mating X Alcohol, which is me just having some fun of my own. By the way, I made that shirt too. You can buy yours at the Top Cow online store!

http://www.thetopcowstore.com/ProductDetails.asp?ProductCode=TTSHIRT

PREDATOR MQ-9 REAPER (DRONE)

Featured in the first chapter heavily is the Predator MQ-9 Reaper, the current workhorse of the Air Force and the one you see predominantly on those YouTube videos. The interesting thing about this Reaper is it's based on designs from over 15 years ago. What they have now is far more insidious! The Drones were originally exclusively used for reconnaissance but very quickly adopted weapons systems. Drone technology is getting smaller and smaller. Remote control bullets with facial recognition software are just around the corner. Pretty soon, if not already, they'll have insect sized Drones that can be remotely controlled and flown under doors or through small cracks in windows. The applications are endless. My father was in the Air Force and I will never forget when I was a kid he told me that the payload storage compartment on the top of the Space Shuttles was conveniently sized so that it could also hold an ICBM nuclear missile. I've never thought of the Space Shuttles as being weaponized, but you can see the potential.

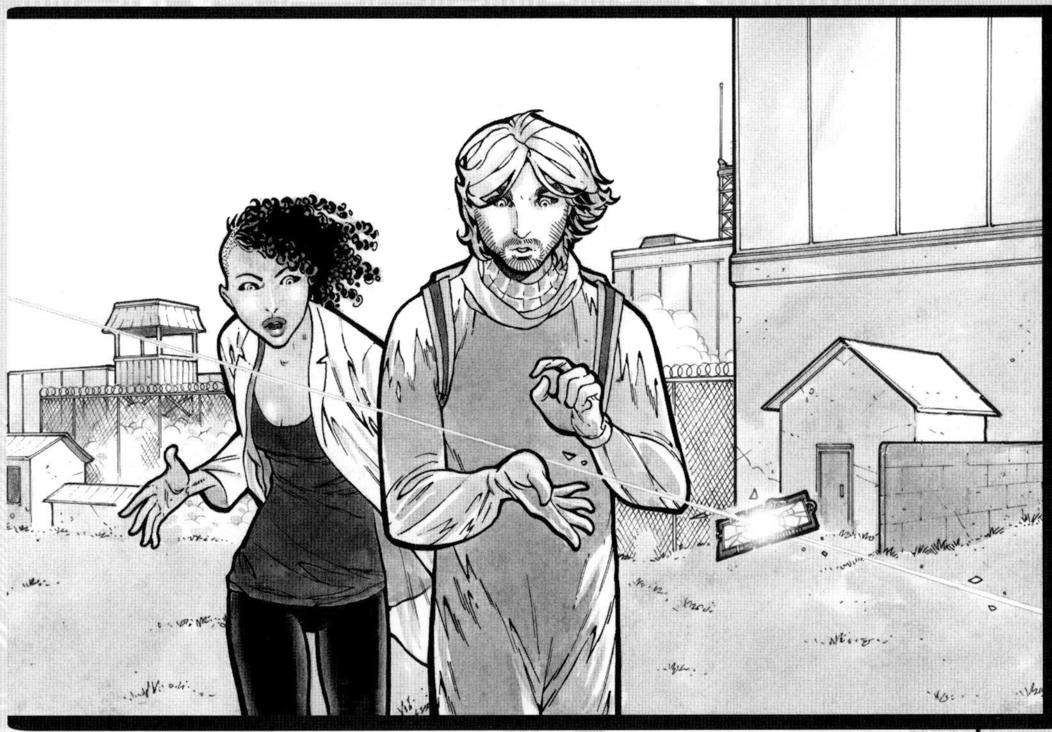

THREAT ASSESSMENT/RISK REDUCTION

Military analysts do this from the comfort of their offices all over the world (there's a large cluster in Washington, D.C.) pretty much 24/7. They use whatever information they have based on ground intelligence, local media, photographs, and other surveillance of key decision makers in these "rogue" nations. In the history of the US, we were more on the conservative, even isolationist side of this pre WW2. Vietnam and the Cold War seem to have changed all that and once something changes in the "culture" of the military it's hard to change it back. Look at WW2; we entered that war late and ONLY after the Japanese bombed Pearl Harbor. I often wonder if the Japanese had not done that and we had not entered the war until even later if the UK would have fallen to the Nazis. It's certainly patriotic for us to all think that the US won WW2, but without Britain staving off the Germans for as long as they did, I doubt our victories would have mattered. On the opposite end of that spectrum is the Second Iraq war where the analysts concocted fictitious weapons of mass destruction to fit the agenda. I'm no Saddam supporter and I'm glad he's dead, but these wars are a mess and they were started under false pretense.

Colin Powell, who gave the final speech to the UN about the WMD in Iraq pre-invasion, has regrets. Check this youtube video:

http://www.youtube.com/watch?v=2ZTLmOoPzjs

There are lots of books on threat analysis and risk reduction. One of the most interesting ones I've read is called *SMALL WAR MANUAL AND MARINE CORPS MILITARY OPERATIONS OTHER THAN WAR DOCTRINE*. No one can question whether or not the Nazis were a real threat, but what about all of the other little battles we've been in? It's available as a free PDF here:

http://www.au.af.mil/au/awc/awcgate/awc-ntel.htm

STRATEGY VERSUS TACTICS

This is just a pet peeve of mine. People use these words interchangeably but they mean different things.

http://www.diffen.com/difference/Strategy_vs_Tactic

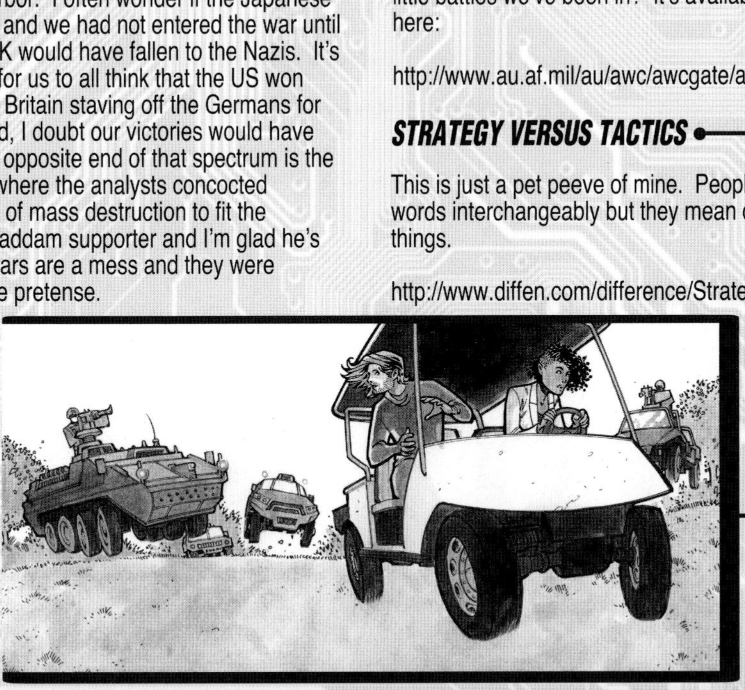

RULES OF ENGAGEMENT (ROE) AND ESCALATION OF FORCE (EOF)

There could not be a more controversial topic in military circles and oversight committees than these two. We don't want to kill civilians, especially kids, but what do you do when your enemy hides among the civilians and fires at you from residential buildings full of people that have nothing to do with the conflict? The first link below talks about Marines that were killed because they were not allowed to fire back WHILE UNDER FIRE. The others talk about rules of engagement, self-defense, and how EOF is allowed. These are dense, sometimes boring reads but skim through them and pay special attention to the "scenarios" they list. This is certainly not a unique problem for the US. The last two links I list here are from the UK and the Philippines and their regulations. I found the Philippine one especially interesting; it's very different from what you read in the US and UK ones.

http://www.breitbart.com/Big-Peace/2012/09/14/Oppressive-rules-of-engagement
http://info.publicintelligence.net/USArmy-ROE-Vignettes.pdf
http://www.usnwc.edu/getattachment/7b0d0f70-bb07-48f2-af0a-7474e92d0bb0/San-Remo-ROE-Handbook
http://www.direct.gov.uk/prod_consum_dg/groups/dg_digitalassets/@dg/@en/documents/digitalasset/dg_191634.pdf
http://www.afp.mil.ph/pdf/Human%20Rights%20Based%20Intelligence%20Operations.pdf

MILITARY GOLF COURSES

I have nothing against golf, but it never ceases to amaze me how large and beautiful military golf courses are. The Naval one in Hawaii is considered one of the best courses in the world. I set up the course in this issue as a contrast to specialized engineering equipment that taxpayers bitch about incessantly. There certainly is wasteful spending, but people never seem to understand research and development costs. They get ANGRY about big pharmaceutical companies charging so much for new drugs being released, but in many cases these drugs took decades to develop and there were 15 other failed drugs that led up to it. Again, not defending any particular company, action, or product, but be informed before you bitch...and don't trust what people say. Do your own research.

http://www.militarygolfcourseguide.com/

CARBON NANOFIBERS •

These make steel rebar look like glass. Incredibly hard with insane tensile strength, carbon nanofibers are pretty cool. In the script it talks about David blowing through the wall, possibly with some hand carried C4 or something. The first link below shows how much TNT or C4 or more concentrated explosives it would actually take to blow through walls. It also shows who in the chain of command has the authority to set mines and other such stuff, so it's pretty interesting. The second link leads to a manufacturer of carbon nanofibers, in case you wanted to buy some! The idea of David using explosives to get through the wall was an afterthought for me, but I found the research interesting. Ultimately, if you look at a map of Fort Meade and follow the southeast corner there is a huge wooded area after the wall so they'd have a long walk through dense forest. I'd always planned on the Drone escape from before the first chapter was written.

http://www.globalsecurity.org/military/library/policy/army/fm/3-06-11/ch8.htm
http://www.sigmaaldrich.com/materials-science/nanomaterials/carbon-nanofibers.html

NATIONAL SECURITY ASSET •

I'll have to admit here I've made some of this up. There's not a lot online about human assets. This link below shows how the US government classifies its national infrastructure assets, including technology, and how they prioritize their protection, etc. It's a dense read, but it doesn't say that humans are NOT classified as assets. The 1,247 people since 1945 thing I made up as a post WW2 number. It is 100% true though that these high-end research scientists are closely guarded and monitored by the government. What is more dangerous, a partially damaged device (like a crashed helicopter) that a country would have to reverse engineer or a scientist who could teach others how to build it…and other things? Sharing classified information is treason and can be capitally punished. If there is "imminent clear and present danger" to the "security of the USA" the government can pretty much do whatever they want. The second link shows how the government will "safeguard" classified information.

http://www.fas.org/sgp/crs/homesec/RL33648.pdf
http://www.fas.org/sgp/isoo/safeguard.html

NON-LETHAL BEAN BAG ROUNDS •

On the Live Fire Range is the same Metalstorm device we saw in the earlier chapters that David had his epiphany about. I wanted to come full circle with it and was happy with how that came out. His comment "funsies" when he shot at the helicopter with the bean bag rounds is something the inimitable Jenni Cheung says regularly, so thought I would steal that. I was trying to convey that he is not really taking this all that seriously. David is showing off a bit and is oddly detached from the gravity of his pursuit, so when you get to the epilogue pages, it gives that final scene a stronger punch in the gut. Hopefully we pulled that off.

LIGHT CHAMELEON CLOAK AND EMP GRENADE

Sometimes you just have to show off some cool tech. Their use here at the end was a setup/payoff situation for the story.

MQ-9 REAPER ESCAPE

This ending was always planned, but I needed to make sure it was feasible. In researching the Drones this big one has a 3,500 lb. payload capacity. They can easily carry two people. I've yet to hear or read anything about it, but I think they could easily be used to retrieve stranded or injured personnel. The first link has the specs for the Reaper. The second one has the Department of Homeland Security's annual budget. I didn't make that part up. There is NO question that there are Drones flying over U.S. airspace right now either performing surveillance or protecting our borders. The University of TX professor hacking the Drone is true as well. That's the third link.

http://www.af.mil/information/factsheets/fact sheet.asp?id=6405
http://www.whitehouse.gov/sites/default/files /omb/budget/fy2013/assets/homeland.pdf
http://www.npr.org/2012/07/08/156459939/h acking-drones-and-the-dangers-it-presents

AFTER THE WALL

Rahsan and I talked about showing how they escape the country and I went as far as mapping out exactly how they did it. It's not as hard as you might think. The Canadian border is 5,525 miles long and the Mexican border is 1,933.4 miles long. People move across the borders pretty regularly. Ultimately, I left this out of the issue for space reasons and figured we could tell some of it in future flashbacks or maintain that escaping the base and lab were the hard part. The other thing I left out was David's finances. In the story it's discussed how his housing, food, etc are all cared for and that everything is provided for him. So what does a guy like that do with his money? Well, David just stuck it in an offshore account. I can bring that into the story if I ever need to.

Well lads and lasses, that's it! Thanks again for picking up *Think Tank* volume one. We hope to see you back for issue 5 where we take a look at specialized weapons designed to target specific genetic structures, be it an individual or a group. As always, if you like the book we'd appreciate it if you recommended *Think Tank* to a friend.

Carpe Diem!

Matt Hawkins
@topcowmatt

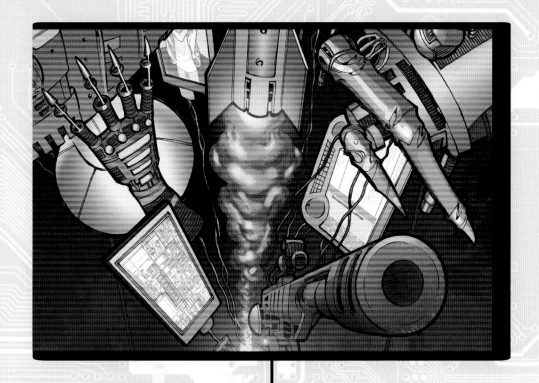

BONUS PREVIEW

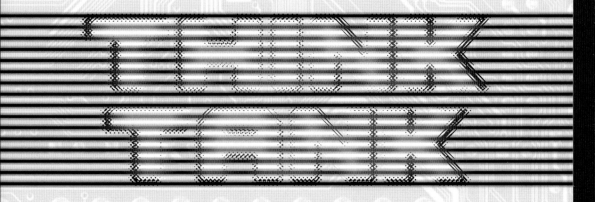

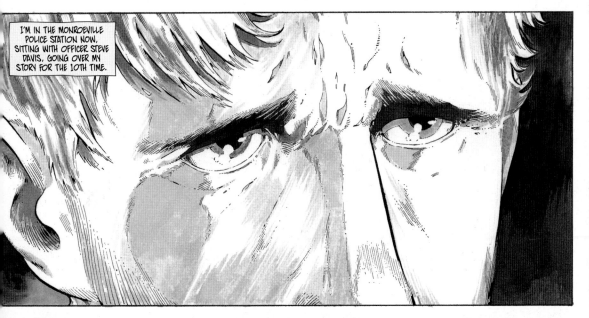

I'M IN THE MONROEVILLE POLICE STATION NOW, SITTING WITH OFFICER STEVE DAVIS, GOING OVER MY STORY FOR THE 10TH TIME.

NOW I'M AT THE FORBES REGIONAL HOSPITAL HEARING MY SON'S HEARTBEAT FOR THE FIRST TIME.

NOW I'M IN THE BASEMENT OF THE HOUSE, A HALF MILE FROM WHERE I GREW UP, HOLDING A BOX OF MY FATHER'S CRIMES.

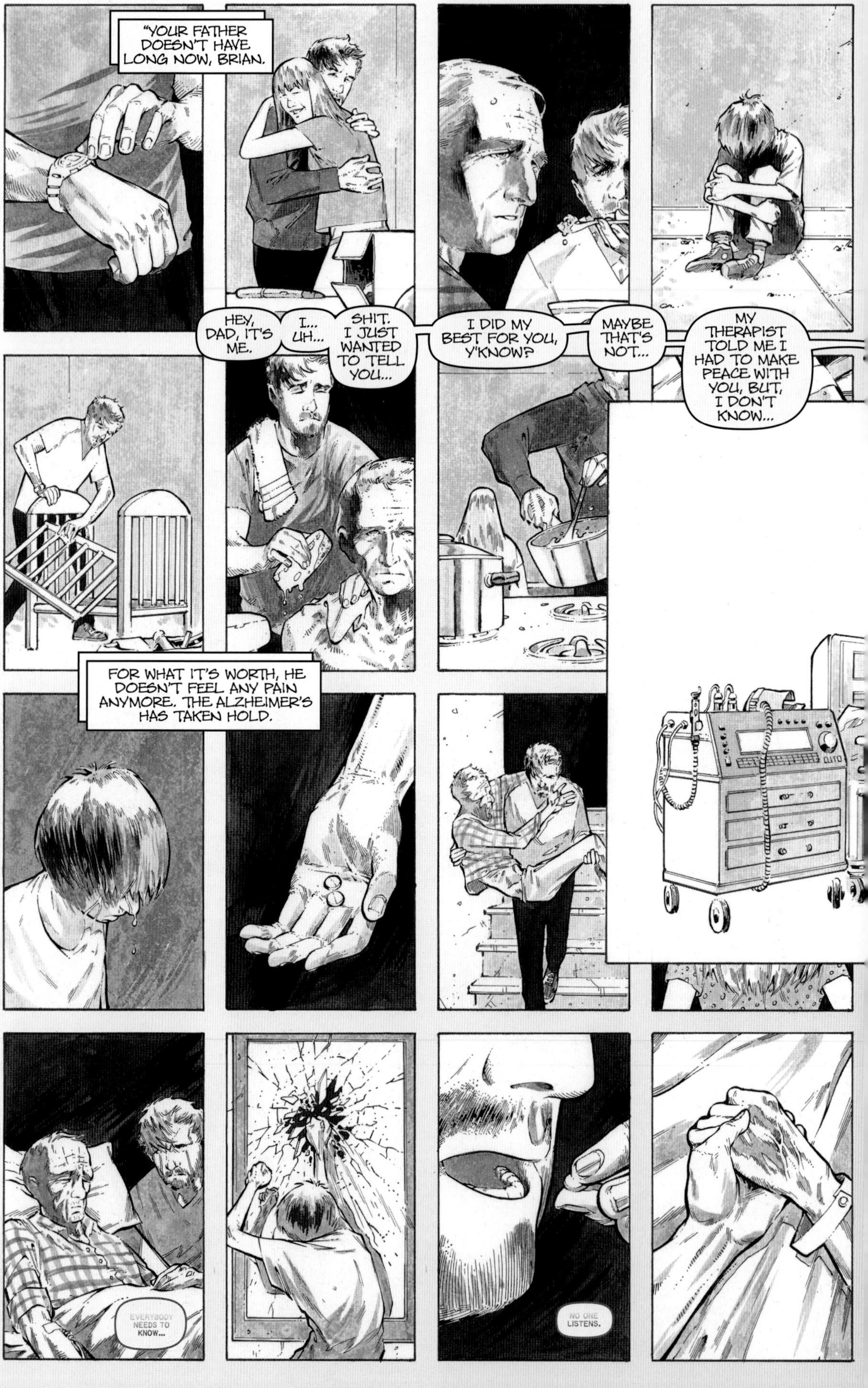
"YOUR FATHER DOESN'T HAVE LONG NOW, BRIAN.
HEY, DAD, IT'S ME.
I... UH...
SHIT. I JUST WANTED TO TELL YOU...
I DID MY BEST FOR YOU, Y'KNOW?
MAYBE THAT'S NOT...
MY THERAPIST TOLD ME I HAD TO MAKE PEACE WITH YOU, BUT, I DON'T KNOW...
FOR WHAT IT'S WORTH, HE DOESN'T FEEL ANY PAIN ANYMORE. THE ALZHEIMER'S HAS TAKEN HOLD.
EVERYBODY NEEDS TO KNOW...
NO ONE LISTENS.

YOU NEED TO SAY GOODBYE.

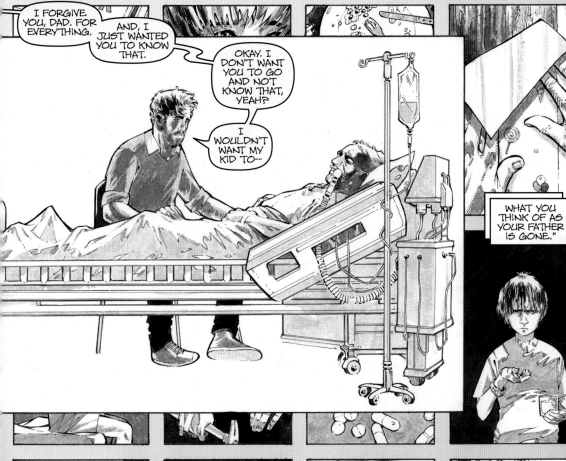

I FORGIVE YOU, DAD. FOR EVERYTHING. AND, I JUST WANTED YOU TO KNOW THAT.

OKAY. I DON'T WANT YOU TO GO AND NOT KNOW THAT, YEAH?

I WOULDN'T WANT MY KID TO--

WHAT YOU THINK OF AS YOUR FATHER IS GONE."

EVERYBODY.

NO ONE COMES. NOBODY CARES.

NO GOOD FOR NOTHING SON.

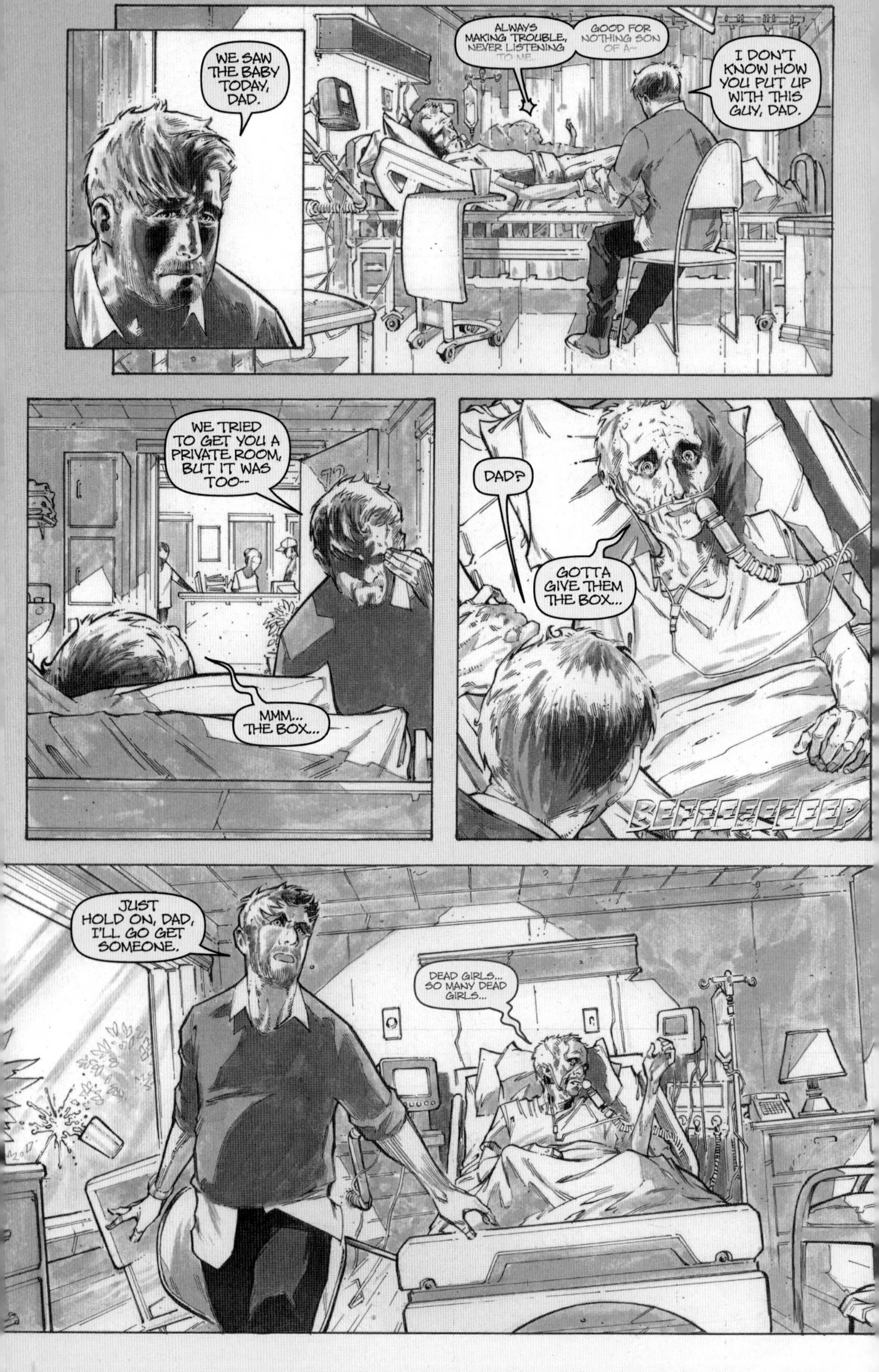
WE SAW THE BABY TODAY, DAD.
ALWAYS MAKING TROUBLE, NEVER LISTENING TO ME...
GOOD FOR NOTHING SON OF A--
I DON'T KNOW HOW YOU PUT UP WITH THIS GUY, DAD.
WE TRIED TO GET YOU A PRIVATE ROOM, BUT IT WAS TOO--
MMM... THE BOX...
DAD?
GOTTA GIVE THEM THE BOX...
JUST HOLD ON, DAD, I'LL GO GET SOMEONE.
DEAD GIRLS... SO MANY DEAD GIRLS...

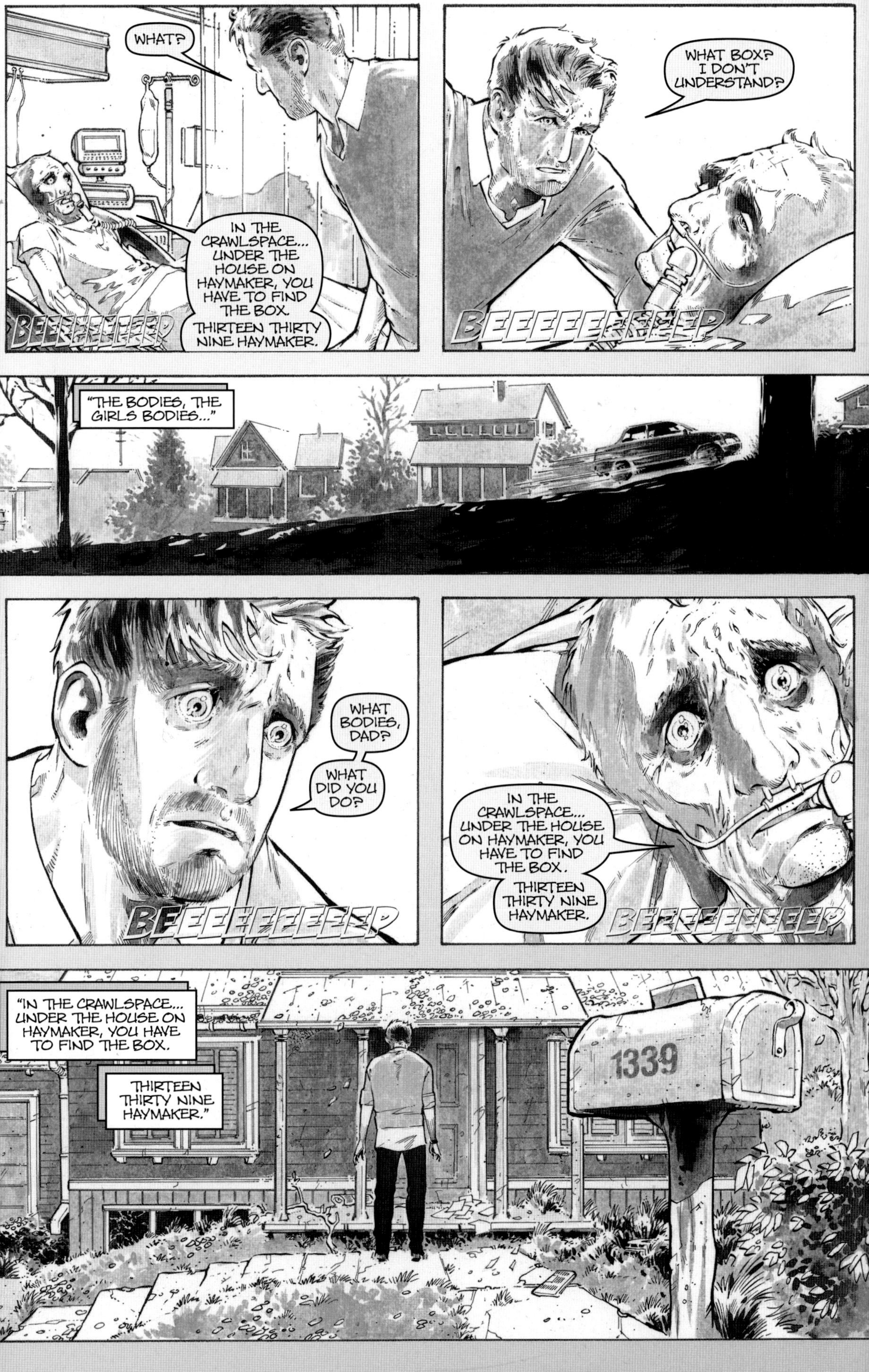
WHAT?
IN THE CRAWLSPACE... UNDER THE HOUSE ON HAYMAKER, YOU HAVE TO FIND THE BOX.
THIRTEEN THIRTY NINE HAYMAKER.
BEEEEEEEEP
WHAT BOX? I DON'T UNDERSTAND?
BEEEEEEEEEEP
"THE BODIES, THE GIRLS BODIES..."
WHAT BODIES, DAD?
WHAT DID YOU DO?
BEEEEEEEEEP
IN THE CRAWLSPACE... UNDER THE HOUSE ON HAYMAKER, YOU HAVE TO FIND THE BOX.
THIRTEEN THIRTY NINE HAYMAKER.
BEEEEEEEEEP
"IN THE CRAWLSPACE... UNDER THE HOUSE ON HAYMAKER, YOU HAVE TO FIND THE BOX.
THIRTEEN THIRTY NINE HAYMAKER."
1339

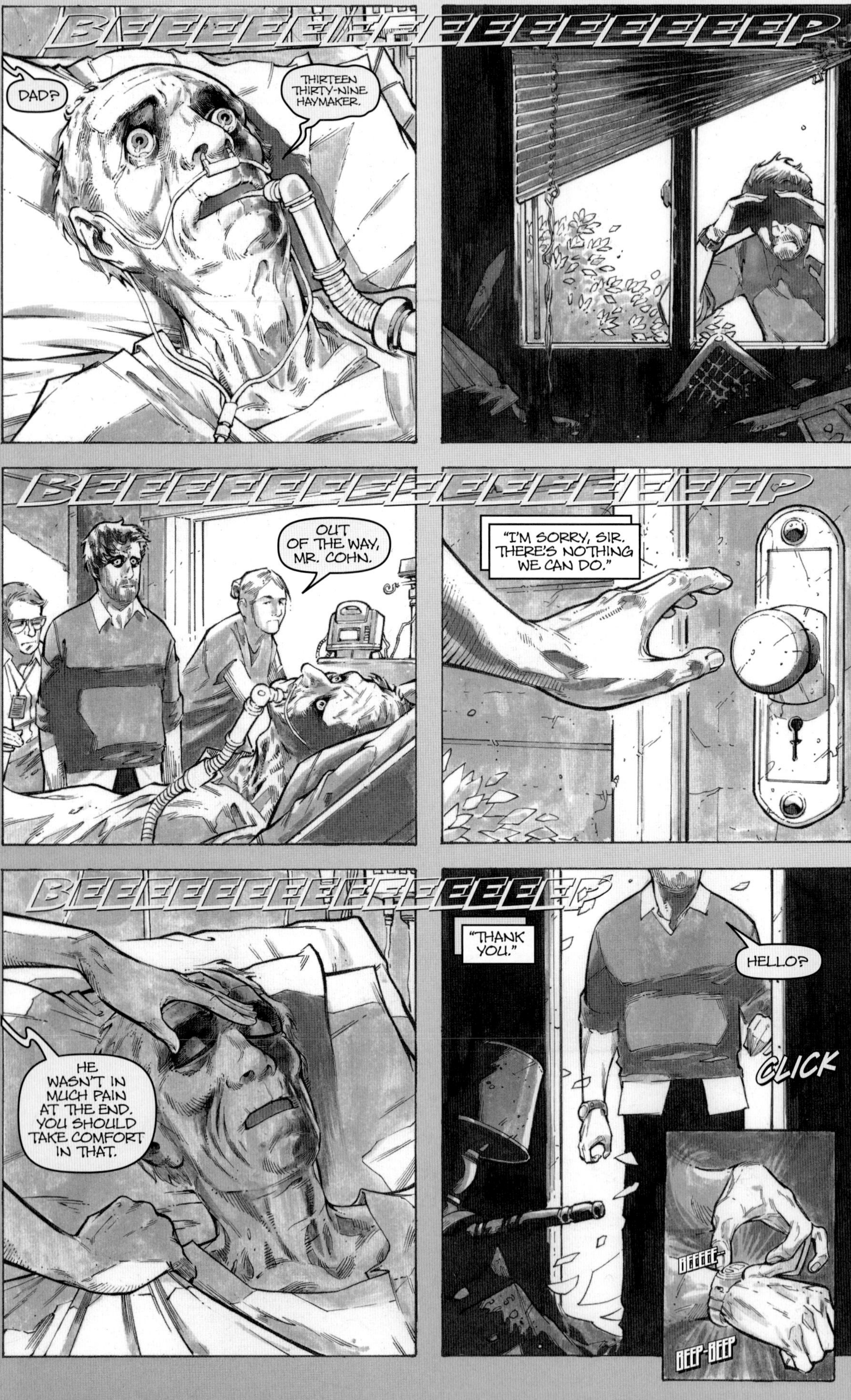
BEEEEEEEEEEEEEEEEEEEEP
DAD?
THIRTEEN THIRTY-NINE HAYMAKER.
BEEEEEEEEEEEEEEEEEEEEP
OUT OF THE WAY, MR. COHN.
"I'M SORRY, SIR. THERE'S NOTHING WE CAN DO."
BEEEEEEEEEEEEEEEEEEEP
HE WASN'T IN MUCH PAIN AT THE END. YOU SHOULD TAKE COMFORT IN THAT.
"THANK YOU."
HELLO?
CLICK
BEEEEE-
BEEP-BEEP

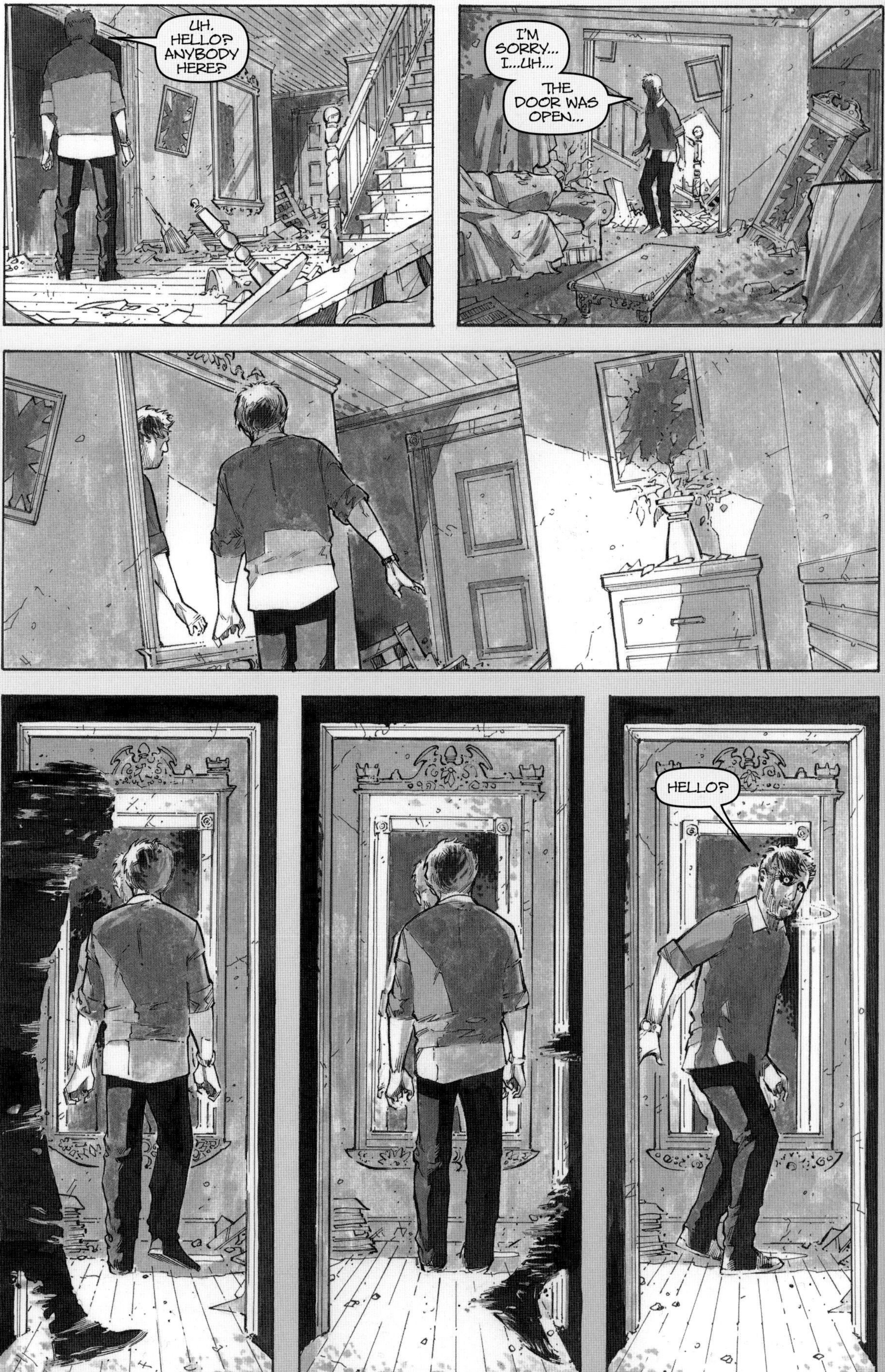
UH. HELLO? ANYBODY HERE?
I'M SORRY... I...UH...
THE DOOR WAS OPEN...
HELLO?

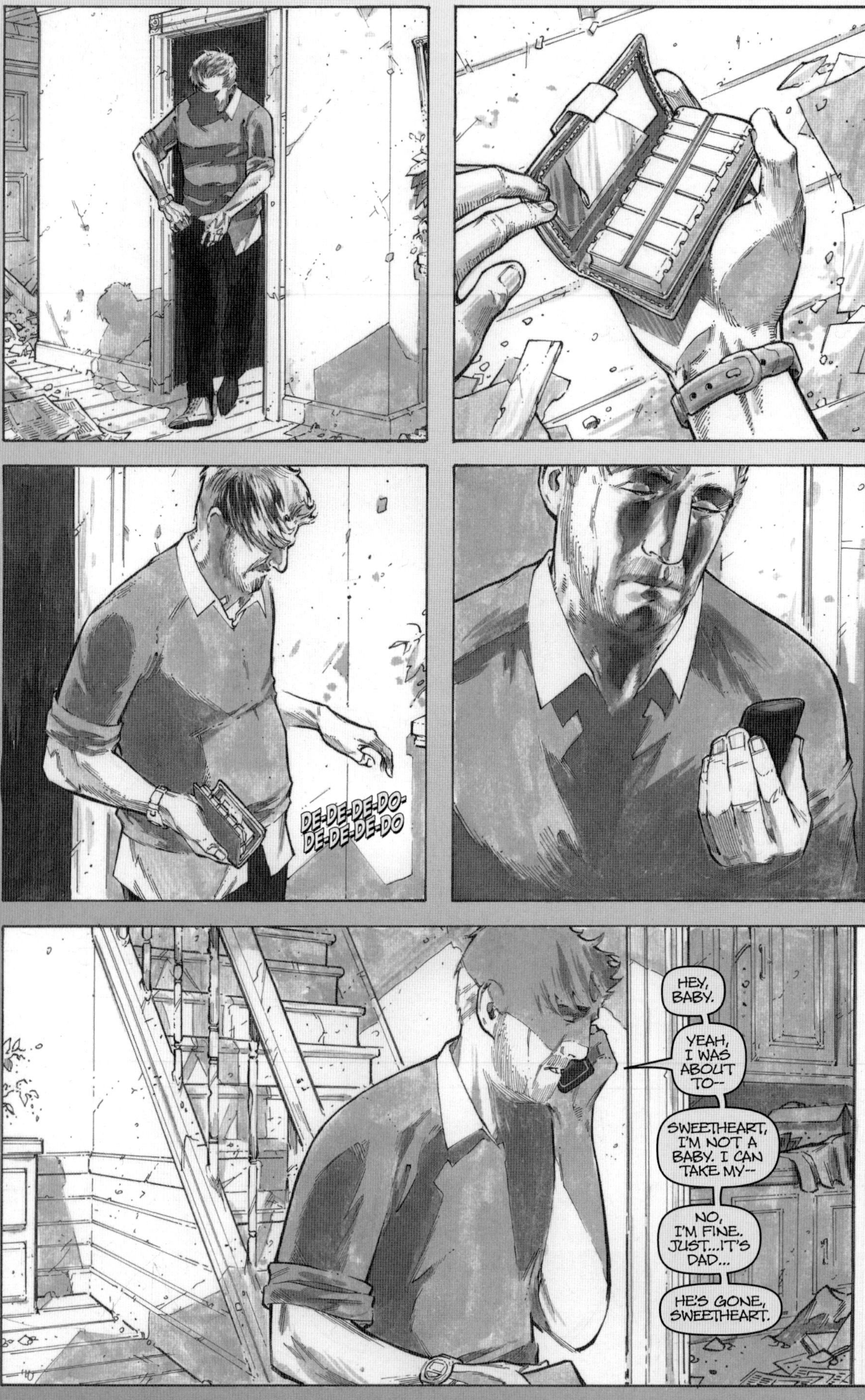
DE-DE-DE-DO-
DE-DE-DE-DO
HEY, BABY.
YEAH, I WAS ABOUT TO--
SWEETHEART, I'M NOT A BABY. I CAN TAKE MY--
NO, I'M FINE. JUST...IT'S DAD...
HE'S GONE, SWEETHEART.

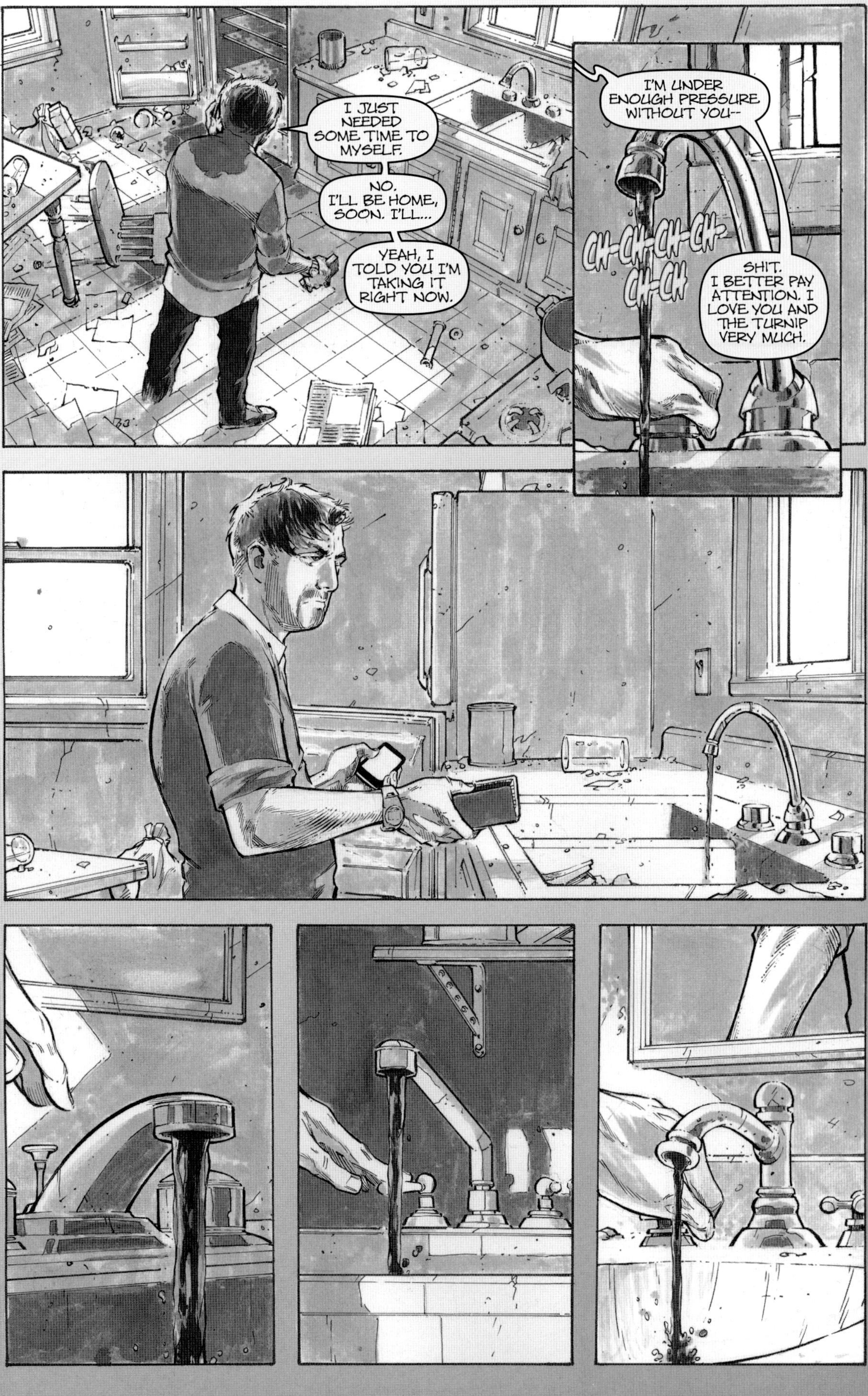
I JUST NEEDED SOME TIME TO MYSELF.
NO. I'LL BE HOME, SOON. I'LL...
YEAH, I TOLD YOU I'M TAKING IT RIGHT NOW.
I'M UNDER ENOUGH PRESSURE WITHOUT YOU--
CH-CH-CH-CH-CH-CH
SHIT. I BETTER PAY ATTENTION. I LOVE YOU AND THE TURNIP VERY MUCH.

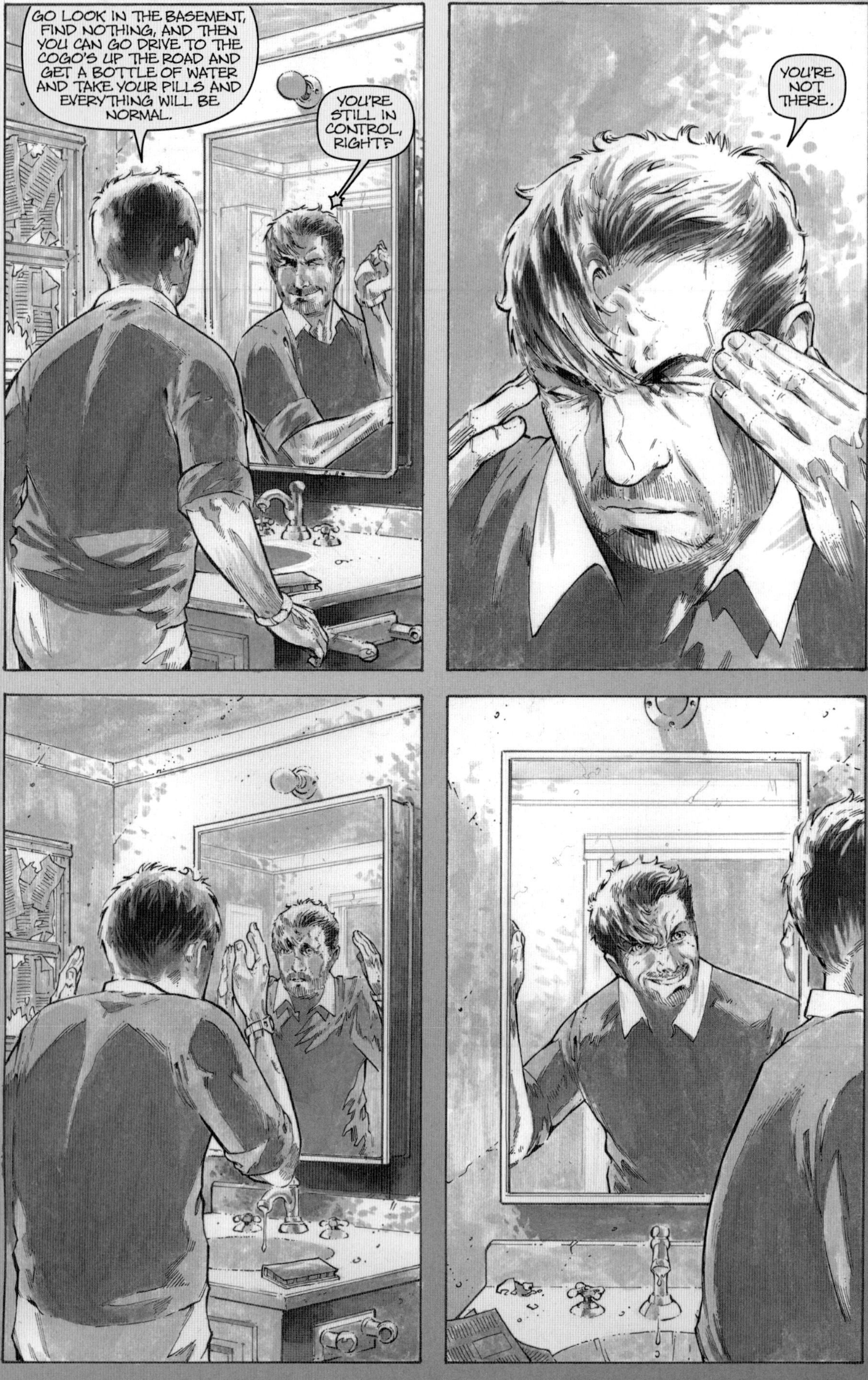
GO LOOK IN THE BASEMENT, FIND NOTHING, AND THEN YOU CAN GO DRIVE TO THE COGO'S UP THE ROAD AND GET A BOTTLE OF WATER AND TAKE YOUR PILLS AND EVERYTHING WILL BE NORMAL.
YOU'RE STILL IN CONTROL, RIGHT?
YOU'RE NOT THERE.

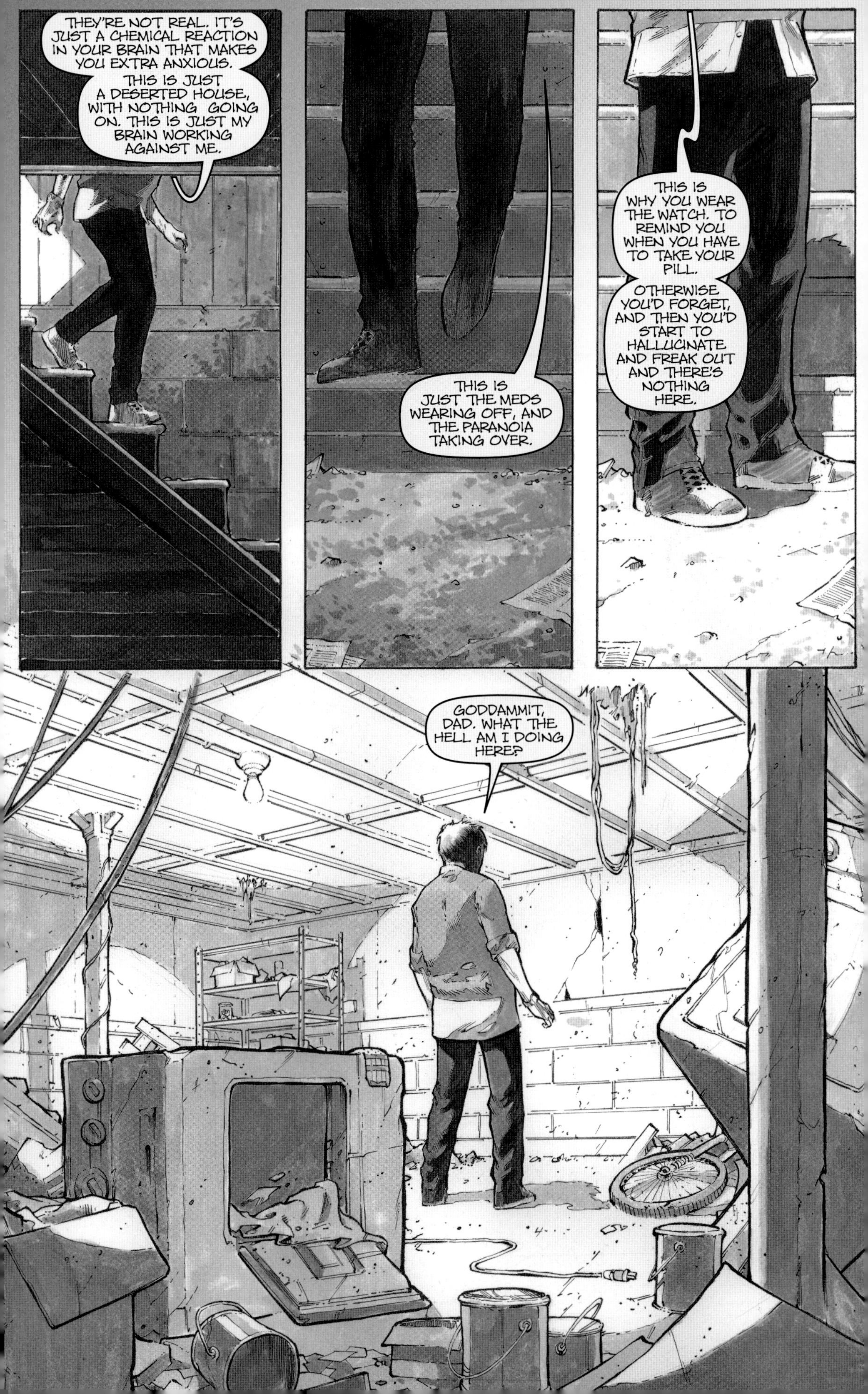
THEY'RE NOT REAL. IT'S JUST A CHEMICAL REACTION IN YOUR BRAIN THAT MAKES YOU EXTRA ANXIOUS.
THIS IS JUST A DESERTED HOUSE, WITH NOTHING GOING ON. THIS IS JUST MY BRAIN WORKING AGAINST ME.
THIS IS JUST THE MEDS WEARING OFF, AND THE PARANOIA TAKING OVER.
THIS IS WHY YOU WEAR THE WATCH. TO REMIND YOU WHEN YOU HAVE TO TAKE YOUR PILL.
OTHERWISE YOU'D FORGET, AND THEN YOU'D START TO HALLUCINATE AND FREAK OUT AND THERE'S NOTHING HERE.
GODDAMMIT, DAD. WHAT THE HELL AM I DOING HERE?

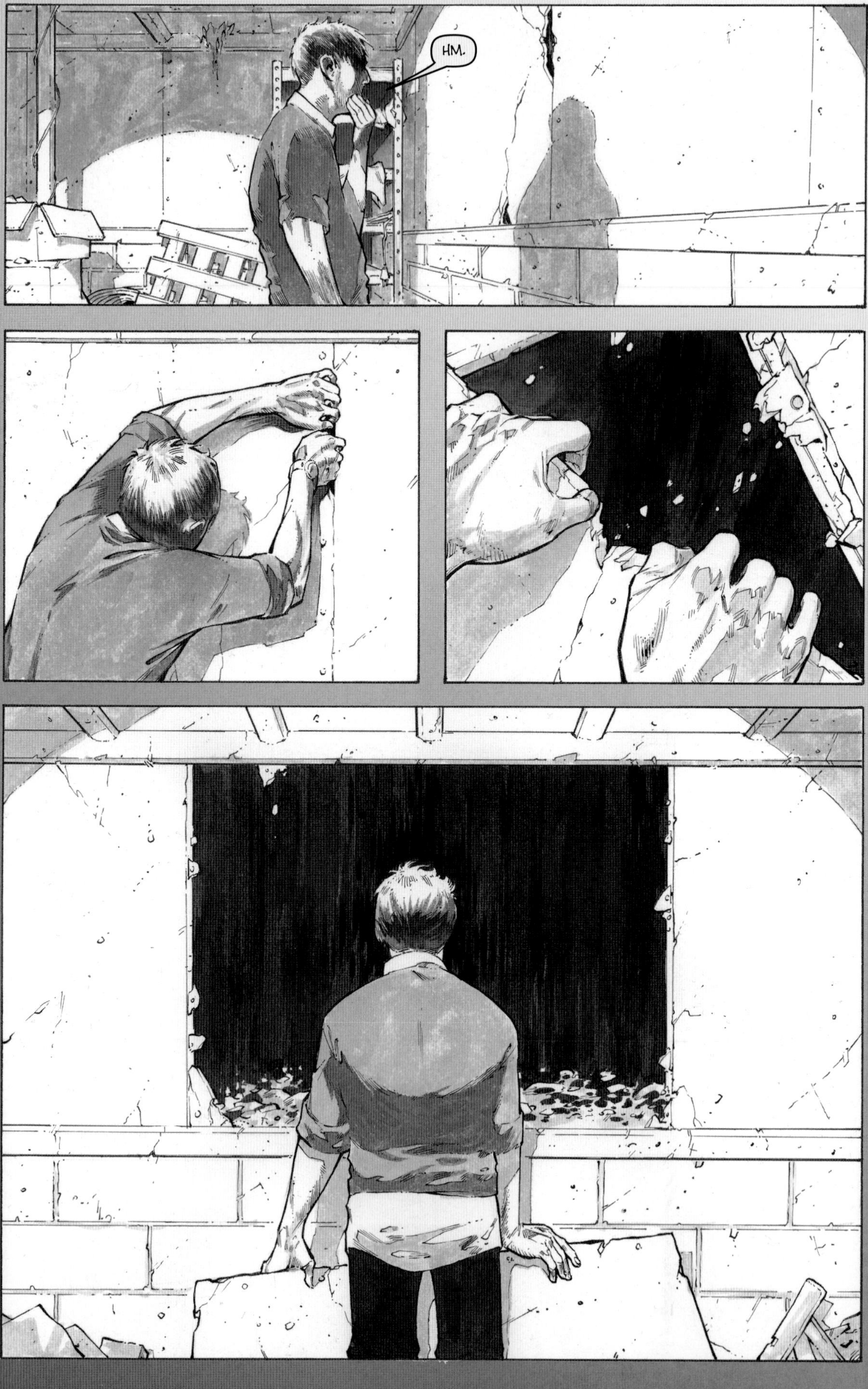
HM.

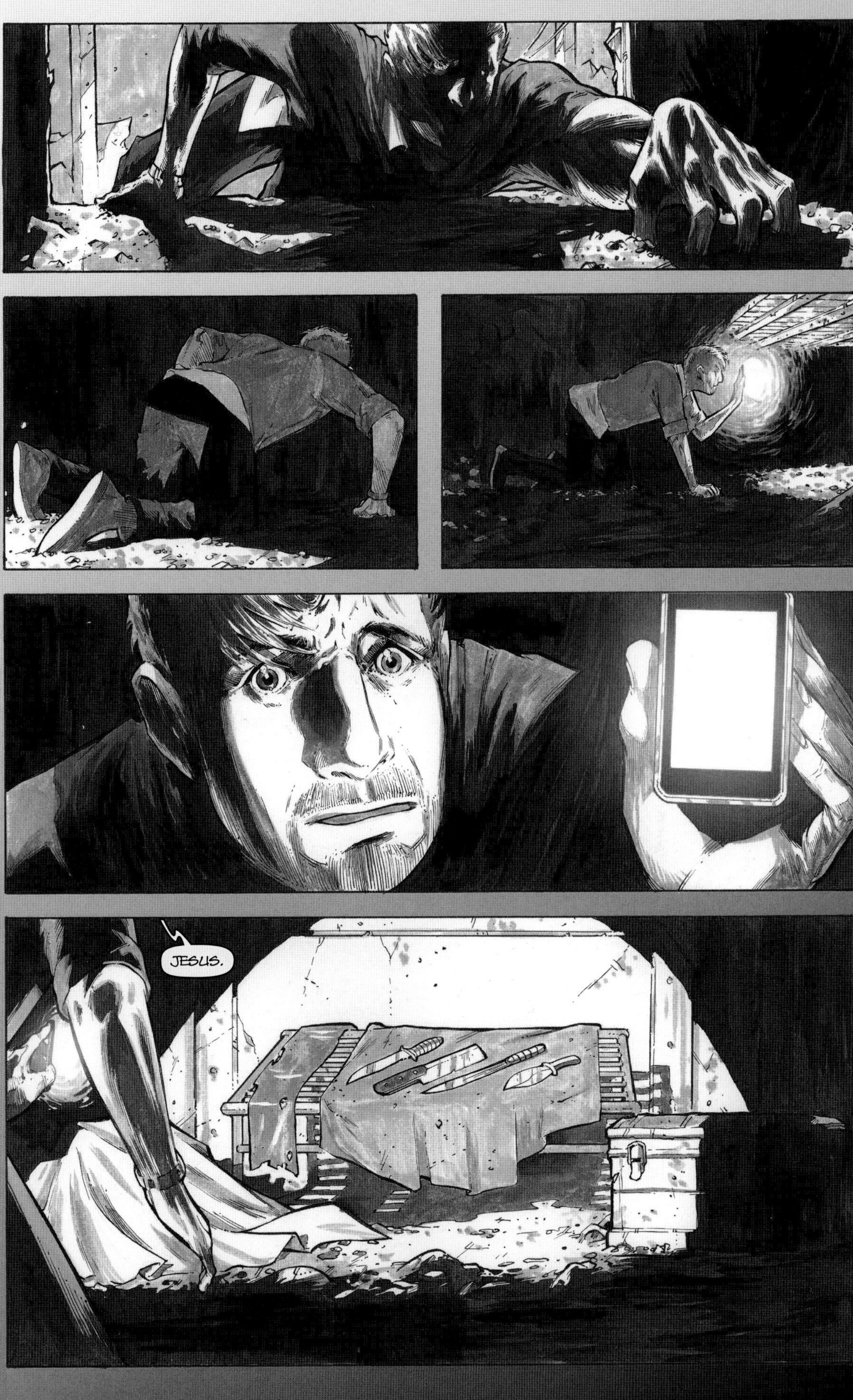
JESUS.

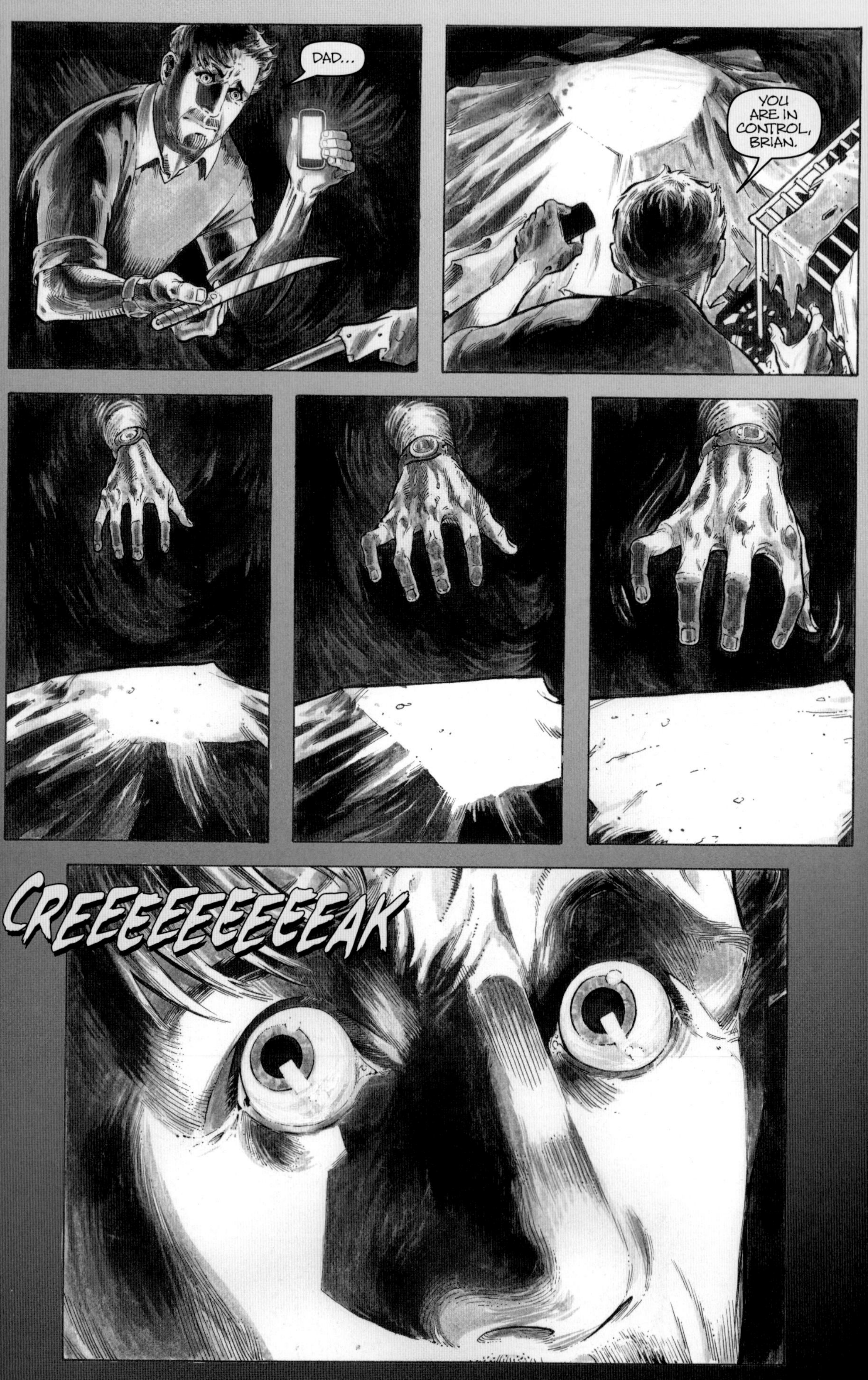
DAD...
YOU ARE IN CONTROL, BRIAN.
CREEEEEEEEEEAK

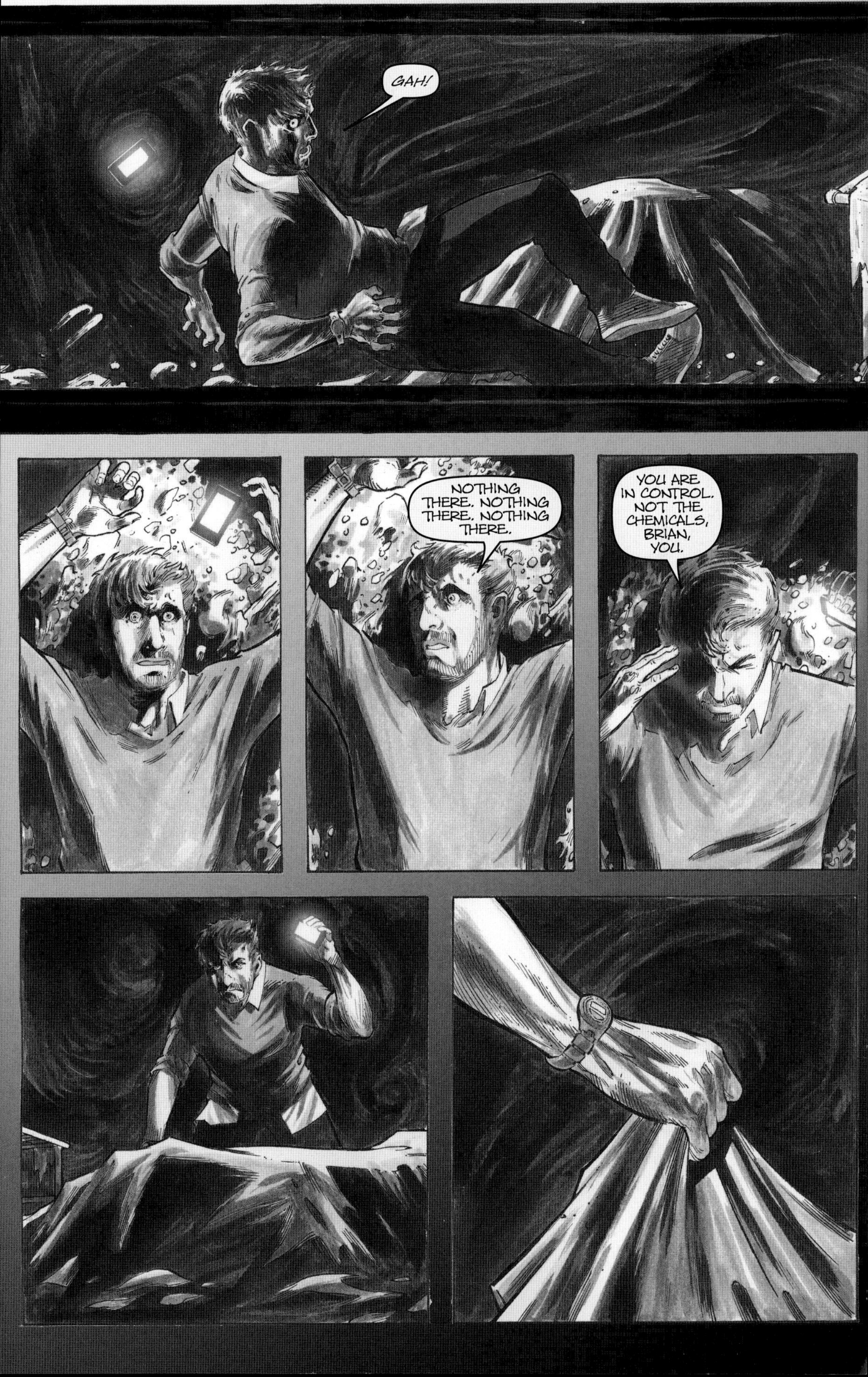
GAH!
NOTHING THERE. NOTHING THERE. NOTHING THERE.
YOU ARE IN CONTROL. NOT THE CHEMICALS, BRIAN, YOU.

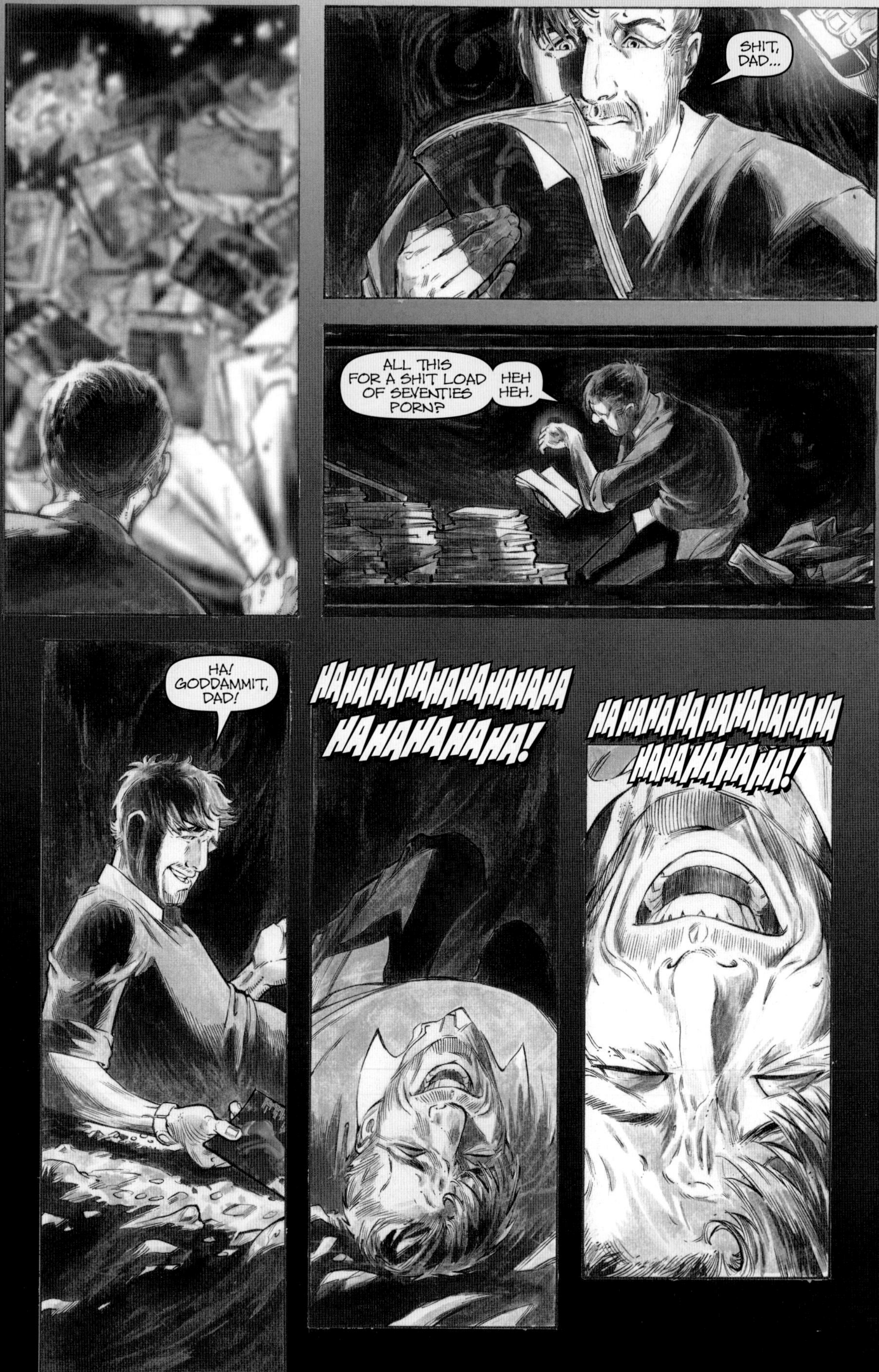
SHIT, DAD...
ALL THIS FOR A SHIT LOAD OF SEVENTIES PORN?
HEH HEH.
HA! GODDAMMIT, DAD!
HAHAHAHAHAHAHAHAHA HAHAHAHAHA!
HAHAHAHAHAHAHAHAHA HAHAHAHAHA!

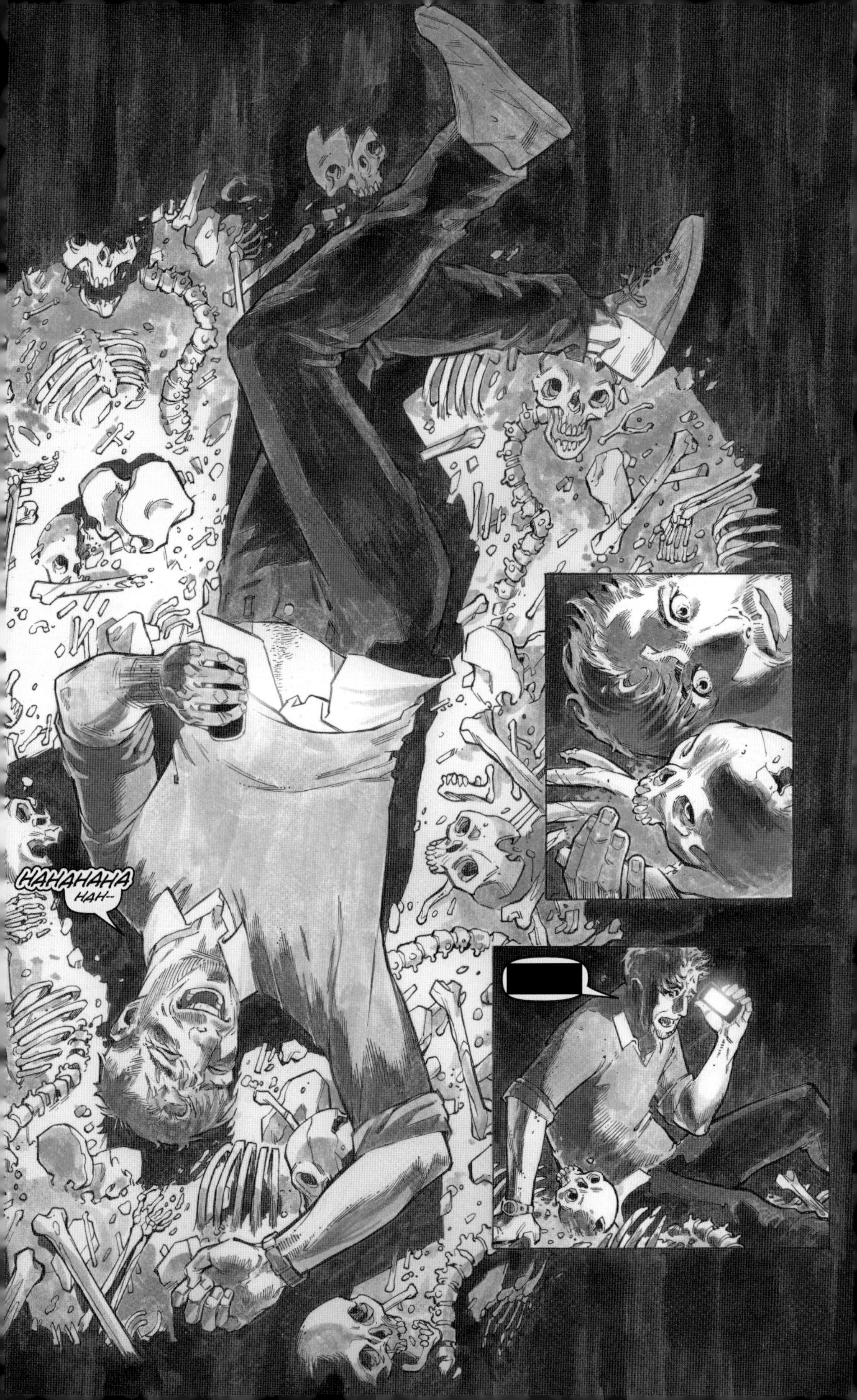
HAHAHAHA HAH--
[redacted]

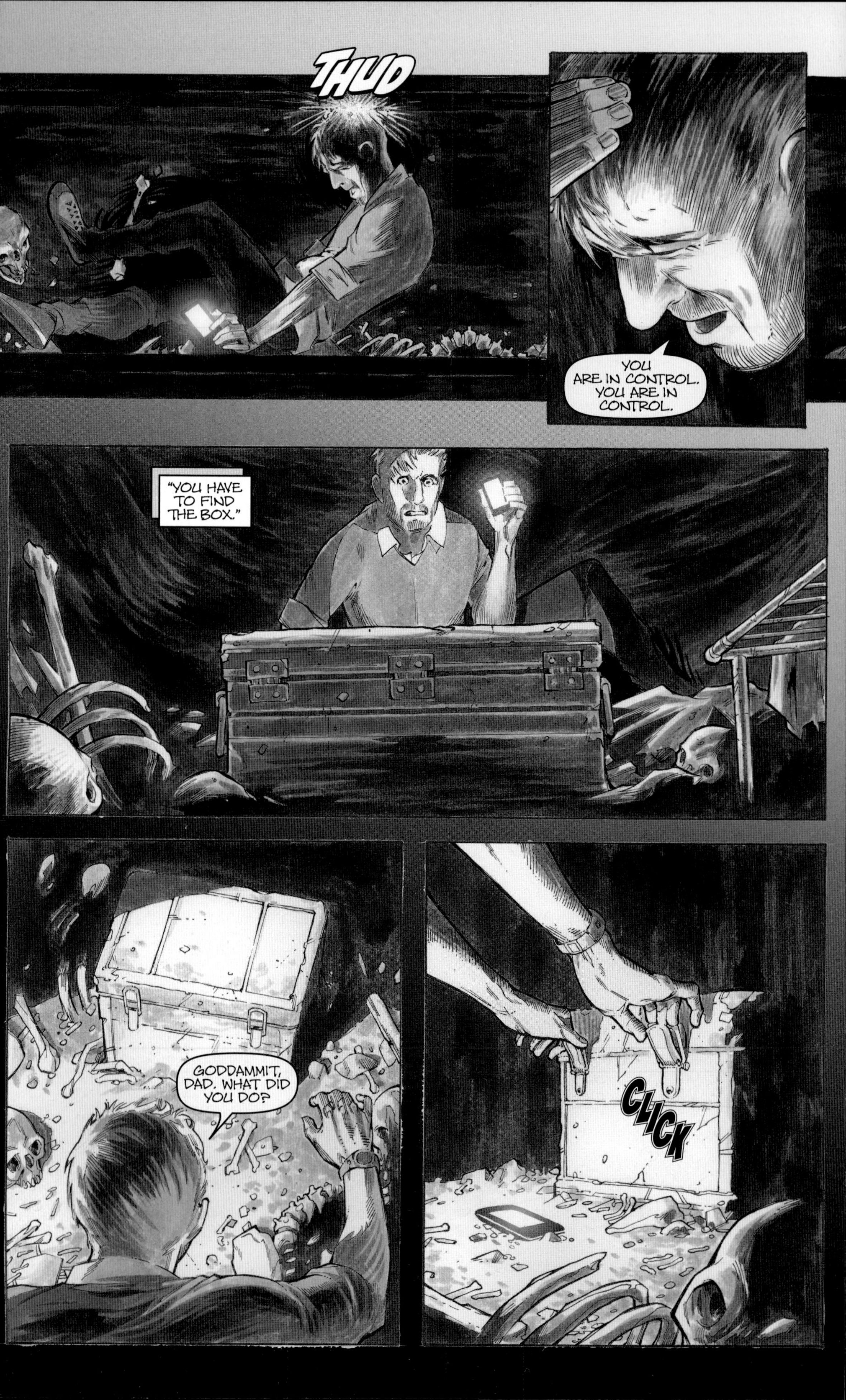
THUD
YOU ARE IN CONTROL. YOU ARE IN CONTROL.
"YOU HAVE TO FIND THE BOX."
GODDAMMIT, DAD. WHAT DID YOU DO?
CLICK

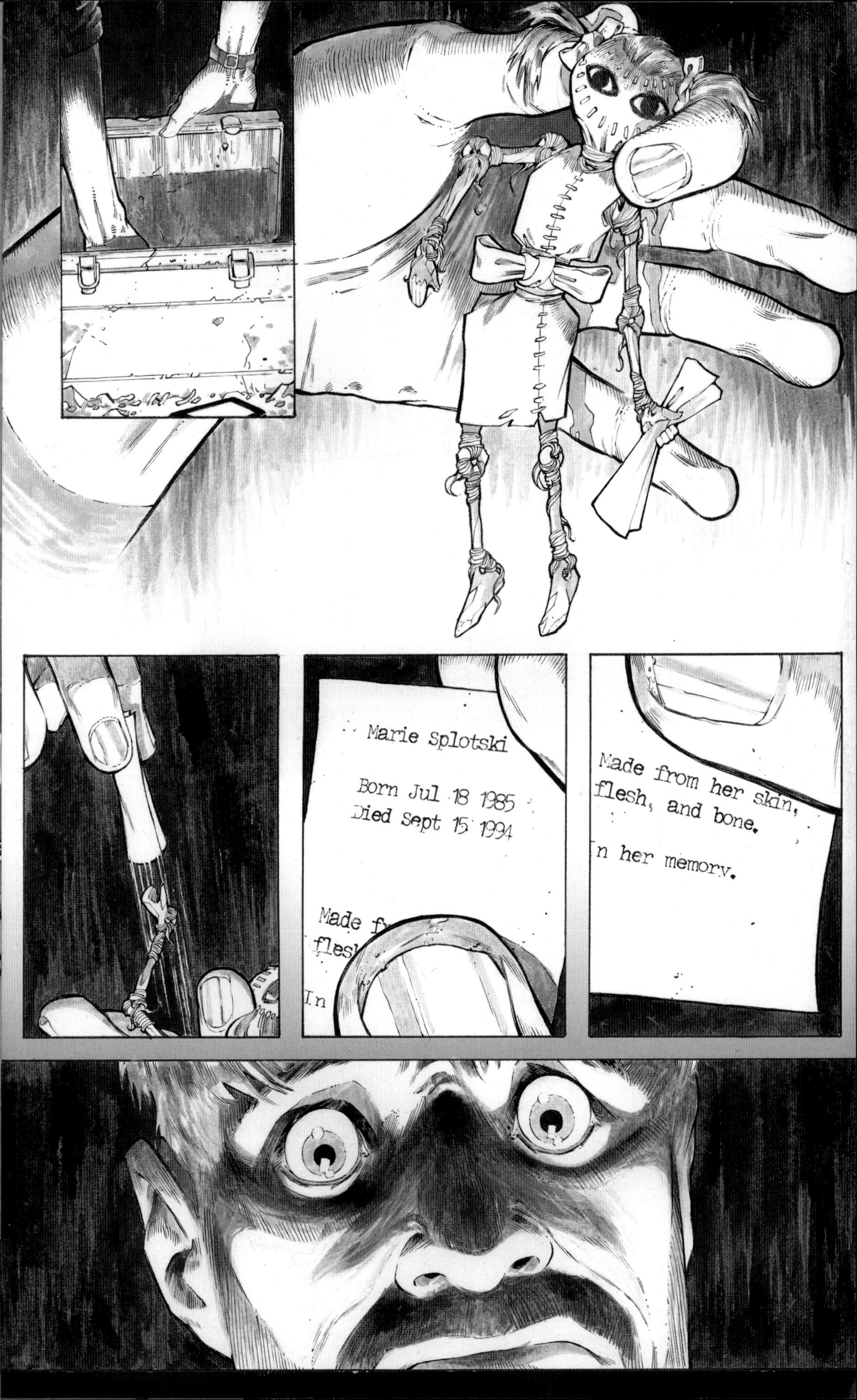
Marie Splotski
Born Jul 18 1985
Died Sept 15 1994
Made f
flesh
In
Made from her skin, flesh, and bone.
In her memory.

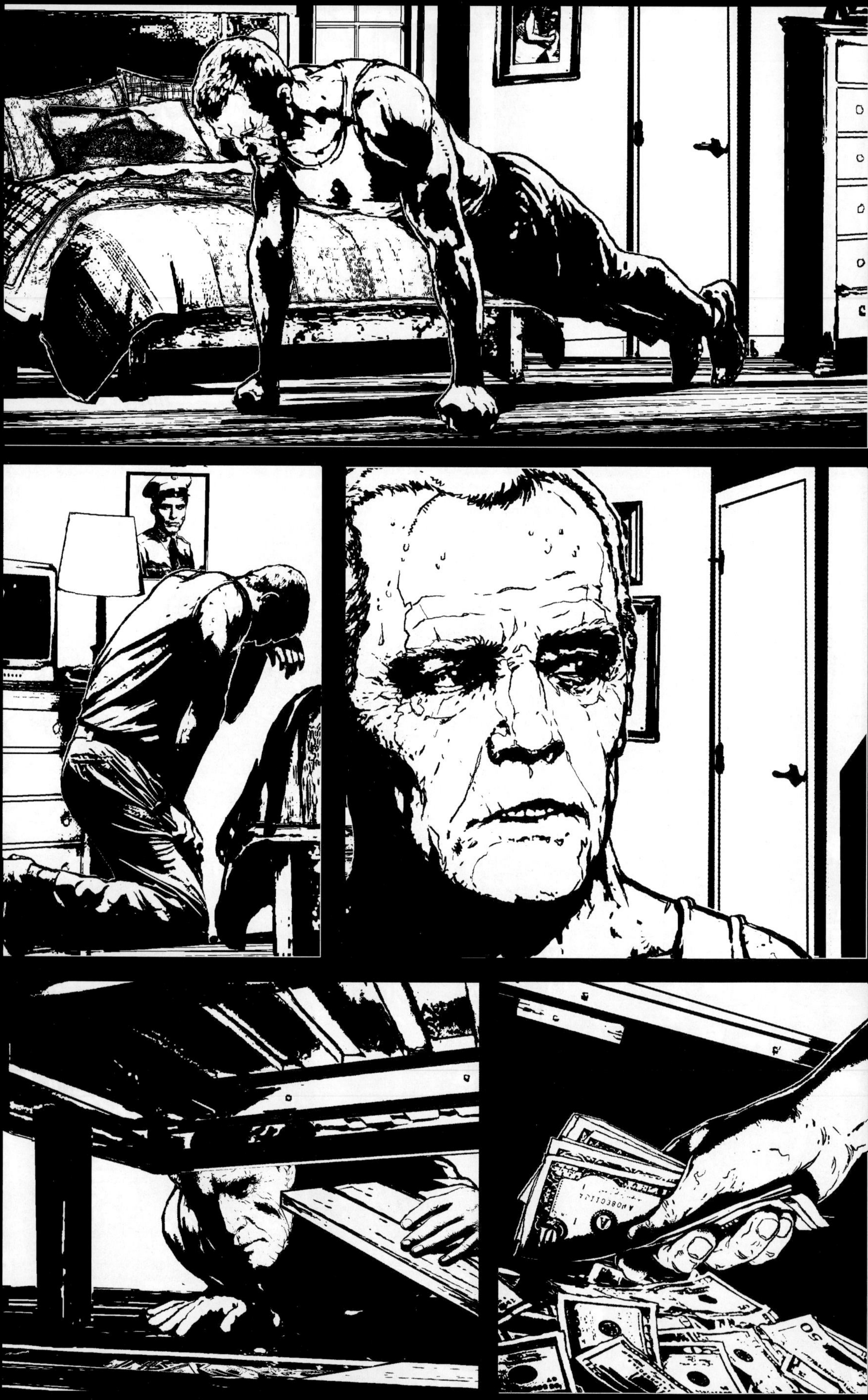

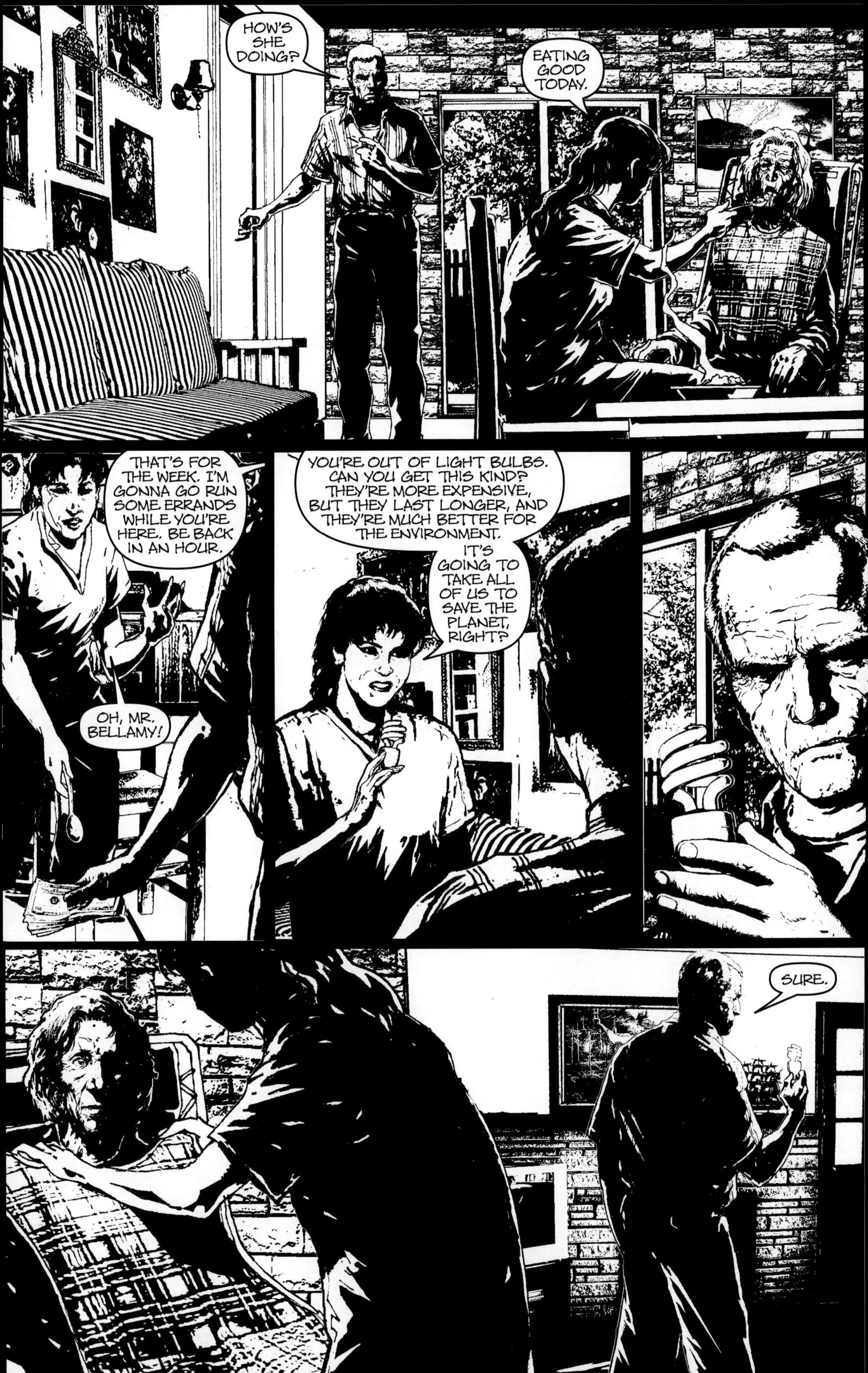

HOW'S SHE DOING?
EATING GOOD TODAY.
THAT'S FOR THE WEEK. I'M GONNA GO RUN SOME ERRANDS WHILE YOU'RE HERE. BE BACK IN AN HOUR.
OH, MR. BELLAMY!
YOU'RE OUT OF LIGHT BULBS. CAN YOU GET THIS KIND? THEY'RE MORE EXPENSIVE, BUT THEY LAST LONGER, AND THEY'RE MUCH BETTER FOR THE ENVIRONMENT.
IT'S GOING TO TAKE ALL OF US TO SAVE THE PLANET, RIGHT?
SURE.

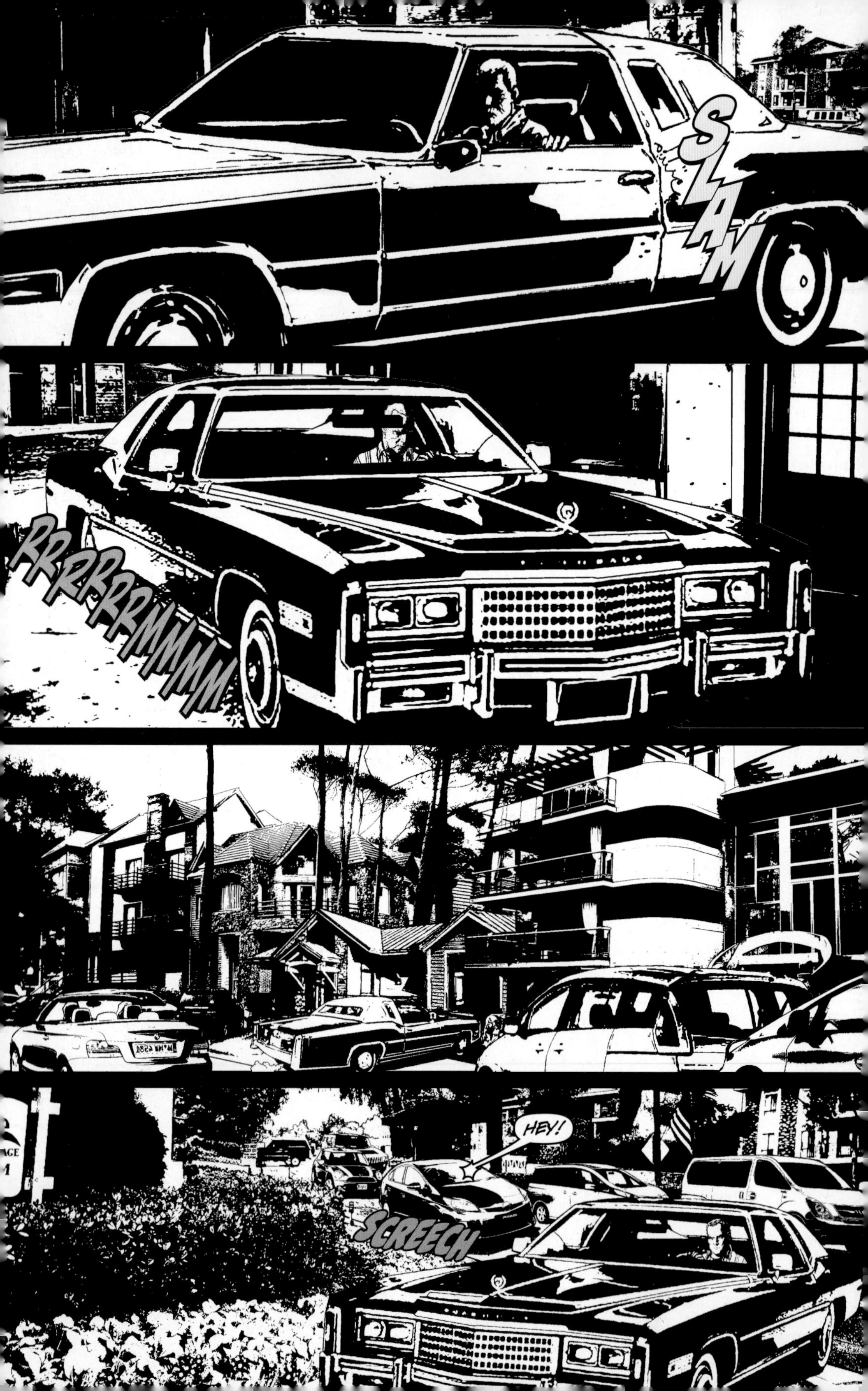
SLAM
RRRRRRMMMMM
HEY!
SCREECH

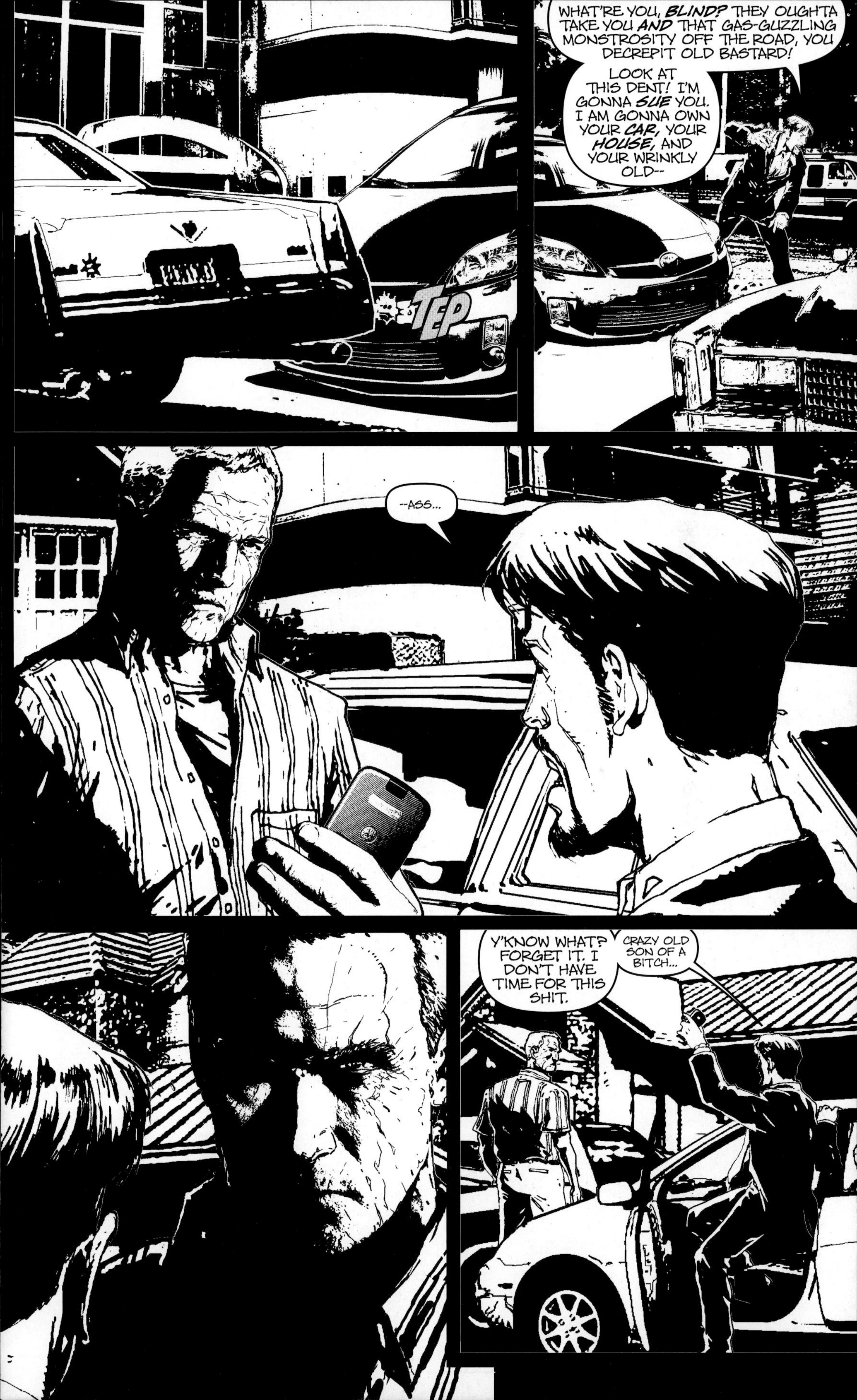
TEP
WHAT'RE YOU, BLIND? THEY OUGHTA TAKE YOU AND THAT GAS-GUZZLING MONSTROSITY OFF THE ROAD, YOU DECREPIT OLD BASTARD!
LOOK AT THIS DENT! I'M GONNA SUE YOU. I AM GONNA OWN YOUR CAR, YOUR HOUSE, AND YOUR WRINKLY OLD--
--ASS...
Y'KNOW WHAT? FORGET IT. I DON'T HAVE TIME FOR THIS SHIT.
CRAZY OLD SON OF A BITCH...

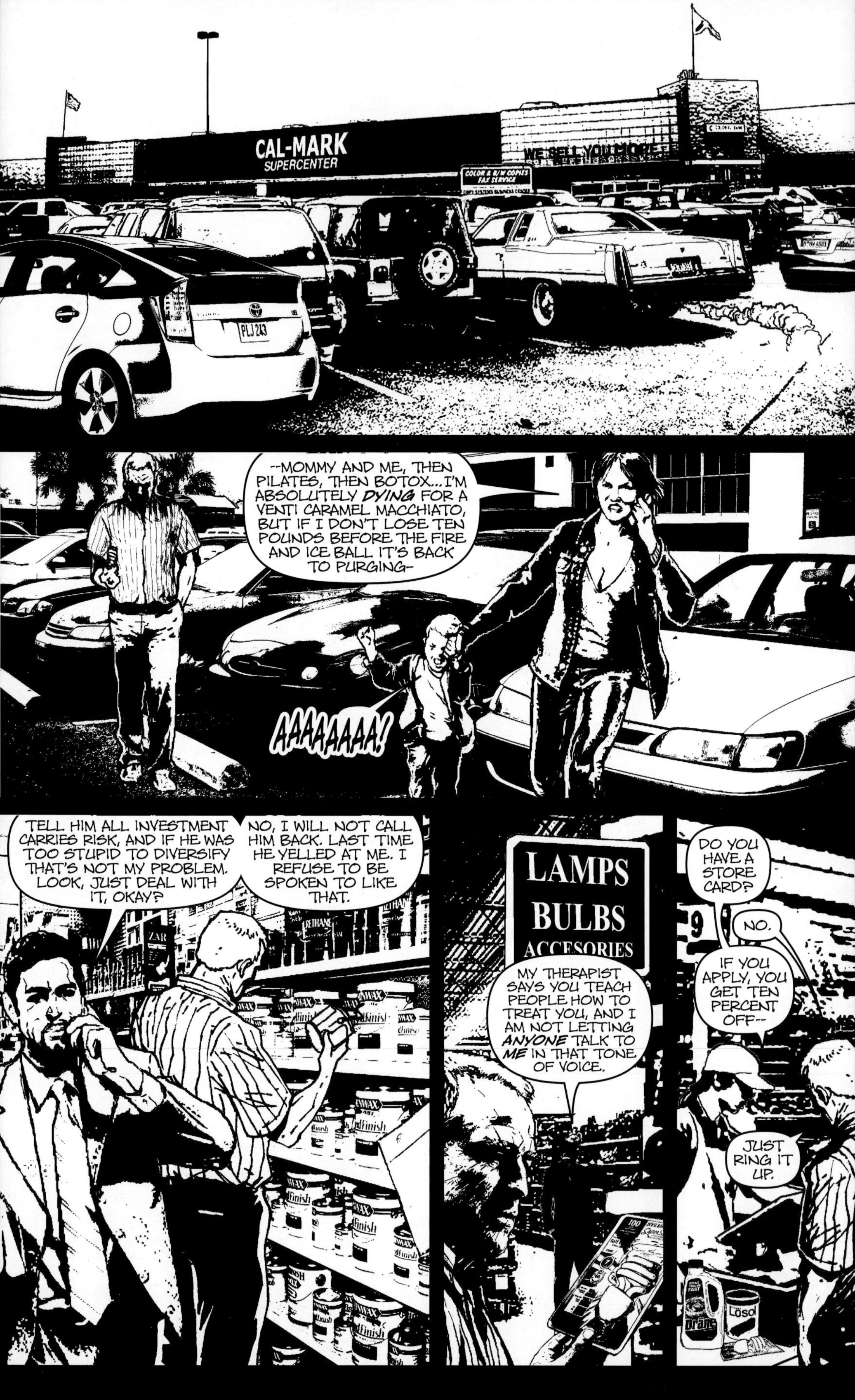
CAL-MARK
SUPERCENTER
WE SELL YOU MORE
COLOR & B/W COPIES FAX SERVICE
PLJ 243
--MOMMY AND ME, THEN PILATES, THEN BOTOX... I'M ABSOLUTELY DYING FOR A VENTI CARAMEL MACCHIATO, BUT IF I DON'T LOSE TEN POUNDS BEFORE THE FIRE AND ICE BALL IT'S BACK TO PURGING-
AAAAAAAA!
TELL HIM ALL INVESTMENT CARRIES RISK, AND IF HE WAS TOO STUPID TO DIVERSIFY THAT'S NOT MY PROBLEM. LOOK, JUST DEAL WITH IT, OKAY?
NO, I WILL NOT CALL HIM BACK. LAST TIME HE YELLED AT ME. I REFUSE TO BE SPOKEN TO LIKE THAT.
LAMPS
BULBS
ACCESORIES
MY THERAPIST SAYS YOU TEACH PEOPLE HOW TO TREAT YOU, AND I AM NOT LETTING ANYONE TALK TO ME IN THAT TONE OF VOICE.
DO YOU HAVE A STORE CARD?
NO.
IF YOU APPLY, YOU GET TEN PERCENT OFF--
JUST RING IT UP.
Drano
Losol

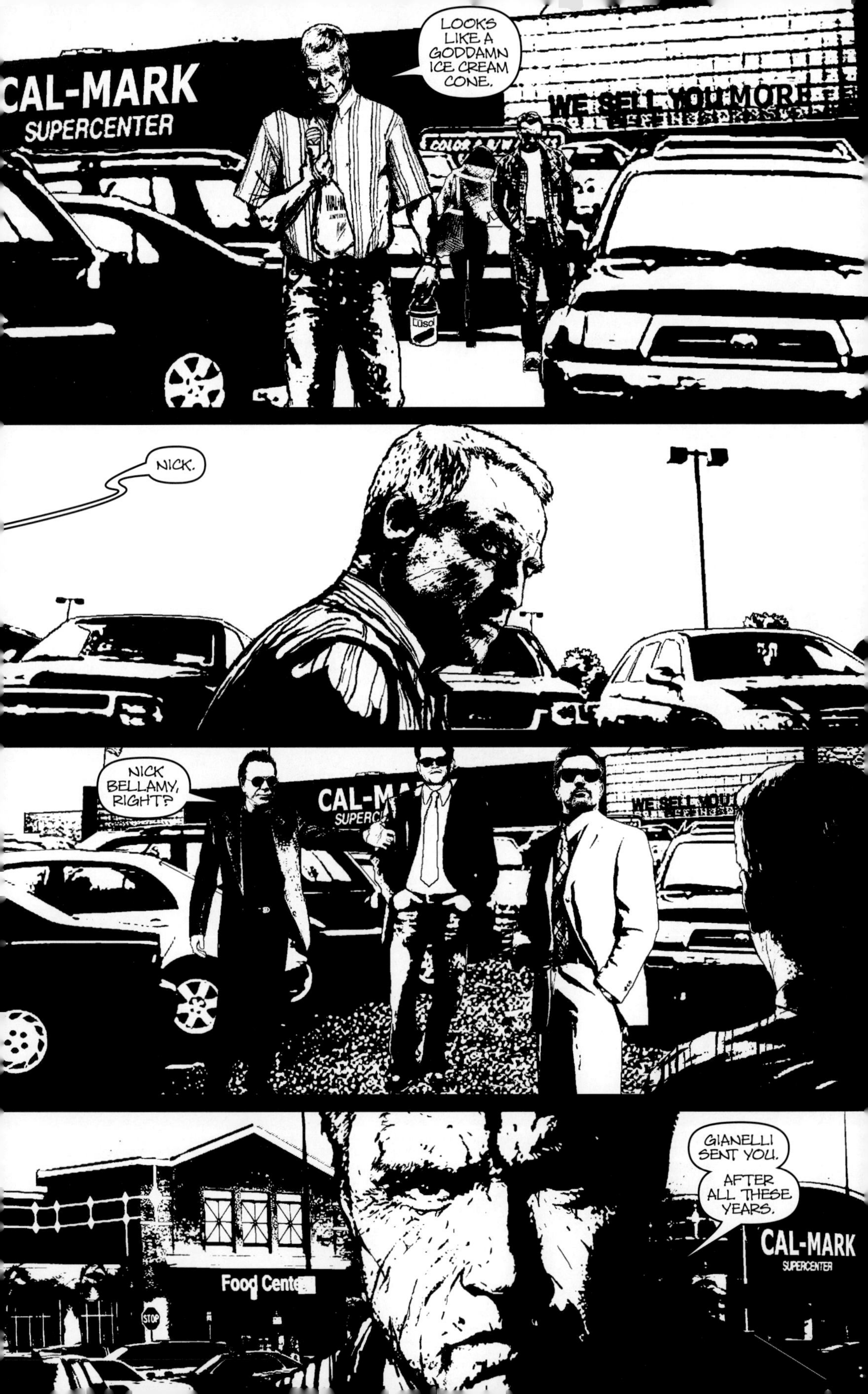
CAL-MARK SUPERCENTER
LOOKS LIKE A GODDAMN ICE CREAM CONE.
WE SELL YOU MORE
NICK.
NICK BELLAMY, RIGHT?
GIANELLI SENT YOU.
AFTER ALL THESE YEARS.
Food Cente
STOP
CAL-MARK SUPERCENTER

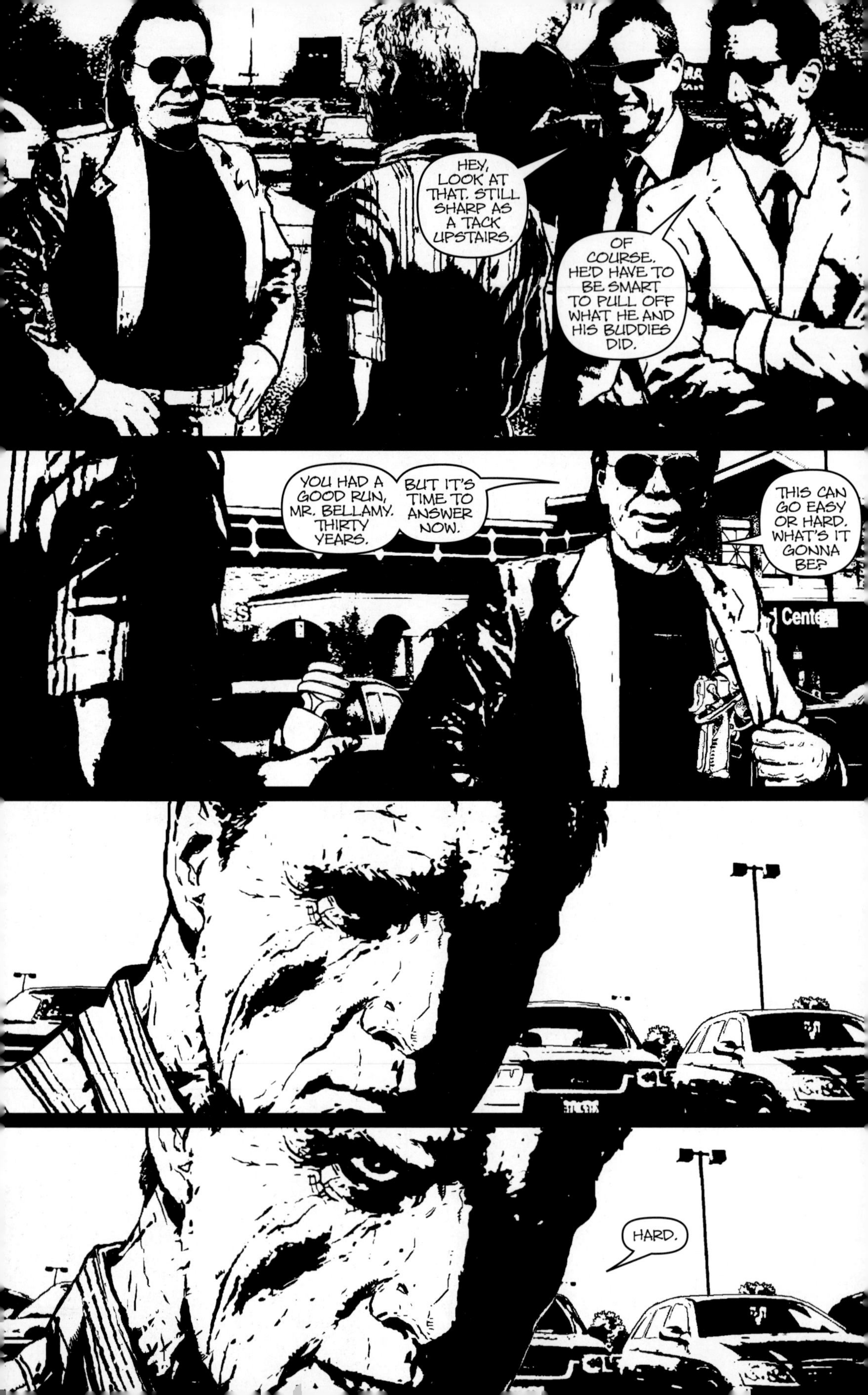
HEY, LOOK AT THAT. STILL SHARP AS A TACK UPSTAIRS.
OF COURSE. HE'D HAVE TO BE SMART TO PULL OFF WHAT HE AND HIS BUDDIES DID.
YOU HAD A GOOD RUN, MR. BELLAMY. THIRTY YEARS.
BUT IT'S TIME TO ANSWER NOW.
THIS CAN GO EASY OR HARD. WHAT'S IT GONNA BE?
HARD.

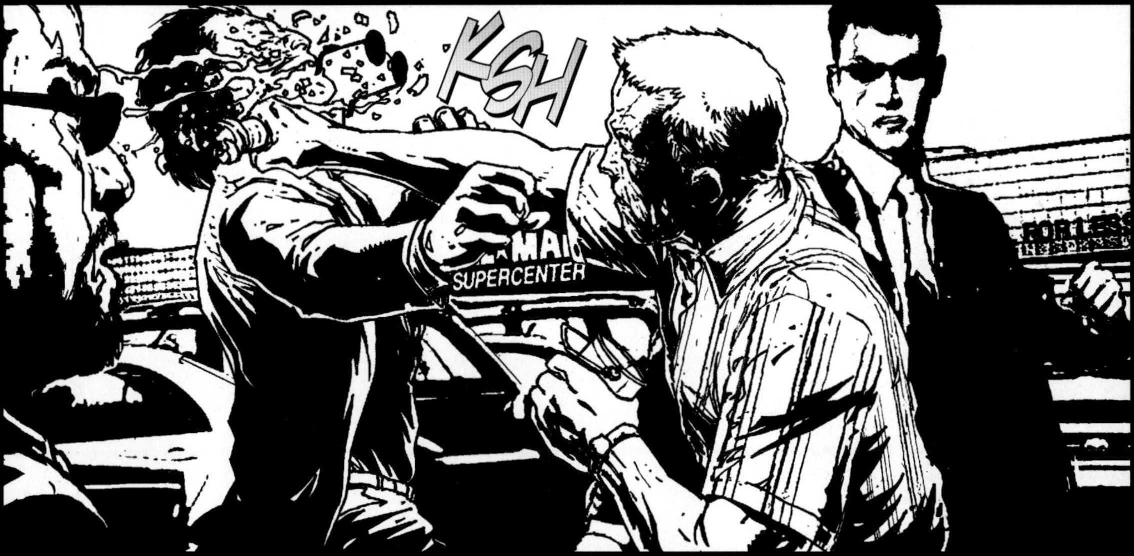
KSH
SUPERCENTER
FOR LESS

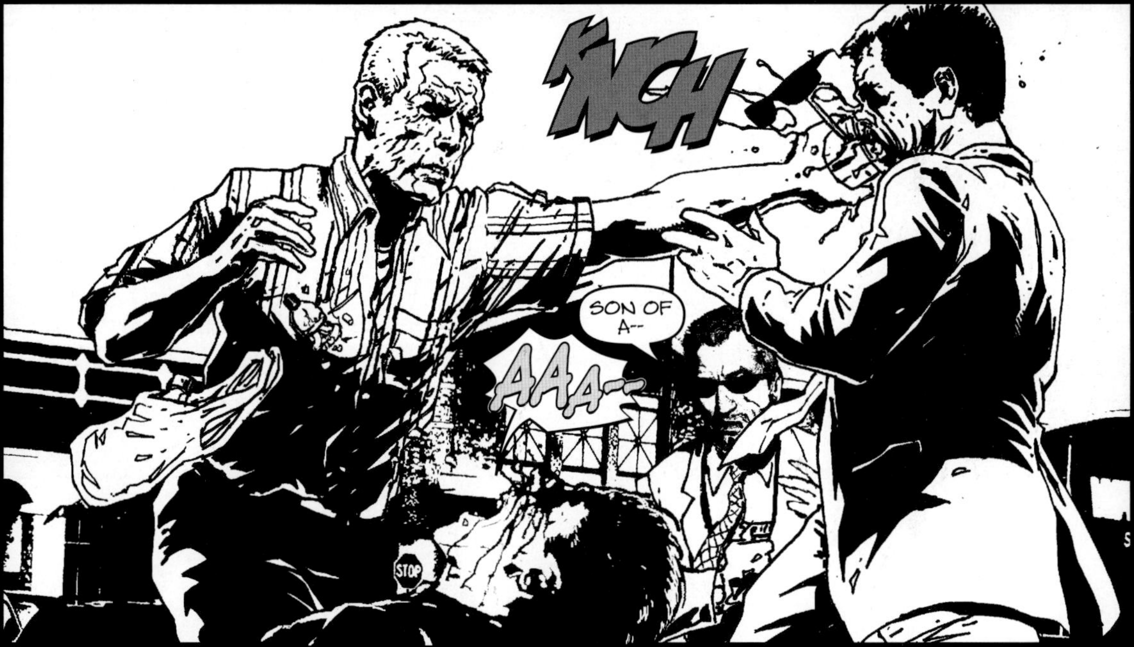
KNCH
SON OF A--
AAA--
STOP

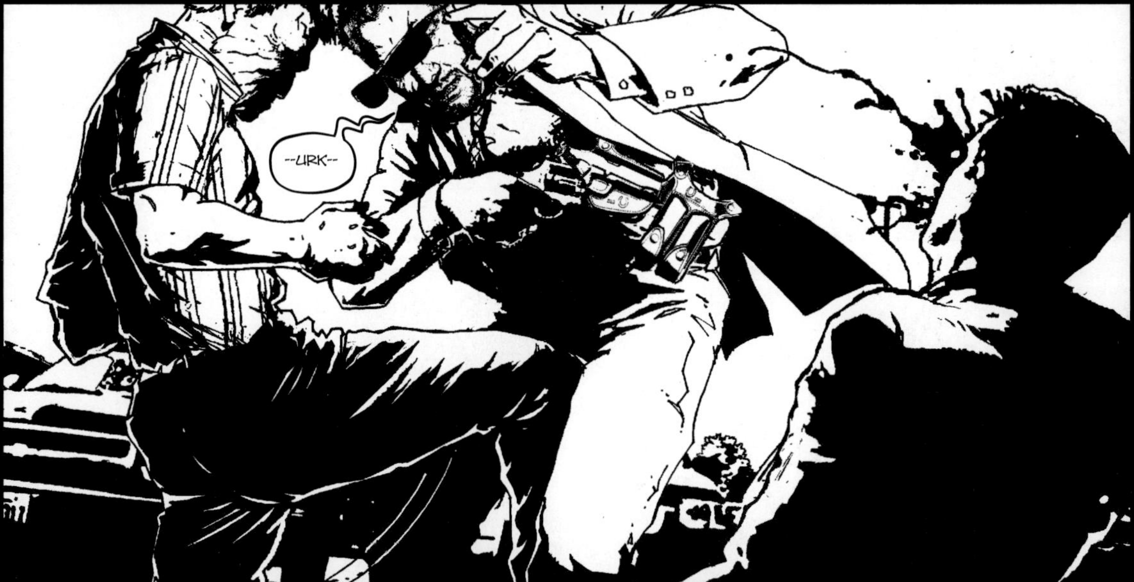
--URK--

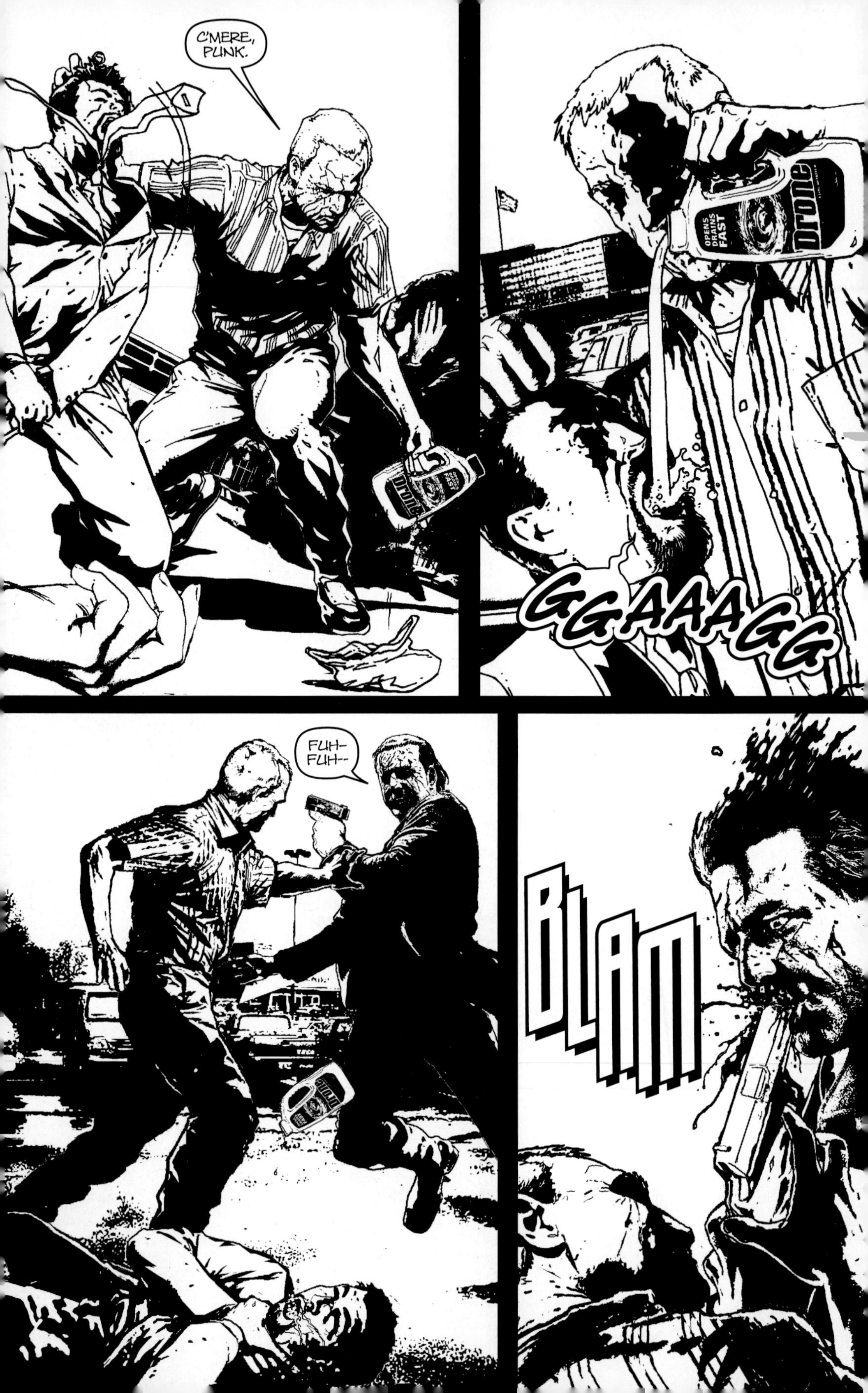
C'MERE, PUNK.
OPENS DRAINS FAST
drone
GGAAAAGG
FUH- FUH--
BLAM

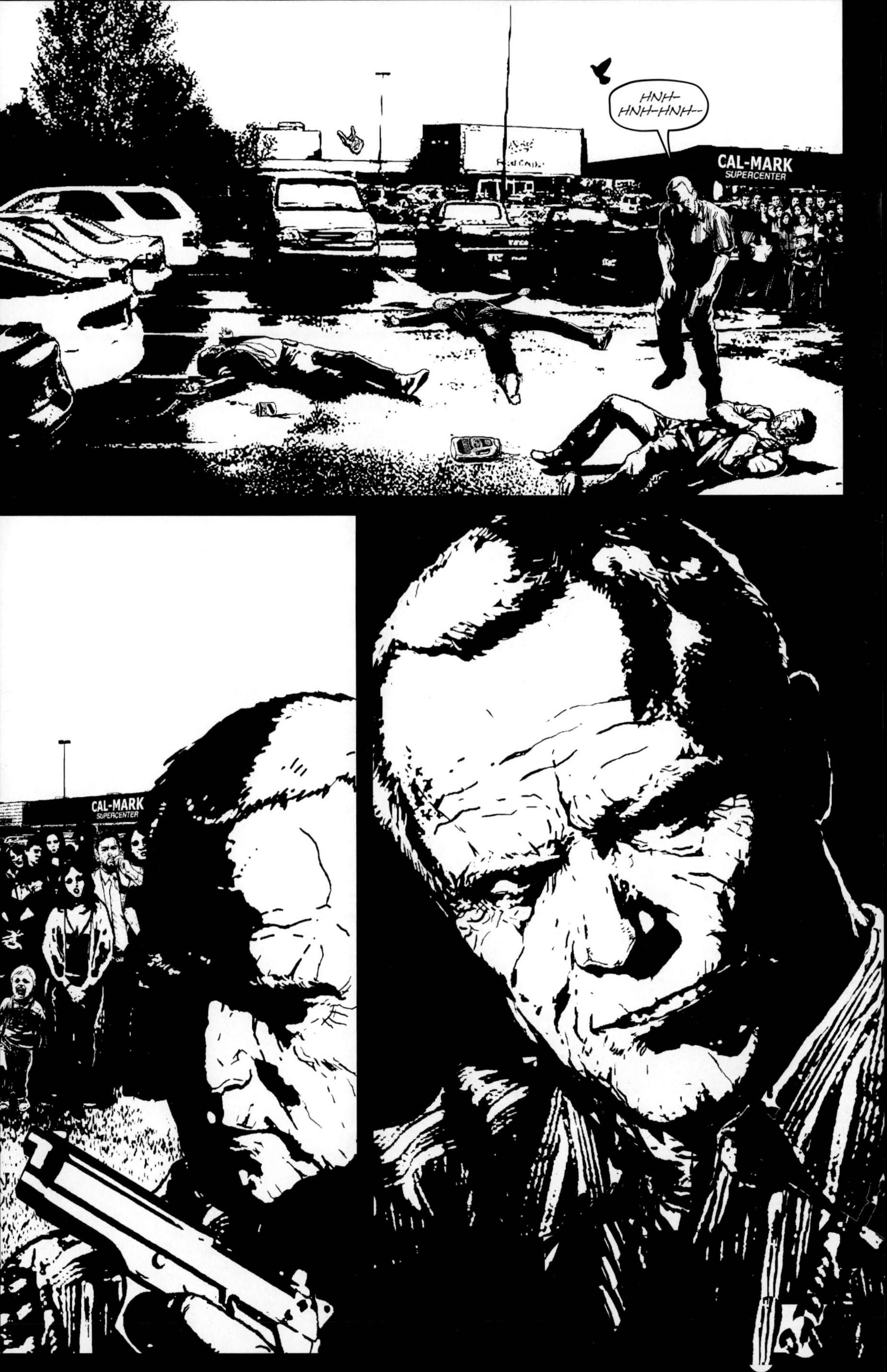
HNH-
HNH-HNH--
CAL-MARK
SUPERCENTER
CAL-MARK
SUPERCENTER

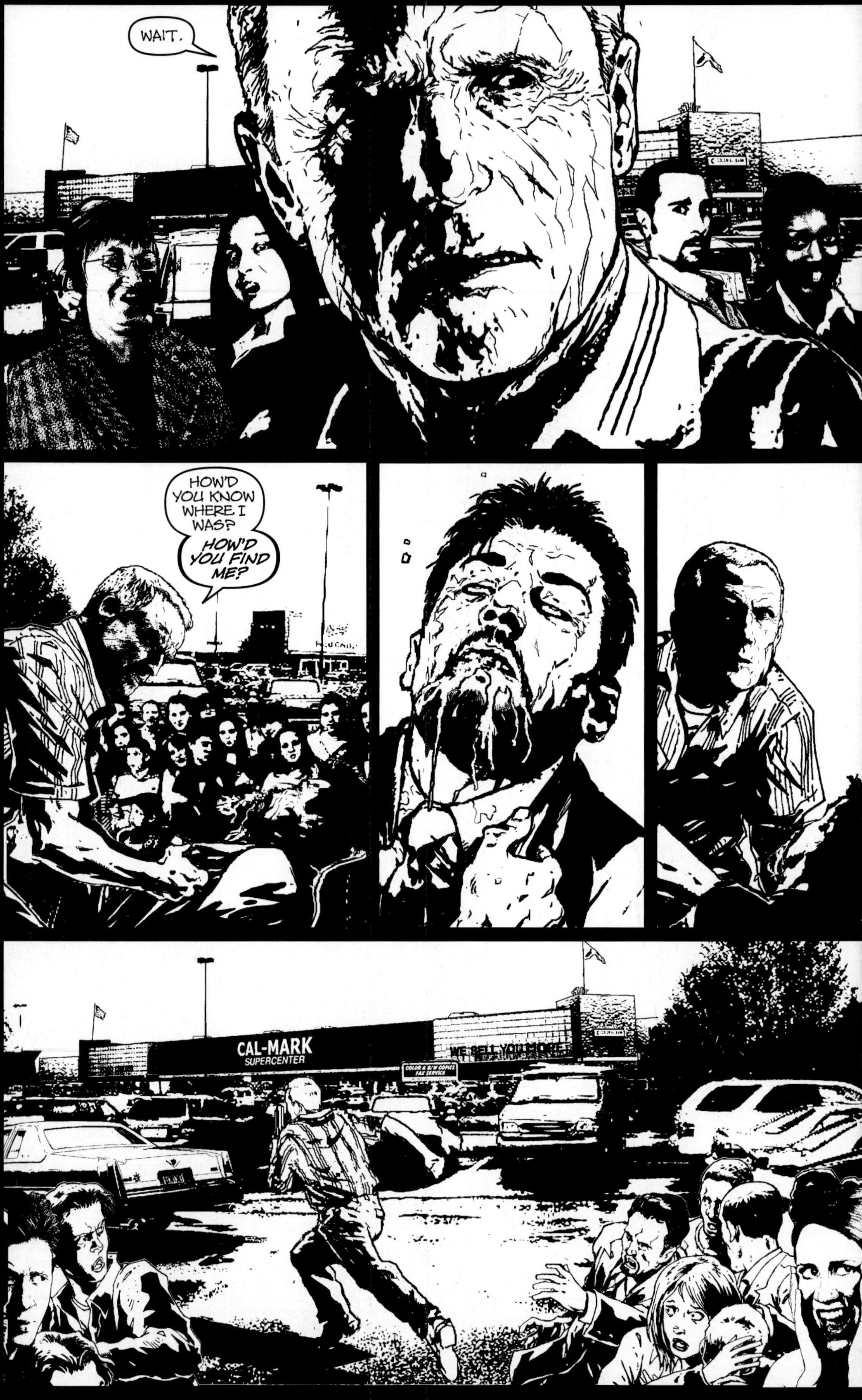
WAIT.
HOW'D YOU KNOW WHERE I WAS?
HOW'D YOU FIND ME?
CAL-MARK
SUPERCENTER
WE SELL YOU MORE
COLOR & B/W COPIES
FAX SERVICE

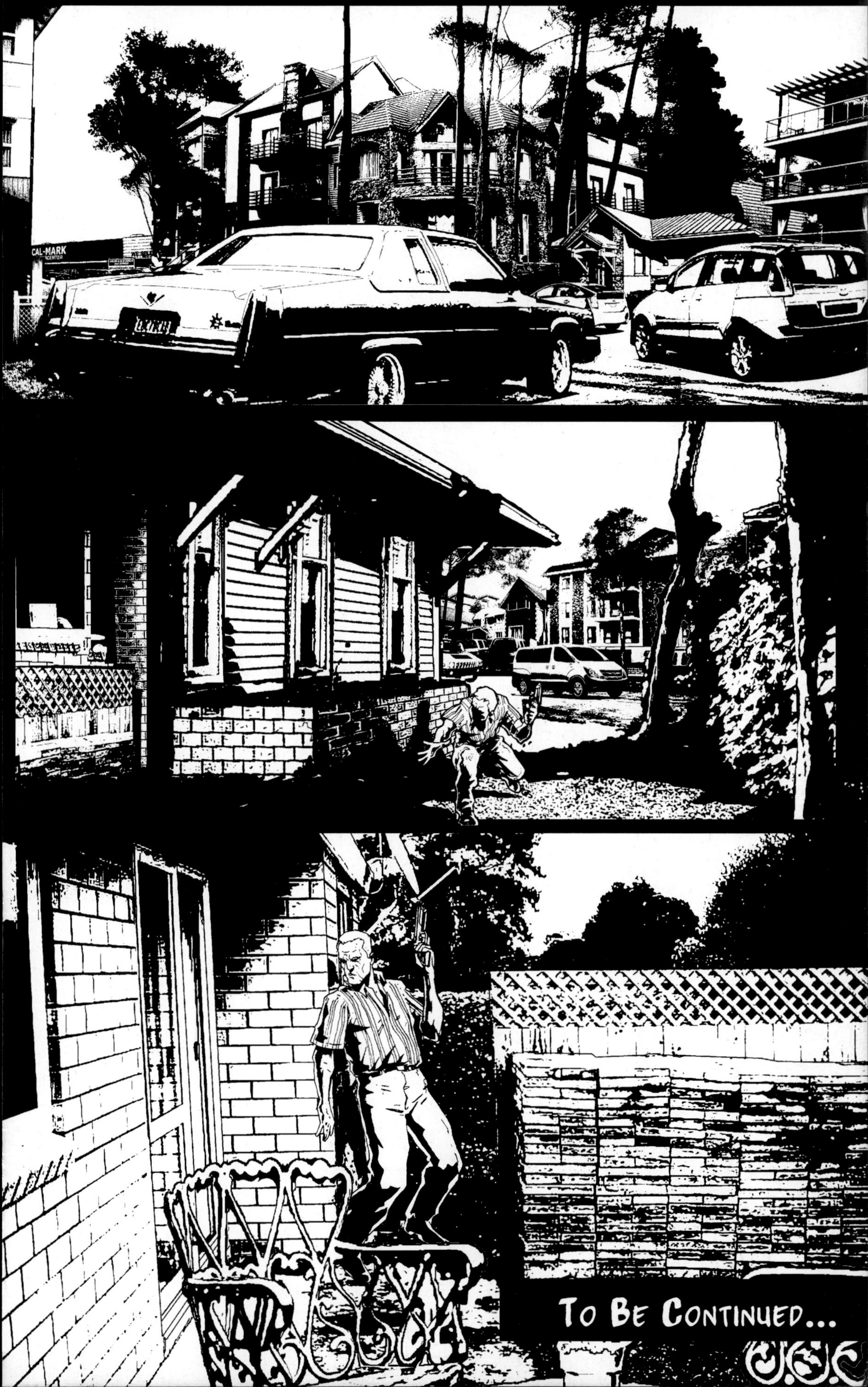
CAL-MARK
To Be Continued...

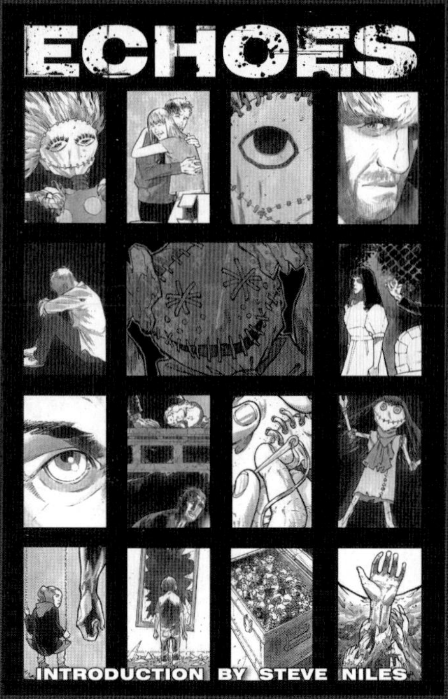
ECHOES
INTRODUCTION BY STEVE NILES

ECHOES

written by *Joshua Hale Fialkov*
art by: *Rahsan Ekedal*

From acclaimed author Joshua Hale Fialkov (*I Vampire, Tumor*) and rising artist Rahsan Ekedal (*Think Tank, Creepy*) a disturbing story of murder and mystery wrapped in questions of sanity. Minotaur Press premieres with a story of madness, family and death. Brian Cohn was learning to deal with the schizophrenia inherited from his father. Supportive wife, new baby on the way, drugs to control the voices. But, when on his father's deathbed he learns that he also inherited the trophies of his father's career as a serial killer, will his madness send him further down into the crawlspace of his father's mind?

ISBN: 978-160706-215-8

[redacted]

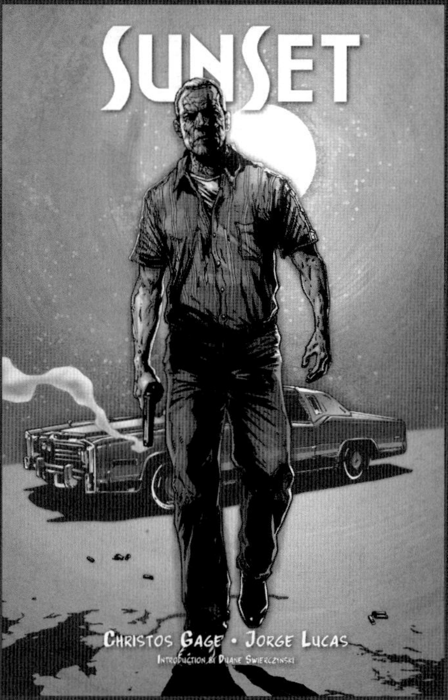
SUNSET
CHRISTOS GAGE • JORGE LUCAS

SUNSET

written by *Christos Gage*
art by: *Jorge Lucas*

In the noir tradition of Chandler and Spillane comes *SUNSET*, a two-fisted tale of revenge and redemption. On the surface, Nick Bellamy looks like any other veteran retiree left behind by a modern world. In reality, Nick is a former enforcer, who stole a fortune and years of freedom from his former mob boss. Now, in the twilight of his life, Nick will lose everything he cares about except two things: revenge... and the chance to die with his guns blazing.

Writer Christos Gage (*Avengers Academy, GI Joe: Cobra*) and artist Jorge Lucas (*The Darkness*) hits hard with Minotaur Press's first original graphic novel that will make you forget all about your Prius and organic whole-grain trans-fat-free diet.

ISBN: 978-1-60706-573-9